THE WANDERINGS
OF A SPIRITUALIST

by Sir Arthur Conan Doyle
creator of Sherlock Holmes

Ronin Publishing, Inc ● Box 1035 Berkeley CA 947091

Published by
Ronin Publishing, Inc.
Post Office Box 1035
Berkeley, California 94701

Wanderings of a Spiritualist
ISBN: 0-914171-23-2
this edition Copyright © 1988 by Ronin Publishing
(first published in the USA in 1921 by G. Doran Company)

First Ronin printing 1988
Printed in the United States of America

Ronin Credits
Project Editors: Sebastian Orfali and Beverly Potter
Editorial Consultant: Peter Beren
Cover Design: Brian Groppe

TO MY WIFE
THIS MEMORIAL OF A JOURNEY WHICH HER HELP AND PRESENCE CHANGED FROM A DUTY TO A PLEASURE

A. C. D.

July 18, 1921

Introduction

by Colin Wilson

Conan Doyle became a convert to ' Spiritualism' in 1915, at the age of fifty six, and there can be no doubt that his conversion caused an enormous damage to his reputation. One critic asked mockingly: 'Oh dear, what would Sherlock Holmes have said?' And old friends like Winston Churchill and King George V simply felt that he had become childishly credulous. It was almost certainly his conversion that prevented from receiving a peerage.

When we look at matter from Conan Doyle's point of view, we can see that all this was totally unfair. For when Doyle accepted the evidence for life after death in 1915, he had been a member of the Society for Psychical research for twenty years, and had not been convinced. The Society was basically a group of philosophers and scientists who felt that the evidence for the ' paranormal ' deserved careful study, and many of its finest intellects remained total sceptics. For the greater part of his life, Doyle was as skeptical as the rest.

But let us start this story at the beginning - that extraordinary ' invasion of the spirit people ' that began at Hydesville, New York, in March 1848. The Fox family, which included two teenage daughters, was kept awake for night after night by banging noises. One night, twelve year old Kate began snapping her fingers, and the bangs and raps imitated her. Neighbors were called in to witness the phenomena, and one of them begin asking the invisible presence questions, and asking it to answer in a code of knocks; it claimed to be the spirit of a pedlar who had been murdered and buried in the basement. (In fact, when the basement was excavated in 1904, a skeleton and a pedlar's tin box were found.) The children were separated and sent to stay with relatives; the rapping noises followed them , and developed into conventional ' poltergeist' occurrences - objects flying through the air. Eventually on instructions from the 'spirits', the first Spiritualist' church was founded in Rochester.

And within ten years, Spiritualism had spread all over the world, and 'mediums' were causing tables to float into the air and ghostly presences to communicate with the audience.

Inevitably, scientists thought it was all hysteria and trickery, and when some mediums were caught cheating, most of them decided to look no further. Yet - as in the case of the UFO craze of the 1950s - the evidence refused to go away. This is why the group of Cambridge philosophers decided to found a research society in 1882 to try to discover once and for all whether the whole thing was a fraud. Those early pioneers - like Henry Sidgwick, Frederick Myers, Arthur Balfour, John Ruskin, Lewis Carroll, Lord Tennyson - hoped that the problem of life after death would yield up its secrets just as nature itself had yielded up so many secrets in the 19th century. But the Sphinx remained inscrutable. And most sensible people eventually decided it didn't matter much anyway.

This was Conan Doyle's attitude until 1915. During the war, the Doyles were looking after a sick girl named Lilly Loder-Symonds, who used to amuse herself by practising automatic writing. The Doyles treated it as a joke until one day the writing announced that something terrible was about to happen, which would have a great influence on the war; that day, a German submarine sank the passenger ship , as a result of which America entered the war. In April 1915, Mrs. Doyle's brother, Malcolm Leckie, was killed at Mons. Soon after, Lilly's hand began to write in Malcolm Leckie's handwriting. Doyle began to put questions, and the handwriting replied. What finally convinced Doyle was when 'Leckie' answered correctly a question about a private conversation he had had with Doyle, and which no one else knew about. From know on, Doyle was convinced that human beings can survive death. He announced his conviction in a book called <u>The New Revolution</u> in 1918, and experienced a sudden slump in his popularity. In 1927, his final book about Sherlock Homes, <u>The Casebook</u>, was received with hostility. And a final novel about Professor Challenger - he of <u>The Lost World</u> - was met with open derision, for <u>The Land of Mist</u> described Challenger's conversion to Spiritualism after the death of his wife.

The present book, which appeared in 1921, makes us aware of the difficulties faced by Doyle. In the opening pages he describes how, after a seance in Wales, he cried: 'My God, if only they knew - if only they could know.' And the many accounts of seances that followed are highly convincing - to the converted. To most of us, they seem quite fascinating - for this is a highly readable and entertaining book - yet somehow irrelevant to real life, as if they had been invented by the author of <u>The Maracot Deep</u>

Now it so happens that my own position is far from that of sceptic. When I was asked to write a book about 'the occult' in 1968, I accepted in a fairly light hearted spirit, convinced that most of it would turn out to be self deception and wishful thinking. Then, like anyone who takes the trouble to study the subject with an open mind, I realized that the evidence for the 'paranormal' is as strong ads the evidence for quasars and black holes - perhaps stronger. And when I came to write a full length book called <u>Afterlife</u>, I had to end by admitting that this also applies to the evidence for life after death. So in a sense, I am a 'convert'. In another sense, I don't give a damn. For me, the great problems of human existence are the problems raised by the great 'Outsider' artists and philosophers. To tell me - as Conan Doyles does - that the answer to these problems is that we shall continue to live after death is somehow too crude and simplistic. The real problem is that if the immense unplumbed depths of the human mind, and the strange powers we all possess without being aware of them - the power, for example, that Proust glimpsed when he tasted a cake dipped in tea, and suddenly 'ceased to feel mediocre, accidental, mortal.' What Doyle has to say is relevant to these questions - which is why I am delighted that this book is being reprinted - but in my own opinion it is only part of the answer.

CONTENTS

CONTENTS

CONTENTS

CONTENTS

ILLUSTRATIONS

Photo: Stirling, Melbourne.

ON THE WARPATH IN AUSTRALIA, 1920-21.

THE WANDERINGS OF
A SPIRITUALIST

"Aggressive fighting for the right is the noblest sport the world affords."

THEODORE ROOSEVELT.

THE WANDERINGS OF A SPIRITUALIST

CHAPTER I

THIS is an account of the wanderings of a spiritualist, geographical and speculative. Should the reader have no interest in psychic things—if indeed any human being can be so foolish as not to be interested in his own nature and fate,—then this is the place to put the book down. It were better also to end the matter now if you have no patience with a go-as-you-please style of narrative, which founds itself upon the conviction that thought may be as interesting as action, and which is bound by its very nature to be intensely personal. I write a record of what absorbs my mind which may be very different from that which appeals to yours. But if you are content to come with me upon these terms then let us start with my apologies in advance for the pages which may bore you, and with my hopes that some may compensate you by pleasure or by profit.

[15]

THE WANDERINGS OF A SPIRITUALIST

I write these lines with a pad upon my knee, heaving upon the long roll of the Indian Ocean, running large and grey under a grey streaked sky, with the rain-swept hills of Ceylon, just one shade greyer, lining the Eastern skyline. So under many difficulties it will be carried on, which may explain if it does not excuse any slurring of a style, which is at its best but plain English.

There was one memorable night when I walked forth with my head throbbing and my whole frame quivering from the villa of Mr. Southey at Merthyr. Behind me the brazen glare of Dowlais iron-works lit up the sky, and in front twinkled the many lights of the Welsh town. For two hours my wife and I had sat within listening to the whispering voices of the dead, voices which are so full of earnest life, and of desperate endeavours to pierce the barrier of our dull senses. They had quivered and wavered around us, giving us pet names, sweet sacred things, the intimate talk of the olden time. Graceful lights, signs of spirit power had hovered over us in the darkness. It was a different and a wonderful world. Now with those voices still haunting our memories we had slipped out into the material world—a world of glaring iron-works and of twinkling cottage windows. As I looked down on it all I grasped my wife's hand in the darkness and I cried aloud, "My God, if they only knew—if they could only know!" Perhaps in that cry, wrung from my very soul, lay the inception of my voyage to the other side of the world. The wish to serve was strong upon us both. God had given us wonderful signs, and they were surely not for ourselves alone.

HOW THIS BOOK WAS WRITTEN.

THE WANDERINGS OF A SPIRITUALIST

I had already done the little I might. From the moment that I had understood the overwhelming importance of this subject, and realised how utterly it must change and chasten the whole thought of the world when it is whole-heartedly accepted, I felt it good to work in the matter and understood that all other work which I had ever done, or could ever do, was as nothing compared to this. Therefore, from the time that I had finished the history of the Great War on which I was engaged, I was ready to turn all my remaining energies of voice or hand to the one great end. At first I had little of my own to narrate, and my task was simply to expound the spiritual philosophy as worked out by the thoughts and experiences of others, showing folk, so far as I was able, that the superficial and ignorant view taken of it in the ordinary newspapers did not touch the heart of the matter. My own experiences were limited and inconclusive, so that it was the evidence of others which I quoted. But as I went forward signs were given in profusion to me also, such signs as were far above all error or deception, so that I was able to speak with that more vibrant note which comes not from belief or faith, but from personal experience and knowledge. I had found that the wonderful literature of Spiritualism did not reach the people, and that the press was so full of would-be jocosities and shallow difficulties that the public were utterly misled. Only one way was left, which was to speak to the people face to face. This was the task upon which I set forth, and it had led me to nearly every considerable city of Great Britain from Aberdeen to Torquay. Everywhere I found interest, though it

[17]

varied from the heavier spirit of the sleepy cathedral towns to the brisk reality of centres of life and work like Glasgow or Wolverhampton. Many a time my halls were packed, and there were as many outside as inside the building. I have no eloquence and make profession of none, but I am audible and I say no more than I mean and can prove, so that my audiences felt that it was indeed truth so far as I could see it, which I conveyed. Their earnestness and receptiveness were my great help and reward in my venture. Those who had no knowledge of what my views were assembled often outside my halls, waving banners and distributing tracts, but never once in the course of addressing 150,000 people, did I have disturbance in my hall. I tried, while never flinching from truth, to put my views in such a way as to hurt no one's feelings, and although I have had clergymen of many denominations as my chairmen, I have had thanks from them and no remonstrance. My enemies used to follow and address meetings, as they had every right to do, in the same towns. It is curious that the most persistent of these enemies were Jesuits on the one side and Evangelical sects of the Plymouth Brethren type upon the other. I suppose the literal interpretation of the Old Testament was the common bond.

However, this is digression, and when the digressions are taken out of this book there will not be much left. I get back to the fact that the overwhelming effect of the Merthyr Séance and of others like it, made my wife and myself feel that when we had done what we could in Britain we must go forth to further fields. Then came the direct invitation from Spiritual bodies in Australia. I had spent some never-to-be-forgotten days with Australian troops at the very crisis of the war. My heart was much with them. If my message could indeed bring consolation to bruised hearts and to bewildered minds—and I had boxes full of letters to show that it did—then to whom should I carry it rather than to those who had fought so splendidly and lost so heavily in the common cause? I was a little weary also after three years of incessant controversy, speaking often five times a week, and continually endeavouring to uphold the cause in the press. The long voyage presented attractions, even if there was hard work at the end of it. There were difficulties in the way. Three children, boys of eleven and nine, with a girl of seven, all devotedly attached to their home and their parents, could not easily be left behind. If they came a maid was also necessary. The pressure upon me of correspondence and interviews would be so great that my old friend and secretary, Major Wood, would be also needed. Seven of us in all therefore, and a cheque of sixteen hundred pounds drawn for our return tickets, apart from outfit, before a penny could be entered on the credit side. However, Mr. Carlyle Smythe, the best agent in Australia, had taken the matter up and I felt that we were in good hands. The lectures would be numerous, controversies severe, the weather at its hottest, and my own age over sixty. But there are compensating forces, and I was constantly aware of their presence. I may count our adventures as actually beginning from the luncheon which was given us in farewell a week or so before our sailing by the Spiritualists of England. Harry Engholm, most unselfish of men, and a born organiser among our most unorganised crowd, had the matter in hand, so it was bound to be a success. There was sitting room at the Holborn Restaurant for 290 people, and it was all taken up three weeks before the event. The secretary said that he could have filled the Albert Hall. It was an impressive example of the solidity of the movement showing itself for the moment round us, but really round the cause. There were peers, doctors, clergymen, officers of both services, and, above all, those splendid lower middle class folk, if one talks in our material earth terms, who are the spiritual peers of the nation. Many professional mediums were there also, and I was honoured by their presence, for as I said in my remarks, I consider that in these days of doubt and sorrow, a genuine professional medium is the most useful member of the whole community. Alas! how few they are! Four photographic mediums do I know in all Britain, with about twelve physical phenomena mediums and as many really reliable clairvoyants. What are these among so many? But there are many amateur mediums of various degrees, and the number tends to increase. Perhaps there will at last be an angel to every church as in the days of John. I see dimly the time when two congregations, the living and those who have passed on, shall move forward together with the medium angel as the bridge between them.

It was a wonderful gathering, and I only wish I could think that my own remarks rose to the height of the occasion. However, I did my best and spoke from my heart. I told how the Australian visit had arisen, and I claimed that the message that I would carry was

[20]

the most important that the mind of man could conceive, implying as it did the practical abolition of death, and the reinforcement of our present religious views by the actual experience of those who have made the change from the natural to the spiritual bodies. Speaking of our own experiences, I mentioned that my wife and I had actually spoken face to face beyond all question or doubt with eleven friends or relatives who had passed over, their direct voices being in each case audible, and their conversation characteristic and evidential—in some cases marvellously so. Then with a sudden impulse I called upon those in the audience who were prepared to swear that they had had a similar experience to stand up and testify. It seemed for a moment as if the whole audience were on their feet. *The Times* next day said 250 out of 290 and I am prepared to accept that estimate. Men and women, of all professions and social ranks—I do not think that I exaggerated when I said that it was the most remarkable demonstration that I had ever seen and that nothing like it had ever occurred in the City of London.

It was vain for those journals who tried to minimise it to urge that in a Baptist or a Unitarian assembly all would have stood up to testify to their own faith. No doubt they would, but this was not a case of faith, it was a case of bearing witness to fact. There were people of all creeds, Church, dissent, Unitarian and ex-materialists. They were testifying to an actual objective experience as they might have testified to having seen the lions in Trafalgar Square. If such a public agreement of evidence does not establish a fact then it is indeed impossible, as Professor Challis remarked long ago, to prove a thing by any human testimony whatever. I confess that I was amazed. When I remember how many years it was before I myself got any final personal proofs I should have thought that the vast majority of Spiritualists were going rather upon the evidence of others than upon their own. And yet 250 out of 290 had actually joined hands across the border. I had no idea that the direct proof was so widely spread.

I have always held that people insist too much upon direct proof. What direct proof have we of most of the great facts of Science? We simply take the word of those who have examined. How many of us have, for example, seen the rings of Saturn? We are assured that they are there, and we accept the assurance. Strong telescopes are rare, and so we do not all expect to see the rings with our own eyes. In the same way strong mediums are rare, and we cannot all expect to experience the higher psychic results. But if the assurance of those who have carefully experimented, of the Barretts, the Hares, the Crookes, the Wallaces, the Lodges and the Lombrosos, is not enough, then it is manifest that we are dealing with this matter on different terms to those which we apply to all the other affairs of science. It would of course be different if there were a school of patient investigators who had gone equally deeply into the matter and come to opposite conclusions. Then we should certainly have to find the path of truth by individual effort. But such a school does not exist. Only the ignorant and inexperienced are in total opposition, and the humblest witness who has really sought the evidence has more weight than they.

After the luncheon my wife made the final preparations—and only ladies can tell what it means to fit out six people with tropical and semi-tropical outfits which will enable them for eight months to stand inspection in public. I employed the time by running down to Devonshire to give addresses at Exeter and Torquay, with admirable audiences at both. Good Evan Powell had come down to give me a last séance, and I had the joy of a few last words with my arisen son, who blessed me on my mission and assured me that I would indeed bring solace to bruised hearts. The words he uttered were a quotation from my London speech at which Powell had not been present, nor had the verbatim account of it appeared anywhere at that time. It was one more sign of how closely our words and actions are noted from the other side. Powell was tired, having given a sitting the night before, so the proceedings were short, a few floating lights, my son and my sister's son to me, one or two greetings to other sitters, and it was over.

Whilst in Exeter I had a discussion with those who would break away from Christianity. They are a strong body within the movement, and how can Christians be surprised at it when they remember that for seventy years they have had nothing but contempt and abuse for the true light-bearers of the world? Is there at the present moment one single bishop, or one head of a Free Church, who has the first idea of psychic truth? Dr. Parker had, in his day, so too Archdeacons Wilberforce and Colley, Mr. Haweis and a few others. General Booth has also testified to spiritual communion with the dead. But what have Spiritualists had in the main save misrepresentation and persecution? Hence the movement has admittedly, so far as it is an organised religion—and it has already 360 churches and 1,000 building funds—taken a purely Unitarian turn. This involves no disrespect towards Him Whom they look upon as the greatest Spirit who ever trod the earth, but only a deep desire to communicate direct without intermediary with that tremendous centre of force from and to whom all things radiate or return. They are very earnest and good men, these organised religious Spiritualists, and for the most part, so far as my experience goes, are converts from materialism who, having in their materialistic days said very properly that they would believe nothing which could not be proved to them, are ready now with Thomas to be absolutely wholehearted when the proof of survival and spirit communion has actually reached them. There, however, the proof ends, nor will they go further than the proof extends, as otherwise their original principles would be gone. Therefore they are Unitarians with a breadth of vision which includes Christ, Krishna, Buddha and all the other great spirits whom God has sent to direct different lines of spiritual evolution which correspond to the different needs of the various races of mankind. Our information from the beyond is that this evolution is continued beyond the grave, and very far on until all details being gradually merged, they become one as children of God. With a deep reverence for Christ it is undeniable that the organised Spiritualist does not accept vicarious atonement nor original

THE GOD-SPEED LUNCHEON IN LONDON.
On this occasion 250 out of 290 guests rose as testimony that they were in personal touch with their dead.

sin, and believes that a man reaps as he sows with no one but himself to pull out the weeds. It seems to me the more virile and manly doctrine, and as to the texts which seem to say otherwise, we cannot deny that the New Testament has been doctored again and again in order to square the record of the Scriptures with the practice of the Church. Professor Nestle, in the preface to a work on theology (I write far from books of reference), remarks that there were actually officials named "Correctores," who were appointed at the time of the Council of Nicæa for this purpose, and St. Jerome, when he constructed the Vulgate, complains to Pope Damasus that it is practically a new book that he is making, putting any sin arising upon the Pope's head. In the face of such facts we can only accept the spirit of the New Testament fortified with common sense, and using such interpretation as brings most spiritual strength to each of us. Personally, I accept the view of the organised Spiritual religion, for it removes difficulties which formerly stood between me and the whole Christian system, but I would not say or do anything which would abash those others who are getting real spiritual help from any sort of Christian belief. The gaining of spirituality and widening of the personality are the aims of life, and how it is done is the business of the individual. Every creed has produced its saints and has to that extent justified its existence. I like the Unitarian position of the main Spiritual body, however, because it links the movement up with the other great creeds of the world and makes it more accessible to the Jew, the Mohammedan or the Buddhist. It is far too big to be confined within the palings of Christianity.

Here is a little bit of authentic teaching from the other side which bears upon the question. I take it from the remarkable record of Mr. Miller of Belfast, whose dialogues with his son after the death of the latter seem to me to be as certainly true as any case which has come to my notice. On asking the young soldier some question about the exact position of Christ in religion he modestly protested that such a subject was above his head, and asked leave to bring his higher guide to answer the question. Using a fresh voice and in a new and more weighty manner the medium then said :—

"I wish to answer your question. Jesus the Christ is the proper designation. Jesus was perfect humanity. Christ was the God idea in Him. Jesus, on account of His purity, manifested in the highest degree the psychic powers which resulted in His miracles. Jesus never preached the blood of the lamb. The disciples after His ascension forgot the message in admiration of the man. The Christ is in every human being, and so are the psychic forces which were used by Jesus. If the same attention were given to spiritual development which you give to the comfort and growth of your material bodies your progress in spiritual life would be rapid and would be characterised by the same works as were performed by Jesus. The one essential thing for all on earth to strive after is a fuller knowledge and growth in spiritual living."

I think that the phrase, "In their admiration of the

man they forgot His message," is as pregnant a one as I ever heard.

To come back then to the discussion at Exeter, what I said then and feel now is that every Spiritualist is free to find his own path, and that as a matter of fact his typical path is a Unitarian one, but that this in no way obscures the fact that our greatest leaders, Lodge, Barrett, Ellis Powell, Tweedale, are devoted sons of the Church, that our literature is full of Christian aspiration, and that our greatest prophet, Vale Owen, is a priest of a particularly sacerdotal turn of mind. We are in a transition stage, and have not yet found any common theological position, or any common position at all, save that the dead carry on, that they do not change, that they can under proper physical conditions communicate with us, and that there are many physical signs by which they make their presence known to us. That is our common ground, and all beyond that is matter of individual observation and inference. Therefore, we are not in a position to take on any anti-Christian agitation, for it would be against the conscience of the greater part of our own people.

Well, it is clear that if I do not begin my book I shall finish it before I have begun, so let me end this chapter by saying that in despite of all superstition we started for Australia in the good ship "Naldera" (Capt. Lewellin, R.N.R.), on Friday, August 13th, 1920. As we carried two bishops in addition to our ominous dates we were foredoomed by every nautical tradition. Our party were my dear, splendid wife, who has shared both my evidence and my convictions. She it is who, by breaking up her household, leaving her beloved

[27]

home, breaking the schooling of her children, and venturing out upon a sea voyage, which of all things she hates, has made the real sacrifice for the cause. As to me, I am fond of change and adventure, and heartily agree with President Roosevelt when he said that the grandest sport upon earth is to champion an unpopular cause which you know to be true. With us were Denis, Malcolm and Baby, concerning whom I wrote the "Three of them" sketches some years ago. In their train was Jakeman, most faithful of maids, and in mine Major Wood, who has been mixed up in my life ever since as young men we played both cricket and football in the same team. Such was the little party who set forth to try and blow that smouldering glow of truth which already existed in Australia, into a more lively flame.

CHAPTER II

WE had a favourable journey across the Bay and came
without adventure to Gibraltar, that strange crag,
Arabic by name, African in type, Spanish by right, and
British by might. I trust that my whole record has
shown me to be a loyal son of the Empire, and I recognise that we must have a secure line of communications with the East, but if any change could give us
Ceuta, on the opposite African coast, instead of this
outlying corner of proud old Spain, it would be good
policy as well as good morality to make the change.
I wonder how we should like it if the French held a
garrison at Mount St. Michael in Cornwall, which
would be a very similar situation. Is it worth having
a latent enemy who at any time might become an active
one, or is it wiser to hold them to us by the memory of
a great voluntary act of justice? They would pay,

of course, for all quays, breakwaters and improvements, which would give us the money to turn Ceuta into a worthy substitute, which could be held without offending the pride of a great nation, as old and proud as ourselves. The whole lesson of this great war is that no nation can do what is unjust with impunity, and that sooner or later one's sin will find one out. How successful seemed all the scheming of Frederick of Prussia! But what of Silesia and of Poland now? Only on justice can you build with a permanent foundation, and there is no justice in our tenure of Gibraltar. We had only an hour ashore, a great joy to the children, and carried away a vague impression of grey-shirted Tommies, swarthy loungers, one long, cobble-stoned street, scarlet blossoms, and a fine Governor's house, in which I picture that brave old warrior, Smith-Dorrien, writing a book which will set all the critics talking, and the military clubs buzzing a year or two from now. I do not know if he was really forced to fight at Le Cateau, though our sympathies must always go to the man who fights, but I do feel that if he had had his way and straightened the salient of Ypres, there would have been a mighty saving of blood and tears. There were sentimental reasons against it, but I can think of no material ones—certainly none which were worth all the casualties of the Salient. I had only one look at the place, and that by night, but never shall I forget the murderous loop, outlined by star shells, nor the horrible noises which rose up from that place of wrath and misery.

On August 19th we were running up the eastern Spanish coast, a most desolate country of high bare cliffs and barren uplands, studded with aged towers which told of pirate raids of old. These Mediterranean shore dwellers must have had a hellish life, when the Barbary Rover was afloat, and they might be wakened any night by the Moslem yell. Truly, if the object of human life was chastening by suffering, then we have given it to each other in full measure. If this were the only life I do not know how the hypothesis of the goodness of God could be sustained, since our history has been one hardly broken record of recurring miseries, war, famine, and disease, from the ice to the equator. I should still be a materialist, as I was of yore, if it were not for the comfort and teaching from beyond, which tells me that this is the worst—far the worst—and that by its standard everything else becomes most gloriously better, so long as we help to make it so. "If the boys knew what it was like over here," said a dead soldier, "they would just jump for it." He added however, "If they did that they would surely miss it." We cannot bluff Providence, or short-circuit things to our liking.

We got ashore once more at Marseilles. I saw converted German merchant ships, with names like "Burgomeister Müller," in the harbour, and railway trucks with "Mainz-Cöln" still marked upon their flanks—part of the captured loot. Germany, that name of terror, how short is the time since we watched you well-nigh all-powerful, mighty on land, dangerous on the sea, conquering the world with your commerce and threatening it with your arms! You had everything, numbers, discipline, knowledge, industry, bravery, organisation, all in the highest—such an engine as the world has never seen. And now—Ichabod! Ichabod! Your warships lie under the waves, your liners fly the flags of your enemies, your mother Rhine on either bank hears the bugles of your invaders. What was wanting in you to bring you to such a pass? Was it not spirituality? Had not your churches become as much a department of State as the Post Office, where every priest and pastor was in State pay, and said that which the State ordained? All other life was at its highest, but spiritual life was dead, and because it was dead all the rest had taken on evil activities which could only lead to dissolution and corruption. Had Germany obeyed the moral law would she not now be great and flourishing, instead of the ruin which we see? Was ever such an object lesson in sin and its consequence placed before the world? But let us look to it, for we also have our lesson to learn, and our punishment is surely waiting if we do not learn it. If now after such years we sink back into old ruts and do not make an earnest effort for real religion and real active morality, then we cumber the ground, and it is time that we were swept away, for no greater chance of reform can ever come to us.

I saw some of the Senegal troops in the streets of Marseilles—a whole battalion of them marching down for re-embarkation. They are fierce, hard soldiers, by the look of them, for the negro is a natural fighter, as the prize ring shows, and these have long service training upon the top of this racial pugnacity. They look pure savages, with the tribal cuts still upon their faces, and I do not wonder that the Germans objected to them, though we cannot doubt that the Germans would themselves have used their Askaris in Europe as well as in Africa if they could have done so. The men who had as allies the murderers of the Armenians would not stick at trifles. I said during the war, and I can clearly see now, that the way in which the war was fought will prove hardly second to the war itself as a misfortune to the human race. A clean war could end in a clean peace. But how can we ever forget the poison gas, the Zeppelin bombardments of helpless cities, the submarine murders, the scattering of disease germs, and all the other atrocities of Germany? No water of oblivion can ever wash her clean. She had one chance, and only one. It was to at once admit it all herself and to set to work purging her national guilt by punishing guilty individuals. Perhaps she may even now save herself and clear the moral atmosphere of the world by doing this. But time passes and the signs are against it. There can be no real peace in the world until voluntary reparation has been made. Forced reparation can only make things worse, for it cannot satisfy us, and it must embitter them. I long for real peace, and should love to see our Spiritualist bodies lead the van. But the time is not yet and it is realities we need, not phrases.

Old travellers say that they never remember the Mediterranean so hot. We went down it with a following breeze which just neutralised our own head wind, the result being a quivering tropical heat. With the Red Sea before us it was no joke to start our trials so soon, and already the children began to wilt. However, Major Wood kept them at work for the forenoons and discipline still flourished. On the third day out we were south of Crete, and saw an island lying there which is surely the same in the lee of which Paul's galley took refuge when Euroclydon was behaving so badly. I had been asked to address the first-class passengers upon psychic religion that evening, and it was strange indeed to speak in those waters, for I knew well that however ill my little pip-squeak might compare with that mighty voice, yet it was still the same battle of the unseen against the material, raging now as it did 2,000 years ago. Some 200 of the passengers, with the Bishop of Kwang-Si, turned up, and a better audience one could not wish, though the acoustic properties of the saloon were abominable. However, I got it across, though I was as wet as if I had fallen overboard when I had finished. I was pleased to learn afterwards that among the most keen of my audience were every coloured man and woman on the ship, Parsees, Hindoos, Japanese and Mohammedans.

"Do you believe it is true?" they were asked next day.

"We *know* that it is true," was the answer, and it came from a lady with a red caste-mark like a wafer upon her forehead. So far as I could learn she spoke for all the Eastern folk.

And the others? At least I set them talking and thinking. I heard next morning of a queue of six waiting at the barber's all deep in theological discussion, with the barber himself, razor in hand, joining warmly in. "There has never been so much religion talked on a P. & O. ship since the line was started," said one old traveller. It was all good-humoured and could do no harm. Before we had reached Port Said all my books on the subject were lent out to eager readers, and I was being led aside into remote corners and cross-questioned all day. I have a number of good psychic photographs with me, some of them of my own taking, and all of them guaranteed, and I find these valuable as making folk realise that my words do in truth represent realities. I have the famous fairy photos also, which will appear in England in the Christmas number of the *Strand*. I feel as if it were a delay-action mine which I had left behind me. I can imagine the cry of "Fake!" which will arise. But they will stand investigation. It has of course nothing to do with Spiritualism proper, but everything which can shake the mind out of narrow material grooves and make it realise that endless worlds surround us, separated only by difference of vibration, must work in the general direction of truth.

"Difference of Vibration"—I have been trying lately to get behind mere words and to realise more clearly what this may mean. It is a fascinating and fruitful line of thought. It begins with my electric fan whizzing over my head. As it starts with slow vibration I see the little propellers. Soon they become a dim mist, and finally I can see them no more. But they are there. At any moment, by slowing the movement, I can bring them back to my vision. Why do I not see it all the time? Because the impression is so fast that my retina has not time to register it. Can we not imagine then that some objects may emit the usual light waves, long enough and slow enough to leave a picture, but that other objects may send waves which are short and steep, and therefore make so swift an impression that it is not recorded? That, so far as I can follow it, is what we mean by an object with a higher rate of vibration. It is but a feeling out into the dark, but it is a hypothesis which may serve us to carry on with, though the clairvoyant seems to be not a person with a better developed physical retina, but rather one who has the power to use that which corresponds with the retina in their own etheric bodies which are in harmony with etheric waves from outside. When a man can walk round a room and examine the pictures with the back of his head, as Tom Tyrrell has done, it is clear that it is not his physical retina which is working. In countless cases inquirers into magnetic phenomena have caused their subjects to read with various parts of their bodies. It is the other body, the etheric body, the "spiritual" body of Paul, which lies behind all such phenomena—that body which is loose with all of us in sleep, but only exceptionally in waking hours. Once we fully understand the existence of that deathless etheric body, merged in our own but occasionally de-tachable, we have mastered many a problem and solved many a ghost story.

However, I must get back to my Cretan lecture. The bishop was interested, and I lent him one of the Rev. Charles Tweedale's pamphlets next day, which shows how sadly Christianity has wandered away from its early faith of spiritual gifts and Communion of Saints. Both have now become words instead of things, save among our ranks. The bishop is a good fellow, red and rough like a Boer farmer, but healthy, breezy, and Apostolic. "Do mention his kind grey eyes," says my wife. He may die a martyr yet in that inland diocese of China—and he would not shrink from it. Meanwhile, apart from his dogma, which must be desperately difficult to explain to an educated Chinaman, he must always be a centre of civilisation and social effort. A splendid fellow—but he suffers from what all bishops and all cardinals and all Popes suffer from, and that is superannuation. A physiologist has said that few men can ever entertain a new idea after fifty. How then can any church progress when all its leaders are over that age? This is why Christianity has stagnated and degenerated. If here and there one had a new idea, how could it survive the pressure of the others? It is hopeless. In this particular question of psychic religion the whole order is an inversion, for the people are ahead of the clergy and the clergy of the bishops. But when the laymen lead strongly enough the others will follow unless they wish to see the whole Church organisation dissolve.

He was very interesting upon the state of Christianity in China. Protestantism, thanks to the joint British and American Missions, is gaining upon Roman Catholicism, and has now far outstripped it, but the Roman Catholic organisations are very wealthy on account of ancient valuable concessions and well-invested funds. In case of a Bolshevist movement that may be a source of danger, as it gives a reason for attack. The Bishop made the very striking remark that if the whites cleared right out of China all the Christian Churches of divers creeds would within a generation merge into one creed. "What have we to do," they say, "with these old historical quarrels which are hardly intelligible to us? We are all followers of Christ, and that is enough." Truly, the converted seem far ahead of those who converted them. It is the priesthoods, the organisations, the funds and the vested interests which prevent the Churches from being united. In the meanwhile ninety per cent. of our population shows what it thinks by never entering into a church at all. Personally, I can never remember since I reached manhood feeling myself the better for having gone into one. And yet I have been an earnest seeker for truth. Verily, there is something deep down which is rotten. It is want of fact, want of reality, words instead of things. Only last Sunday I shuddered as I listened to the hymns, and it amazed me to look around and see the composed faces of those who were singing them. Do they think what they are saying, or does Faith atrophy some part of the brain? We are "born through water and blood into the true church." We drink precious blood. "He hath broken the teeth in their jaw." Can such phrases really mean anything to any thoughtful man? If not, why continue them? You will have your churches empty while you do. People will not argue about it—they will, and do, simply stay away. And the clergy go on stating and re-stating incredible unproved things, while neglecting and railing at those which could be proved and believed. On our lines those nine out of ten could be forced back to a reconsideration of their position, even though that position would not square with all the doctrines of present-day Christianity, which would, I think, have offended the early Christians as much as it does the earnest thinkers of to-day.

Port Said came at last, and we entered the Suez Canal. It is a shocking thing that the entrance to this, one of the most magnificent of the works of man, are flanked by great sky advertisements of various brands of whisky. The sale of whisky may or may not be a tolerable thing, but its flaunting advertisements, Dewar, Johnny Walker, and the rest, have surely long been intolerable. If anything would make me a total prohibitionist those would. They are shameless. I do not know if some middle way could be found by which light alcoholic drinks could remain—so light that drunkenness would be hardly possible—but if this cannot be done, then let us follow the noble example of America. It is indeed shameful to see at the very point of the world where some noble sentiment might best be expressed these huge reminders of that which has led to so much misery and crime. To a Frenchman it must seem even worse than to us, while what the abstemious Mohammedan can think is beyond my imagination. In that direction at least the religion of Mohammed has done better than that of Christ. If all those Esquimaux, South Sea Islanders and others who have been converted to Christianity and then debauched by drink, had followed the prophet instead, it cannot be denied that their development would have been a happier and a higher one, though the cast-iron doctrines and dogmas of the Moslem have dangers of their own.

Has France ever had the credit she deserves for the splendid faith with which she followed that great beneficent genius Lesseps in his wonderful work? It is beautiful from end to end, French in its neatness, its order, its exquisite finish. Truly the opposition of our people, both experts and public, was a disgrace to us, though it sinks into insignificance when compared with our colossal national stupidity over the Channel tunnel. When our descendants compute the sums spent in shipping and transhipping in the great war, the waste of merchant ships and convoys, the sufferings of the wounded, the delay in reinforcements, the dependence upon the weather, they will agree that our sin had found us out and that we have paid a fitting price for our stupidity. Unhappily, it was not our blind guides who paid it, but it was the soldier and sailor and taxpayer, for the nation always pays collectively for the individual blunder. Would a hundred million pounds cover the cost of that one? Well can I remember how a year before war was declared, seeing clearly what was coming, I sent three memoranda to the Naval and Military authorities and to the Imperial Council of Defence pointing out exactly what the situation would be, and especially the danger to our transports. It is admitted now that it was only the strange inaction of the German light forces, and especially their want of comprehension of the possibilities of the submarine, which enabled our Expeditionary Force to get across at all, so that we might have lost the war within the first month. But as to my poor memoranda, which proved so terribly correct, I might as well have dropped them into my own wastepaper basket instead of theirs, and so saved the postage. My only convert was Captain, now General, Swinton, part inventor of the tanks, who acted as Secretary to the Imperial Defence Committee, and who told me at the time that my paper had set him thinking furiously.

Which leads my thoughts to the question of the torpedoing of merchant vessels by submarines. So sure was I that the Germans would do this, that after knocking at official doors in vain, I published a sketch called "Danger," which was written a year before the war, and depicted all that afterwards occurred, even down to such small details as the ships zig-zagging up Channel to escape, and the submarines using their guns to save torpedoes. I felt as if, like Solomon Eagle, I could have marched down Fleet Street with a brazier on my head if I could only call people's attention to the coming danger. I saw naval officers on the point, but they were strangely blind, as is shown by the comments printed at the end of "Danger," which give the opinions of several admirals pooh-poohing my fears. Among others I saw Captain Beatty, as he then was, and found him alive to the possible danger, though he did not suggest a remedy. His quiet, brisk personality impressed me, and I felt that our national brain-errors might perhaps be made good in the end by the grit that is in us. But how hard were our tasks from our want of foresight. Admiral Von Capelle did me the honour to say during the war, in the German Reichstag, that I was the only man who had prophesied the conditions of the great naval war. As a matter of fact, both Fisher and Scott had done so, though they had not given it to the public in the same detail— but nothing had been done. We know now that there was not a single harbour proof against submarines on our whole East Coast. Truly the hand of the Lord was over England. Nothing less could have saved her.

We tied up to the bank soon after entering the Canal, and lay there most of the night while a procession of great ships moving northwards swept silently past us in the ring of vivid light cast by their search-lights and our own. I stayed on deck most of the night to watch them. The silence was impressive—those huge structures sweeping past with only the slow beat of their propellers and the wash of their bow wave on either side. No sooner had one of these great shapes slid past than, looking down the Canal, one saw the brilliant head light of another in the distance. They are only allowed to go at the slowest pace, so that their wash may not wear away the banks. Finally, the last had passed, and we were ourselves able to cast off our warps and push southwards. I remained on deck see-ing the sun rise over the Eastern desert, and then a wonderful slow-moving panorama of Egypt as the bank slid slowly past us. First desert, then green oases, then the long line of rude fortifications from Kantara down-wards, with the camp fires smoking, groups of early busy Tommies and endless dumps of stores. Here and to the south was the point where the Turks with their German leaders attempted the invasion of Egypt, car-rying flat-bottomed boats to ford the Canal. How they were ever allowed to get so far is barely compre-hensible, but how they were ever permitted to get back again across one hundred miles of desert in the face of our cavalry and camelry is altogether beyond me. Even their guns got back untaken. They dropped a number of mines in the Canal, but with true Turkish slovenliness they left on the banks at each point the long bamboos on which they had carried them across the desert, which considerably lessened the work of those who had to sweep them up. The sympathies of the Egyptians seem to have been against us, and yet they have no desire to pass again under the rule of the Turk. Our dominion has had the effect of turning a very poor country into a very rich one, and of securing some sort of justice for the fellah or peasant, but since we get no gratitude and have no trade preference it is a little difficult to see how we are the better for all our labours. So long as the Canal is secure—and it is no one's interest to injure it—we should be better if the country governed itself. We have too many commitments, and if we have to take new ones, such as Mesopotamia, it would be well to get rid of some of the others where our task is reasonably complete. "We never let the youngsters grow up," said a friendly critic. There is, however, I admit, another side to the question, and the idea of permitting a healthy moral place like Port Said to relapse into the hotbed of gambling and syphilis which it used to be, is repugnant to the mind. Which is better—that a race be free, immoral and incompetent, or that it be forced into morality and prosperity? That question meets us at every turn.

The children have been delighted by the fish on the surface of the Canal. Their idea seems to be that the one aim and object of our excursion is to see sharks in the sea and snakes in Australia. We did actually see a shark half ashore upon a sandbank in one of the lower lakes near Suez. It was lashing about with a frantic tail, and so got itself off into deep water. To the west all day we see the very wild and barren country through which our ancestors used to drive upon the overland route when they travelled by land from Cairo to Suez. The smoke of a tiny mail-train marks the general line of that most desolate road. In the evening we were through the Canal and marked the rugged shore upon our left down which the Israelites pursued their way in the direction of Sinai. One wonders how much truth there is in the narrative. On the one hand it is impossible to doubt that something of the sort did occur. On the other, the impossibility of so huge a crowd living on the rare wells of the desert is manifest. But numbers are not the strong point of an Oriental historian. Perhaps a thousand or two may have followed their great leader upon that perilous journey. I have heard that Moses either on his own or through his wife was in touch with Babylonian habits. This would explain those tablets of stone, or of inscribed clay burned into brick which we receive as the Ten Commandments, and which only differ from the moral precepts of other races in the strange limitations and omissions. At least ten new ones have long been needed to include drunkenness, gluttony, pride, envy, bigotry, lying and the rest.

The weather grows hotter and hotter, so that one aged steward who has done 100 voyages declares it to be unique. One passenger has died. Several stewards have collapsed. The wind still keeps behind us. In the midst of all this I had an extensively signed petition from the second class passengers that I should address them. I did so, and spoke on deck for forty minutes to a very attentive audience which included many of the officers of the ship. I hope I got my points across to them. I was a sad example of sweated labour when I had finished. My wife tells me that the people were impressed. As I am never aware of the presence of any individual when I am speaking on this subject I rely upon my wife's very quick and accurate feminine impressions. She sits always beside me, notes everything, gives me her sympathetic atmosphere which is of such psychic importance, and finally reports the result. If any point of mine seems to her to miss its mark I unhesitatingly take it out. It interests me to hear her tell of the half-concealed sneer with which men listen to me, and how it turns into interest, bewilderment and finally something like reverence and awe as their brain gradually realises the proved truth of what I am saying, which upsets the whole philosophy on which their lives are built.

There are several Australian officers on board who are coming from the Russian front full of dreadful stories of Bolshevist atrocities, seen with their own eyes. The executioners were Letts and Chinese, and the instigators renegade Jews, so that the Russians proper seem to have been the more or less innocent dupes. They had dreadful photographs of tortured and mutilated men as corroboration. Surely hell, the place of punishment and purgatorial expiation, is actually upon this earth in such cases. One leader seems to have been a Sadic madman, for after torturing his victims till even the Chinese executioners struck, he would sit playing a violin very exquisitely while he gloated over their agonies. All these Australian boys agree that the matter will burn itself out, and that it will end in an immense massacre of Jews which may involve the whole seven millions now in Russia. God forbid, but the outlook is ominous! I remember a prophecy which I read early in the war that a great figure would arise in the north and have power for six years. If Lenin was the great figure then he has, according to the prophet, about two years more to run. But prophecy is fitful, dangerous work. The way in which the founders of the Christian faith all foretold the imminent end of the world is an example. What they dimly saw was no doubt the destruction of Jerusalem, which seems to have been equally clear to Ezekiel 600 years before, for his picture of cannibalism and dispersion is very exact.

It is wonderful what chances of gaining direct information one has aboard a ship of this sort, with its mixed crowd of passengers, many of them famous in their own lines. I have already alluded to the officers returning from Russia with their prophecies of evil. But there are many other folk with tales of deep interest. There is a Mr. Covell, a solid practical Briton, who may prove to be a great pioneer, for he has made farming pay handsomely in the very heart of the Indian plains. Within a hundred miles of Lucknow he has founded the townlet of Covellpore, where he handles 3,000 acres of wheat and cotton with the aid of about the same number of natives. This is the most practical step I have ever heard of for forming a real indigenous white population in India. His son was with him, going out to carry on the work. Mr. Covell holds that the irrigation of the North West of India is one of the greatest wonders of the world, and Jacob the engineer responsible. I had never heard of him nor, I am ashamed to say, had I heard of Sir Leonard Rogers, who is one of those great men like Sir Ronald Ross, whom the Indian Medical Service throws up. Rogers has reduced the mortality of cholera by intravenous in-

jections of hypertonic saline until it is only 15 per cent.
General Maude, I am informed, would almost certainly
have been saved, had it not been that some false depart-
mental economy had withheld the necessary apparatus.
Leprosy also seems in a fair way to yielding to Rogers'
genius for investigation.

It is sad to hear that this same Indian Medical Service which has produced such giants as Fayrer, Ross,
and Rogers is in a fair way to absolute ruin, because
the conditions are such that good white candidates will
no longer enter it. White doctors do not mind working
with, or even under, natives who have passed the same
British examinations as themselves, but they bar the
native doctor who has got through a native college in
India, and is on a far lower educational level than themselves. To serve under such a man is an impossible
inversion. This is appreciated by the medical authorities at home, the word is given to the students, and the
best men avoid the service. So unless a change is made,
the end is in sight of the grand old service which has
given so much to humanity.

Aden is remarkable only for the huge water tanks
cut to catch rain, and carved out of solid rock. A
whole captive people must have been set to work on so
colossal a task, and one wonders where the poor
wretches got water themselves the while. Their work
is as fresh and efficient as when they left it. No doubt
it was for the watering, not of the population, but of
the Egyptian and other galleys on their way to Punt
and King Solomon's mines. It must be a weary life
for our garrison in such a place. There is strange

fishing, sea snakes, parrot fish and the like. It is their only relaxation, for it is desert all round.

Monsoon and swell and drifting rain in the Indian Ocean. We heard that "thresh of the deep sea rain," of which Kipling sings. Then at last in the early morning the long quay of Bombay, and the wonderful crowd of men of every race who await an incoming steamer. Here at least half our passengers were disgorged, young subalterns, grey colonels, grave administrators, yellow-faced planters, all the fuel which is grown in Britain and consumed in the roaring furnace of India. So devoted to their work, so unthanked and uncomprehended by those for whom they work! They are indeed a splendid set of men, and if they withdrew I wonder how long it would be before the wild men of the frontier would be in Calcutta and Bombay, as the Picts and Scots flowed over Britain when the Roman legions were withdrawn. What view will the coming Labour governments of Britain take of our Imperial commitments? Upon that will depend the future history of great tracts of the globe which might very easily relapse into barbarism.

The ship seemed lonely when our Indian friends were gone, for indeed, the pick of the company went with them. Several pleased me by assuring me as they left that their views of life had been changed since they came on board the "Naldera." To many I gave reading lists that they might look further into the matter for themselves. A little leaven in the great lump, but how can we help leavening it all when we know that, unlike other creeds, no true Spiritualist can ever revert, so that while we continually gain, we never lose. One hears of the converts to various sects, but one does not hear of those who are driven out by their narrow, intolerant doctrines. You can change your mind about faiths, but not about facts, and hence our certain conquest.

One cannot spend even a single long day in India without carrying away a wonderful impression of the gentle dignity of the Indian people. Our motor drivers were extraordinarily intelligent and polite, and all we met gave the same impression.

India may be held by the sword, but it is certainly kept very carefully in the scabbard, for we hardly saw a soldier in the streets of this, its greatest city. I observed some splendid types of manhood, however, among the native police. We lunched at the Taj Mahal Hotel, and got back tired and full of mixed impressions.

Verily the ingenuity of children is wonderful. They have turned their active minds upon the problem of paper currency with fearsome results. Baby writes cheques in quaint ways upon odd bits of paper and brings them to me to be cashed. Malcolm, once known as Dimples, has made a series of pound and five pound notes of his own. The bank they call the money shop. I can trace every sort of atavism, the arboreal, the cave dweller, the adventurous raider, and the tribal instinct in the child, but this development seems a little premature.

Sunday once more and the good Bishop preaching. I wonder more and more what an educated Chinaman would make of such doctrines. To take an example, he has quoted to-day with great approval, the action of Peter in discarding the rite of circumcision as a proof

[49]

of election. That marked, according to the Bishop, the broad comprehensive mind which could not confine the mercies of God to any limited class. And yet when I take up the œcumenical pronouncement from the congress of Anglican bishops which he has just attended, I find that baptism is made the test, even as the Jews made circumcision. Have the bishops not learned that there are millions who revere the memory of Christ, whether they look upon Him as God or man, but who think that baptism is a senseless survival of heathendom, like so many of our religious observances? The idea that the Being who made the milky way can be either placated or incensed by pouring a splash of water over child or adult is an offence to reason, and a slur upon the Divinity.

Two weary days upon the sea with drifting rain showers and wonderful scarlet and green sunsets. Have beguiled the time with W. B. Maxwell's "Lamp and the Mirror." I have long thought that Maxwell was the greatest of British novelists, and this book confirms me in my opinion. Who else could have drawn such fine detail and yet so broad and philosophic a picture? There may have been single books which were better than Maxwell's best—the "Garden of Allah," with its gorgeous oriental colour, would, for example, make a bid for first place, but which of us has so splendid a list of first class serious works as "Mrs. Thompson," "The Rest Cure," "Vivian," "In Cotton Wool," above all, "The Guarded Flame"—classics, every one. Our order of merit will come out very differently in a generation or so to what it stands now, and I shall expect to find my nominee at the top. But

after all, what's the odds? You do your work as well
as you can. You pass. You find other work to do.
How the old work compares with the other fellow's
work can be a matter of small concern.

In Colombo harbour lay H.M.S. "Highflyer," which
we looked upon with the reverence which everybody
and everything which did well in the war deserve from
us—a saucy, rakish, speedy craft. Several other steamers were flying the yellow quarantine flag, but our
captain confided to me that it was a recognised way of
saying "no visitors," and did not necessarily bear any
pathological meaning. As we had nearly two days before we resumed our voyage I was able to give all
our party a long stretch on shore, finally staying with
my wife for the night at the Galle Face Hotel, a place
where the preposterous charges are partly compensated
for by the glorious rollers which break upon the beach
outside. I was interested in the afternoon by a native
conjurer giving us what was practically a private performance of the mango-tree trick. He did it so admirably that I can well understand those who think that
it is an occult process. I watched the man narrowly,
and believe that I solved the little mystery, though even
now I cannot be sure. In doing it he began by laying
several objects out in a casual way while hunting in
his bag for his mango seed. These were small odds
and ends including a little rag doll, very rudely fash-
ioned, about six or eight inches long. One got accus-
tomed to the presence of these things and ceased to
remark them. He showed the seed and passed it for
examination, a sort of large Brazil nut. He then laid
it among some loose earth, poured some water on it,

covered it with a handkerchief, and crooned over it. In about a minute he exhibited the same, or another seed, the capsule burst, and a light green leaf protruding. I took it in my hands, and it was certainly a real bursting mango seed, but clearly it had been palmed and substituted for the other. He then buried it again and kept raising the handkerchief upon his own side, and scrabbling about with his long brown fingers underneath its cover. Then he suddenly whisked off the handkerchief and there was the plant, a foot or so high, with thick foliage and blossoms, its root well planted in the earth. It was certainly very startling.

My explanation is that by a miracle of packing the whole of the plant had been compressed into the rag doll, or little cloth cylinder already mentioned. The scrabbling of the hands under the cloth was to smooth out the leaves after it was freed from this covering. I observed that the leaves were still rather crumpled, and that there were dark specks of fungi which would not be there if the plant were straight from nature's manufactory. But it was wonderfully done when you consider that the man was squatting in our midst, we standing in a semi-circle around him, with no adventitious aid whatever. I do not believe that the famous Mr. Maskeleyne or any of those otherwise conjurers who are good enough occasionally to put Lodge, Crookes and Lombroso in their places, could have wrought a better illusion.

The fellow had a cobra with him which he challenged me to pick up. I did so and gazed into its strange eyes, which some devilry of man's had turned to a lapis lazuli blue. The juggler said it was the result of its skin-sloughing, but I have my doubts. The poison bag had, I suppose, been extracted, but the man seemed nervous and slipped his brown hand between my own and the swaying venomous head with its peculiar flattened hood. It is a fearsome beast, and I can realise what was told me by a lover of animals that the snake was the one creature from which he could get no return of affection. I remember that I once had three in my employ when the "Speckled Band" was produced in London, fine, lively rock pythons, and yet in spite of this profusion of realism I had the experience of reading a review which, after duly slating the play, wound up with the scathing sentence, "The performance ended with the production of a palpably artificial serpent." Such is the reward of virtue. Afterwards when the necessities of several travelling companies compelled us to use dummy snakes we produced a much more realistic effect. The real article either hung down like a pudgy yellow bell rope, or else when his tail was pinched, endeavoured to squirm back and get level with the stage carpenter, who pinched him, which was not in the plot. The latter individual had no doubts at all as to the dummy being an improvement upon the real.

Never, save on the west coast of Africa, have I seen "the league-long roller thundering on the shore," as here, where the Indian Ocean with its thousand leagues of momentum hits the western coast of Ceylon. It looks smooth out at sea, and then you are surprised to observe that a good-sized boat had suddenly vanished. Then it scoops upwards once more on the smooth arch of the billow, disappearing on the further slope. The native catamarans are almost invisible, so that you see a row of standing figures from time to time on the crest of the waves. I cannot think that any craft in the world would come through rough water as these catamarans with their long outriggers can do. Man has made few more simple and more effective inventions, and if I were a younger man I would endeavour to introduce them to Brighton beach, as once I introduced ski to Switzerland, or auto-wheels to the British roads. I have other work to do now, but why does not some sportsman take the model, have it made in England, and then give an exhibition in a gale of wind on the south coast. It would teach our fishermen some possibilities of which they are ignorant.

As I stood in a sandy cove one of them came flying in, a group of natives rushing out and pulling it up on the beach. The craft consists only of two planks edgewise and lengthwise. In the nine-inch slit between them lay a number of great twelve-pound fish, like cod, and tied to the side of the boat was a ten-foot swordfish. To catch that creature while standing on a couple of floating planks must have been sport indeed, and yet the craft is so ingenious that to a man who can at a pinch swim for it, there is very small element of danger. The really great men of our race, the inventor of the wheel, the inventor of the lever, the inventor of the catamaran are all lost in the mists of the past, but ethnologists have found that the cubic capacity of the neolithic brain is as great as our own.

There are two robbers' castles, as the unhappy visitor calls them, facing the glorious sea, the one Galle Face, the other the Mount Lavinia Hotel. They are con-

nected by an eight-mile road, which has all the colour
and life and variety of the East for every inch of the
way. In that glorious sun, under the blue arch of such
a sky, and with the tropical trees and flowers around,
the poverty of these people is very different from the
poverty of a London slum. Is there in all God's world
such a life as that, and can it really be God's world
while we suffer it to exist! Surely, it is a palpable
truth that no one has a right to luxuries until every one
has been provided with necessities, and among such
necessities a decent environment is the first. If we had
spent money to fight slumland as we spent it to fight
Germany, what a different England it would be. The
world moves all the same, and we have eternity before
us. But some folk need it.

A doctor came up to me in the hotel and told me that
he was practising there, and had come recently from
England. He had lost his son in the war, and had
himself become unsettled. Being a Spiritualist he
went to Mrs. Brittain, the medium, who told him that
his boy had a message for him which was that he
would do very well in Colombo. He had himself
thought of Ceylon, but Mrs. B. had no means of know-
ing that. He had obeyed the advice thus given, and
was glad that he had done so. How much people may
miss by cutting themselves away from these ministers
of grace! In all this opposition to Spiritualism the
punishment continually fits the crime.

Once again we shed passengers and proceeded in
chastened mood with empty decks where once it was
hard to move. Among others, good Bishop Banister of
Kwang-si had gone. I care little for his sacramental

and vicarious doctrines, but I am very sure that wherever his robust, kindly, sincere personality may dwell is bound to be a centre of the true missionary effort—the effort which makes for the real original teaching of his Master, submission to God and goodwill to our fellow-men.

Now we are on the last lap with nothing but a clear stretch of salt water between our prow and West Australia. Our mission from being a sort of dream takes concrete form and involves definite plans. Meanwhile we plough our way through a deep blue sea with the wind continually against us. I have not seen really calm water since we left the Canal. We carry on with the usual routine of ship sports, which include an England and Australia cricket match, in which I have the honour of captaining England, a proper ending for a long if mediocre career as a cricketer. We lost by one run, which was not bad considering our limited numbers.

Posers of all sorts are brought to me by thoughtful inquirers, which I answer when I can. Often I can't. One which is a most reasonable objection has given me a day's thought. If, as is certain, we can remember in our next life the more important incidents of this one, why is it that in this one we can remember nothing of that previous spiritual career, which must have existed since nothing can be born in time for eternity. Our friends on the other side cannot help us there, nor can even such extended spiritual visions as those of Vale Owen clear it up. On the whole we must admit that our Theosophical friends, with whom we quarrel for their absence of evidence, have the best attempt at an explanation. I imagine that man's soul has a cycle which is complete in itself, and all of which is continuous and self conscious. This begins with earth life. Then at last a point is reached, it may be a reincarnation, and a new cycle is commenced, the old one being closed to our memory until we have reached some lofty height in our further journey. Pure speculation, I admit, but it would cover what we know and give us a working hypothesis. I can never excite myself much about the reincarnation idea, for if it be so, it occurs seldom, and at long intervals, with ten years spent in the other spheres for one spent here, so that even admitting all that is said by its supporters it is not of such great importance. At the present rate of change this world will be as strange as another sphere by the time we are due to tread the old stage once more. It is only fair to say that though many spiritualists oppose it, there is a strong body, including the whole French Allan Kardec school, who support it. Those who have passed over may well be divided upon the subject since it concerns their far future and is a matter of speculation to them as to us.

Thrasher whales and sperm whales were seen which aroused the old whaling thrill in my heart. It was the more valuable Greenland whale which I helped to catch, while these creatures are those which dear old Frank Bullen, a childlike sailor to the last, described in his "Cruise of the Cachelot." How is it that sailors write such perfect English. There are Bullen and Conrad, both of whom served before the mast—the two purest stylists of their generation. So was Loti in France. There are some essays of Bullen's, especially a description of a calm in the tropics, and again of "Sunrise seen from the Crow's Nest," which have not been matched in our time for perfection of imagery and diction. They are both in his "Idyls of the Sea." If there is compensation in the beyond—and I know that there is—then Frank Bullen is in great peace, for his whole earthly life was one succession of troubles. When I think of his cruel stepmother, his dreadful childhood, his life on a Yankee blood ship, his struggles as a tradesman, his bankruptcy, his sordid worries, and finally, his prolonged ill-health, I marvel at the unequal distribution of such burdens. He was the best singer of a chanty that I have ever heard, and I can hear him now with his rich baritone voice trolling out "Sally Brown" or "Stormalong." May I hear him once again! Our dear ones tell us that there is no great gap between what pleases us here and that which will please us in the beyond. Our own brains, had we ever used them in the matter, should have instructed us that all evolution, spiritual as well as material, must be gradual. Indeed, once one knows psychic truth, one can, reasoning backwards, perceive that we should un-aided have come to the same conclusions, but since we have all been deliberately trained not to use our reason in religious matters, it is no wonder that we have made rather a hash of it. Surely it is clear enough that in the case of an artist the artistic nature is part of the man himself. Therefore, if he survives it must survive. But if it survives it must have means of expression, or it is a senseless thing. But means of expression im-plies appreciation from others and a life on the general lines of this one. So also of the drama, music, science

[58]

and literature, if we carry on they carry on, and they cannot carry on without actual expression and a public to be served.

To the east of us and just beyond the horizon lie the Cocos Islands, where Ross established his strange little kingdom, and where the *Emden* met its end—a glorious one, as every fair minded man must admit. I have seen her stern post since then in the hall of the Federal Parliament at Melbourne, like some fossil monster, once a terror and now for children to gaze at. As to the Cocos Islands, the highest point is, I understand, about twenty feet, and tidal waves are not unknown upon the Pacific, so that the community holds its tenure at very short and sudden notice to quit.

On the morning of September 17th a low coast line appeared upon the port bow—Australia at last. It was the edge of the West Australian State. The evening before a wireless had reached me from the spiritualists of Perth saying that they welcomed us and our message. It was a kind thought and a helpful one. We were hardly moored in the port of Fremantle, which is about ten miles from the capital, when a deputation of these good, kind people was aboard, bearing great bunches of wild flowers, most of which were new to us. Their faces fell when they learned that I must go on in the ship and that there was very little chance of my being able to address them. They are only connected with the other States by one long thin railway line, 1,200 miles long, with scanty trains which were already engaged, so that unless we stuck to the ship we should have to pass ten days or so before we could

[59]

resume our journey. This argument was unanswerable, and so the idea of a meeting was given up.

These kind people had two motors in attendance, which must, I fear, have been a strain upon their resources, for as in the old days the true believers and practical workers are drawn from the poor and humble. However, they certainly treated us royally, and even the children were packed into the motors. We skirted the Swan River, passed through the very beautiful public park, and, finally, lunched at the busy town, where Bone's store would cut a respectable figure in London, with its many departments and its roof restaurant. It was surprising after our memories of England to note how good and abundant was the food. It is a charming little town, and it was strange, after viewing its settled order, to see the mill where the early settlers not so very long ago had to fight for their lives with the black fellows. Those poor black fellows! Their fate is a dark stain upon Australia. And yet it must in justice to our settlers be admitted that the question was a very difficult one. Was colonisation to be abandoned, or were these brave savages to be overcome? That was really the issue. When they speared the cattle of the settlers what were the settlers to do? Of course, if a reservation could have been opened up, as in the case of the Maoris, that would have been ideal. But the noble Maori is a man with whom one could treat on equal terms and he belonged to a solid race. The Aborigines of Australia were broken wandering tribes, each at war with its neighbours. In a single reservation they would have exterminated each other. It was a piteous tragedy, and yet, even now in retrospect, how difficult it is to point out what could have been done.

The Spiritualists of Perth seem to be a small body, but as earnest as their fellows elsewhere. A masterful looking lady, Mrs. McIlwraith, rules them, and seems fit for the part. They have several mediums developing, but I had no chance of testing their powers. Altogether our encounter with them cheered us on our way. We had the first taste of Australian labour conditions at Fremantle, for the men knocked off at the given hour, refusing to work overtime, with the result that we carried a consignment of tea, meant for their own tea-pots, another thousand miles to Adelaide, and so back by train which must have been paid for out of their own pockets and those of their fellow citizens. Verily, you cannot get past the golden rule, and any breach of it brings its own punishment somehow, somewhere, be the sinner a master or a man.

And now we had to cross the dreaded Bight, where the great waves from the southern ice come rolling up, but our luck was still in, and we went through it without a qualm. Up to Albany one sees the barren irregular coast, and then there were two days of blue water, which brought us at last to Adelaide, our port of debarkation. The hour and the place at last!

CHAPTER III

I was welcomed to Australia by a hospitable letter
from the Premier, Mr. Hughes, who assured me that
he would do what he could to make our visit a pleasant
one, and added, "I hope you will see Australia as it is,
for I want you to tell the world about us. We are a
very young country; we have a very big and very
rich heritage, and the great war has made us realise
that we are Australians, proud to belong to the Empire,
but proud too of our own country."

Apart from Mr. Hughes's kind message, my chief
welcome to the new land came from Sydney, and took
the queer form of two independent challenges to public
debate, one from the Christian Evidence Society, and
the other from the local leader of the Materialists. As
the two positions are mutually destructive, one felt inclined to tell them to fight it out between themselves
and that I would fight the winner. The Christian Evidence Society, is, of course, out of the question, since
they regard a text as an argument, which I can only

accept with many qualifications, so that there is no common basis. The materialist is a more worthy antagonist, for though he is often as bigoted and inaccessible to reason as the worst type of Christian, there is always a leaven of honest, open-minded doubters on whom a debate might make an impression. A debate with them, as I experienced when I met Mr. MacCabe, can only follow one line, they quoting all the real or alleged scandals which have ever been connected with the lowest forms of mediumship, and claiming that the whole cult is comprised therein, to which you counter with your own personal experiences, and with the evidence of the cloud of witnesses who have found the deepest comfort and enlarged knowledge. It is like two boxers each hitting the air, and both returning to their respective corners amid the plaudits of their backers, while the general public is none the better.

Three correspondents headed me off on the ship, and as I gave each of them a long separate interview, I was a tired man before I got ashore. Mr. Carlyle Smythe, my impresario, had also arrived, a small alert competent gentleman, with whom I at once got on pleasant terms, which were never once clouded during our long travels together upon our tour. I was fortunate indeed to have so useful and so entertaining a companion, a musician, a scholar, and a man of many varied experiences. With his help we soon got our stuff through the customs, and made the short train journey which separates the Port of Adelaide from the charming city of that name. By one o'clock we were safely housed in the Grand Central Hotel, with windows in place of port holes, and the roar of the trams to take the place of the murmurs of the great ocean.

The good genius of Adelaide was a figure, already almost legendary, one Colonel Light, who played the part of Romulus and Remus to the infant city. Somewhere in the thirties of last century he chose the site, against strong opposition, and laid out the plan with such skill that in all British and American lands I have seen few such cities, so pretty, so orderly and so self-sufficing. When one sees all the amenities of the place, botanical gardens, zoological gardens, art gallery, museum, university, public library and the rest, it is hard to realise that the whole population is still under three hundred thousand. I do not know whether the press sets the tone to the community or the community to the press, but in any case Adelaide is greatly blessed in this respect, for its two chief papers, the *Register* and the *Advertiser,* under Sir William Sowden and Sir Langdon Bonython respectively, are really excellent, with a world-wide Metropolitan tone.

Their articles upon the subject in which I am particularly interested, though by no means one-sided, were at least informed with knowledge and breadth of mind.

In Adelaide I appreciated, for the first time, the crisis which Australia has been passing through in the shape of a two-years' drought, only recently broken. It seems to have involved all the States and to have caused great losses, amounting to millions of sheep and cattle. The result was that the price of those cattle which survived has risen enormously, and at the time of our visit an absolute record had been established, a bullock having been sold for £41. The normal price would be about

Photo: Stirling, Melbourne.

THE WANDERERS, 1920-21.

£13. Sheep were about £3 each, the normal being fifteen shillings. This had, of course, sent the price of meat soaring with the usual popular unrest and agitation as a result. It was clear, however, that with the heavy rains the prices would fall. These Australian droughts are really terrible things, especially when they come upon newly-opened country and in the hotter regions of Queensland and the North. One lady told us that she had endured a drought in Queensland which lasted so long that children of five had never seen a drop of rain. You could travel a hundred miles and find the brown earth the whole way, with no sign of green anywhere, the sheep eating twigs or gnawing bark until they died. Her brother sold his surviving sheep for one shilling each, and when the drought broke had to restock at 50s. a head. This is a common experience, and all but the man with savings have to take to some subordinate work, ruined men. No doubt, with afforestation, artesian wells, irrigation and water storage things may be modified, but all these things need capital, and capital in these days is hard to seek, nor can it be expected that capitalists will pour their money into States which have wild politicians who talk lightly of past obligations. You cannot tell the investor that he is a bloated incubus one moment, and go hat in hand for further incubation the next. I fear that this grand country as a whole may suffer from the wild ideas of some of its representatives. But under it all lies the solid self-respecting British stuff, which will never repudiate a just debt, however heavily it may press. Australians may groan under the burden, but they should remember that for every pound of taxation they carry the home Briton carries nearly three.

But to return for a moment to the droughts; has any writer of fiction invented or described a more long-drawn agony than that of the man, his nerves the more tired and sensitive from the constant unbroken heat, waiting day after day for the cloud that never comes, while under the glaring sun from the unchanging blue above him, his sheep, which represent all his life's work and his hopes, perish before his eyes? A revolver shot has often ended the long vigil and the pioneer has joined his vanished flocks. I have just come in contact with a case where two young returned soldiers, demobilised from the war and planted on the land, had forty-two cattle given them by the State to stock their little farm. Not a drop of water fell for over a year, the feed failed, and these two warriors of Palestine and Flanders wept at their own helplessness while their little herd died before their eyes. Such are the trials which the Australian farmer has to bear.

While waiting for my first lecture I do what I can to understand the country and its problems. To this end I visited the vineyards and wine plant of a local firm which possesses every factor for success, save the capacity to answer letters. The originator started grape culture as a private hobby about 60 years ago, and now such an industry has risen that this firm alone has £700,000 sunk in the business, and yet it is only one of several. The product can be most excellent, but little or any ever reaches Europe, for it cannot overtake the local demand. The quality was good and purer than the corresponding wines in Europe—especially the champagnes, which seem to be devoid of that poison, whatever it may be, which has for a symptom a dry tongue with internal acidity, driving elderly gentlemen to whisky and soda. The Australian product, taken in moderate doses, seems to have no poisonous quality, and is without that lime-like dryness which appears to be the cause of it. If temperance reform takes the sane course of insisting upon a lowering of the alcohol in our drinks, so that one may be surfeited before one could be drunken, then this question of good mild wines will bulk very largely in the future, and Australia may supply one of the answers. With all my sympathy for the reformers I feel that wine is so useful a social agent that we should not abolish it until we are certain that there is no *via media*. The most pregnant argument upon the subject was the cartoon which showed the husband saying "My dear, it is the anniversary of our wedding. Let us have a second bottle of ginger beer."

We went over the vineyards, ourselves mildly interested in the vines, and the children wildly excited over the possibility of concealed snakes. Then we did the vats and the cellars with their countless bottles. We were taught the secrets of fermentation, how the wonderful Pasteur had discovered that the best and quickest was produced not by the grape itself, as of old, but by the scraped bloom of the grape inserted in the bottle. After viewing the number of times a bottle must be turned, a hundred at least, and the complex processes which lead up to the finished article, I will pay my wine bills in future with a better grace. The place was all polished wood and shining brass, like the fittings of a man-of-war, and a great impression of cleanliness and efficiency was left upon our minds. We only know the Australian wines at present by the rough articles sold in flasks, but when the supply has increased the world will learn that this country has some very different stuff in its cellars, and will try to transport it to their tables.

We had a small meeting of Spiritualists in our hotel sitting-room, under the direction of Mr. Victor Cromer, a local student of the occult, who seems to have considerable psychic power. He has a small circle for psychic development which is on new lines, for the neophytes who are learning clairvoyance sit around in a circle in silence, while Mr. Cromer endeavours by mental effort to build up the thought form of some object, say a tree, in the centre of the room. After a time he asks each of the circle what he or she can see, and has many correct answers. With colours in the same way he can convey impressions to his pupils. It is clear that telepathy is not excluded as an explanation, but the actual effect upon the participants is, according to their own account, visual rather than mental. We had an interesting sitting with a number of these developing mediums present, and much information was given, but little of it could be said to be truly evidential. After seeing such clairvoyance as that of Mr. Tom Tyrell or others at home, when a dozen names and addresses will be given together with the descriptions of those who once owned them, one is spoiled for any lesser display.

There was one man whom I had particularly determined to meet when I came to Australia. This was

THE WANDERINGS OF A SPIRITUALIST

Mr. T. P. Bellchambers, about whom I had read an article in some magazine which showed that he was a sort of humble Jeffries or Thoreau, more lonely than the former, less learned than the latter, who lived among the wild creatures in the back country, and was on such terms with our humble brothers as few men are ever privileged to attain. I had read how the eagle with the broken wing had come to him for succour, and how little birds would sit on the edge of his panni-kin while he drank. Him at all cost would we see. Like the proverbial prophet, no one I met had ever heard of him, but on the third day of our residence there came a journalist bearing with him a rudely dressed, tangle-haired man, collarless and unkempt, with kind, irregular features and clear blue eyes—the eyes of a child. It was the man himself. "He brought me," said he, nodding towards the journalist. "He had to, for I always get bushed in a town."

This rude figure fingering his frayed cap was clearly out of his true picture, and we should have to visit him in his own little clearing to see him as he really was. Meanwhile I wondered whether one who was so near nature might know something of nature's more occult secrets. The dialogue ran like this:

"You who are so near nature must have psychic experiences."

"What's psychic? I live so much in the wild that I don't know much."

"I expect you know plenty we don't know. But I meant spiritual."

"Supernatural?"

"Well, we think it is natural but little understood."

[69]

"You mean fairies and things?"

"Yes, and the dead."

"Well, I guess our fairies would be black fairies."

"Why not?"

"Well, I never saw any."

"I hoped you might."

"No, but I know one thing. The night my mother died I woke to find her hand upon my brow. Oh, there's no doubt. Her hand was heavy on my brow."

"At the time?"

"Yes, at the very hour."

"Well, that was good."

"Animals know more about such things."

"Yes."

"They see something. My dog gets terrified when I see nothing, and there's a place in the bush where my horse shies and sweats, he does, but there's nothing to see."

"Something evil has been done there. I've known many cases."

"I expect that's it."

So ran our dialogue. At the end of it he took a cigar, lighted it at the wrong end, and took himself with his strong simple backwoods atmosphere out of the room. Assuredly I must follow him to the wilds.

Now came the night of my first lecture. It was in the city hall, and every seat was occupied. It was a really magnificent audience of two thousand people, the most representative of the town. I am an embarrassed and an interested witness, so let me for this occasion quote the sympathetic, not to say flattering account of the *Register*.

THE WANDERINGS OF A SPIRITUALIST

"There could not have been a more impressive set of circumstances than those which attended the first Australian lecture by Sir Arthur Conan Doyle at the Adelaide Town Hall on Saturday night, September 25th. The audience, large, representative and thoughtful, was in its calibre and proportions a fitting compliment to a world celebrity and his mission. Many of the intellectual leaders of the city were present—University professors, pulpit personalities, men eminent in business, legislators, every section of the community contributed a quota. It cannot be doubted, of course, that the brilliant literary fame of the lecturer was an attraction added to that strange subject which explored the 'unknown drama of the soul.' Over all, Sir Arthur dominated by his big arresting presence. His face has a rugged, kindly strength, tense and earnest in its grave moments, and full of winning animation when the sun of his rich humour plays on the powerful features.

"It is not altogether a sombre journey he makes among the shadows, but apparently one of happy, as well as tender experiences, so that laughter is not necessarily excluded from the exposition. Do not let that be misunderstood. There was no intrusion of the slightest flippancy—Sir Arthur, the whole time, exhibited that attitude of reverence and humility demanded of one traversing a domain on the borderland of the tremendous. Nothing approaching a theatrical presentation of the case for Spiritualism marred the discourse. It was for the most part a plain statement. First things had to be said, and the explanatory groundwork laid for future development. It was a lucid, illuminating introduction.

"Sir Arthur had a budget of notes, but after he had turned over a few pages he sallied forth with fluent independence under the inspiration of a vast mental store of material. A finger jutted out now and again with a thrust of passionate emphasis, or his big glasses twirled during moments of descriptive ease, and occasionally both hands were held forward as though delivering settled points to the audience for its examination. A clear, well-disciplined voice, excellent diction, and conspicuous sincerity of manner marked the lecture, and no one could have found fault with the way in which Sir Arthur presented his case.

"The lecturer approached the audience in no spirit of impatient dogmatism, but in the capacity of an understanding mind seeking to illumine the darkness of doubt in those who had not shared his great experiences. He did not dictate, but reasoned and pleaded, taking the people into his confidence with strong conviction and a consoling faith. 'I want to speak to you to-night on a subject which concerns the destiny of every man and woman in this room,' began Sir Arthur, bringing everybody at once into an intimate personal circle. 'No doubt the Almighty, by putting an angel in King William Street, could convert every one of you to Spiritualism, but the Almighty law is that we must use our own brains, and find out our own salvation, and it is not made too easy for us.' "

[72]

THE WANDERINGS OF A SPIRITUALIST

It is awkward to include this kindly picture, and yet I do not know how else to give an idea of how the matter seemed to a friendly observer. I had chosen for my theme the scientific aspect of the matter, and I marshalled my witnesses and showed how Professor Mayo corroborated Professor Hare, and Professor Challis Professor Mayo, and Sir William Crookes all his predecessors, while Russell Wallace and Lombroso and Zollner and Barrett, and Lodge, and many more had all after long study assented, and I read the very words of these great men, and showed how bravely they had risked their reputations and careers for what they knew to be the truth. I then showed how the opposition who dared to contradict them were men with no practical experience of it at all. It was wonderful to hear the shout of assent when I said that what struck me most in such a position was its colossal impertinence. That shout told me that my cause was won, and from then onwards the deep silence was only broken by the occasional deep murmur of heart-felt agreement. I told them the evidence that had been granted to me, the coming of my son, the coming of my brother, and their message. "Plough! Plough! others will cast the seed." It is hard to talk of such intimate matters, but they were not given to me for my private comfort alone, but for that of humanity. Nothing could have gone better than this first evening, and though I had no chairman and spoke for ninety minutes without a pause, I was so upheld—there is no other word for the sensation—that I was stronger at the end than when I began. A leading materialist was among my audience. "I am profoundly impressed," said he to

Mr. Smythe, as he passed him in the corridor. That stood out among many kind messages which reached me that night.

My second lecture, two nights later, was on the Religious aspect of the matter. I had shown that the phenomena were nothing, mere material signals to arrest the attention of a material world. I had shown also that the personal benefit, the conquest of death, the Communion of Saints, was a high, but not the highest boon. The real full flower of Spiritualism was what the wisdom of the dead could tell us about their own conditions, their present experiences, their outlook upon the secret of the universe, and the testing of religious truth from the viewpoint of two worlds instead of one. The audience was more silent than before, but the silence was that of suspense, not of dissent, as I showed them from message after message what it was exactly which awaited them in the beyond. Even I, who am oblivious as a rule to my audience, became aware that they were tense with feeling and throbbing with emotion. I showed how there was no conflict with religion, in spite of the misunderstanding of the churches, and that the revelation had come to extend and explain the old, even as the Christ had said that he had much more to tell but could not do it now. "Entirely new ground was traversed," says my kindly chronicler, "and the audience listened throughout with rapt attention. They were obviously impressed by the earnestness of the speaker and his masterly presentation of the theme." I cannot answer for the latter but at least I can for the former, since I speak not of what I think but of what I know. How can a man fail to be earnest then?

THE WANDERINGS OF A SPIRITUALIST

A few days later I followed up the lectures by two exhibitions of psychic pictures and photographs upon a screen. It was certainly an amazing experience for those who imagined that the whole subject was dreamland, and they freely admitted that it staggered them. They might well be surprised, for such a series has never been seen, I believe, before, including as it does choice samples from the very best collections. I showed them the record of miracle after miracle, some of them done under my very eyes, one guaranteed by Russell Wallace, three by Sir William Crookes, one of the Geley series from Paris, two of Dr. Crawford's medium with the ecto-plasm pouring from her, four illustrating the absolutely final Lydia Haig case on the island of Rothesay, several of Mr. Jeffrey's collection and several also of our own Society for the Study of Supernormal Pictures, with the fine photograph of the face within a crystal. No wonder that the audience sat spellbound, while the local press declared that no such exhibition had ever been seen before in Australia. It is almost too overwhelming for immediate propaganda purposes. It has a stunning, dazing effect upon the spectators. Only afterwards, I think, when they come to turn it all over in their minds, do they see that the final proof has been laid before them, which no one with the least sense for evidence could reject. But the sense for evidence is not, alas, a universal human quality.

I am continually aware of direct spirit intervention in my own life. It have put it on record in my "New Revelation" that I was able to say that the turn of the great war would come upon the Piave months before that river was on the Italian war map. This was recorded at the time, before the fulfilment which occurred more than a year later—so it does not depend upon my assertion. Again, I dreamed the name of the ship which was to take us to Australia, rising in the middle of the night and writing it down in pencil on my cheque-book. I wrote *Nadera,* but it was actually *Naldera.* I had never heard that such a ship existed until I visited the P. & O. office, when they told me we should go by the *Osterley,* while I, seeing the *Naldera* upon the list, thought "No, that will be our ship!" So it proved, through no action of our own, and thereby we were saved from quarantine and all manner of annoyance.

Never before have I experienced such direct visible intervention as occurred during my first photographic lecture at Adelaide. I had shown a slide the effect of which depended upon a single spirit face appearing amid a crowd of others. This slide was damp, and as photos under these circumstances always clear from the edges when placed in the lantern, the whole centre was so thickly fogged that I was compelled to admit that I could not myself see the spirit face. Suddenly, as I turned away, rather abashed by my failure, I heard cries of "There it is," and looking up again I saw this single face shining out from the general darkness with so bright and vivid an effect that I never doubted for a moment that the operator was throwing a spot light upon it, my wife sharing my impression. I thought how extraordinarily clever it was that he should pick it out so accurately at the distance. So the matter passed, but next morning Mr. Thomas, the operator, who is not a Spiritualist, came in in great excitement to say that a palpable miracle had been wrought, and that in his great experience of thirty years he had never known a photo dry from the centre, nor, as I understood him, become illuminated in such a fashion. Both my wife and I were surprised to learn that he had thrown no ray upon it. Mr. Thomas told us that several experts among the audience had commented upon the strangeness of the incident. I, therefore, asked Mr. Thomas if he would give me a note as to his own impression, so as to furnish an independent account. This is what he wrote :—

"Hindmarsh Square, Adelaide.

"In Adelaide, on September 28th, I projected a lantern slide containing a group of ladies and gentlemen, and in the centre of the picture, when the slide was reversed, appeared a human face. On the appearance of the picture showing the group the fog incidental to a damp or new slide gradually appeared covering the whole slide, and only after some minutes cleared, and then quite contrary to usual practice did so from a central point just over the face that appeared in the centre, and refused even after that to clear right off to the edge. The general experience is for a slide to clear from the outside edges to a common centre. Your slide cleared only sufficiently in the centre to show the face, and did not, while the slide was on view, clear any more than sufficient to show that face. Thinking that perhaps there might be a scientific explanation to this phenomenon, I hesitated before writing you, and in the meantime I have made several experiments but have not in any one particular experiment obtained the same result. I am very much interested—as are hundreds of others who personally witnessed the phenomenon."

Mr. Thomas, in his account, has missed the self-illuminated appearance of the face, but otherwise he brings out the points. I never gave occasion for the repetition of the phenomenon, for in every case I was careful that the slides were carefully dried beforehand.

So much for the lectures at Adelaide, which were five in all, and left, as I heard from all sides, a deep impression upon the town. Of course, the usual abusive messages poured in, including one which wound up with the hearty words: "May you be struck dead before you leave this Commonwealth." From Melbourne I had news that before our arrival in Australia at a public prayer meeting at the Assembly Hall, Collins Street, a Presbyterian prayed that we might never reach Australia's shores. As we were on the high seas at the time this was clearly a murderous petition, nor could I have believed it if a friend of mine had not actually been present and heard it. On the other hand, we received many letters of sympathy and thanks, which amply atoned. "I feel sure that many mothers, who have lost their sons in the war, will, wherever you go, bless you, as I do, for the help you have given." As this was the object of our journey it could not be denied that we had attained our end. When I say "we," I mean that such letters with inquiries came continually to my wife as well as myself, though she answered them with far greater fullness and clearness than I had time to do.

Hotel life began to tell upon the children, who are like horses with a profusion of oats and no exercise. On the whole they were wonderfully good. When some domestic crisis was passed the small voice of Malcolm, once "Dimples," was heard from the darkness of his bed, saying, "Well, if I am to be good I must have a proper start. Please, mammie, say one, two, three, and away!" When this ceremony had been performed a still smaller voice of Baby asked the same favour, so once more there was a formal start. The result was intermittent, and it is as well. I don't believe in angelic children.

The Adelaide doctors entertained me to dinner, and I was pleased to meet more than one who had been of my time at Edinburgh. They seemed to be a very prosperous body of men. There was much interesting conversation, especially from one elderly professor named Watson, who had known Bully Hayes and other South Sea celebrities in the semi-piratical, black-birding days. He told me one pretty story. They landed upon some outlying island in Carpentaria, peopled by real primitive blacks, who were rounded up by the ship's crew on one of the peninsulas which formed the end of the island. These creatures, the lowest of the human race, huddled together in consternation while the white men trained a large camera upon them. Suddenly three males advanced and made a speech in their own tongue which, when interpreted, proved to be an offer that those three should die in exchange for the lives of the tribe. What could the very highest do more than this, and yet it came from the lowest savages. Truly, we all have something of the divine, and it is the very part which will grow and spread until it has burned out all the rest. "Be a Christ!" said brave old Stead. At the end of countless æons we may all reach that point which not only Stead but St. Paul also has foreshadowed.

I refreshed myself between lectures by going out to

Nature and to Bellchambers. As it was twenty-five miles out in the bush, inaccessible by rail, and only to be approached by motor roads which were in parts like the bed of a torrent, I could not take my wife. though the boys, after the nature of boys, enjoy a journey the more for its roughness. It was a day to remember. I saw lovely South Australia in the full beauty of the spring, the budding girlhood of the year, with all her winsome growing graces upon her. The brilliant yellow wattle was just fading upon the trees, but the sward was covered with star-shaped purple flowers of the knot-grass, and with familiar home flowers, each subtly altered by their transportation. It was wild bush for part of the way, but mostly of the second growth on account of forest fires as much as the woodman's axe. Bellchambers came in to guide us, for there is no one to ask upon these desolate tracks, and it is easy to get bushed. Mr. Waite, the very capable zoologist of the museum, joined the party, and with two such men the conversation soon got to that high nature talk which represents the really permanent things of material life —more lasting than thrones and dynasties. I learned of the strange storks, the "native companions" who meet, 500 at a time, for their stately balls, where in the hush of the bush they advance, retreat, and pirouette in their dignified minuets. I heard of the bower birds, who decorate their homes with devices of glass and pebbles. There was talk, too, of the little red beetles who have such cunning ways that they can fertilise the insectivorous plants without being eaten, and of the great ants who get through galvanised iron by the aid of some acid-squirting insect which they bring with

Photo: W. G. Smith, Adelaide.

BELLCHAMBERS AND THE MALLEE FOWL. "GET ALONG WITH YOU, DO!"

them to the scene of their assault. I heard also of the shark's egg which Mr. Waite had raped from sixty feet deep in Sydney Harbour, descending for the purpose in a diver's suit, for which I raised my hat to him. Deep things came also from Bellchambers's store of knowledge and little glimpses of beautiful humanity from this true gentleman.

"Yes," he said, "I am mostly vegetarian. You see, I know the beasts too well to bring myself to pick their bones. Yes, I'm friends with most of them. Birds have more sense than animals to my mind. They understand you like. They know what you mean. Snakes have least of any. They don't get friendly-like in the same way. But Nature helps the snakes in queer ways. Some of them hatch their own eggs, and when they do Nature raises the temperature of their bodies. That's queer."

I carried away a mixed memory of the things I had seen. A blue-headed wren, an eagle soaring in the distance; a hideous lizard with a huge open mouth; a laughing jackass which refused to laugh; many more or less tame wallabies and kangaroos; a dear little 'possum which got under the back of my coat, and would not come out; noisy mynah birds which fly ahead and warn the game against the hunter. Good little noisy mynah! All my sympathies are with you! I would do the same if I could. This senseless lust for killing is a disgrace to the race. We, of England, cannot preach, for a pheasant battue is about the worst example of it. But do let the creatures alone unless they are surely noxious! When Mr. Bellchambers told us how he had trained two ibises—the old religious variety—and how both had been picked off by some unknown local "sportsman" it made one sad.

We had a touch of comedy, however, when Mr. Bellchambers attempted to expose the egg of the Mallee fowl, which is covered a foot deep in mould. He scraped into the mound with his hands. The cock watched him with an expression which clearly said: "Confound the fellow! What is he up to now?" He then got on the mound, and as quickly as Bellchambers shovelled the earth out he kicked it back again, Bellchambers in his good humoured way crying, "Get along with you, do!" A good husband is the Mallee cock, and looks after the family interests. But what we humans would think if we were born deep underground and had to begin our career by digging our way to the surface, is beyond imagination.

There are quite a clan of Bellchambers living in or near the little pioneer's hut built in a clearing of the bush. Mrs. Bellchambers is of Sussex, as is her husband, and when they heard that we were fresh from Sussex also it was wonderful to see the eager look that came upon their faces, while the bush-born children could scarce understand what it was that shook the solid old folk to their marrow. On the walls were old prints of the Devil's Dyke and Firle Beacon. How strange that old Sussex should be wearing out its very life in its care for the fauna of young Australia. This remarkable man is unpaid with only his scanty holding upon which to depend, and many dumb mouths dependent upon him. I shall rejoice if my efforts in the local press serve to put his affairs upon a more worthy foundation, and to make South Australia realise what a valuable instrument lies to her hand.

Before I left Adelaide I learned many pleasing things about the lectures, which did away with any shadow cast by those numerous correspondents who seemed to think that we were still living under the Mosaic dispensation, and who were so absent-minded that they usually forgot to sign their names. It is a curious difference between the Christian letters of abuse and those of materialists, that the former are usually anonymous and the latter signed. I heard of one man, a lame stockman, who had come 300 miles from the other side of Streaky Bay to attend the whole course, and who declared that he could listen all night. Another seized my hand and cried, "You will never know the good you have done in this town." Well, I hope it was so, but I only regard myself as the plough. Others must follow with the seed. Knowledge, perseverance, sanity, judgment, courage—we ask some qualities from our disciples if they are to do real good. Talking of moral courage I would say that the Governor of South Australia, Sir Archibald Weigall, with Lady Weigall, had no hesitation in coming to support me with their presence. By the end of September this most successful mission in Adelaide was accomplished, and early in October we were on our way to Melbourne, which meant a long night in the train and a few hours of the next morning during which we saw the surface diggings of Ballarat on every side of the railway line, the sandy soil pitted in every direction with the shallow claims of the miners.

CHAPTER IV

ONE cannot help speculating about those great ones
who first carried to the world the Christian revelation.
What were their domestic ties! There is little said
about them, but we should never have known that Peter
had a wife were it not for a chance allusion to his
mother-in-law, just as another chance allusion shows us
that Jesus was one of a numerous family. One thing
can safely be said of Paul, that he was either a bachelor
or else was a domestic bully with a very submissive
wife, or he would never have dared to express his well
known views about women. As to his preaching, he
had a genius for making a clear thing obscure, even as
Jesus had a genius for making an obscure thing clear.
Read the Sermon on the Mount and then a chapter of
Paul as a contrast in styles. Apart from his style one
can reconstruct him as a preacher to the extent that he

[84]

had a powerful voice—no one without one could speak from the historic rocky pulpit on the hill of Mars at Athens, as I ascertained for myself. The slope is downwards, sound ascends, and the whole conditions are abominable. He was certainly long-winded and probably monotonous in his diction, or he could hardly have reduced one of his audience to such a deep sleep that he fell out of the window. We may add that he was a man of brisk courage in an emergency, that he was subject to such sudden trances that he was occasionally unaware himself whether he was normal or not, and that he was probably short-sighted, as he mistook the person who addressed him, and had his letters usually written for him. At least three languages were at his command, he had an intimate and practical knowledge of the occult, and was an authority upon Jewish law—a good array of accomplishments for one man.

There are some points about Paul's august Master which also help in a reconstruction of Himself and His surroundings. That His mother was opposed to His mission is, I think, very probable. Women are dubious about spiritual novelties, and one can well believe that her heart ached to see her noble elder son turn from the sure competence of His father's business at Nazareth to the precarious existence of a wandering preacher. This domestic opposition clouded Him as one can see in the somewhat cold, harsh words which He used to her, and his mode of address which began simply as "Woman." His assertion to the disciples that one who followed His path had to give up his family points to the same thing. No doubt Mary remained with the younger branches at Nazareth while Jesus pursued His ministry, though she came, as any mother would, to be near Him at the end.

Of His own personality we know extraordinarily little, considering the supreme part that He played in the world. That He was a highly trained psychic, or as we should say, medium, is obvious to anyone who studies the miracles, and it is certainly not derogatory to say that they were done along the line of God's law rather than that they were inversions of it. I cannot doubt also that he chose his apostles for their psychic powers—if not, on what possible principle were they selected, since they were neither staunch nor learned? It is clear that Peter and James and John were the inner circle of psychics, since they were assembled both at the transfiguration and at the raising of Jairus' daughter. It is from unlearned open-air men who are near Nature that the highest psychic powers are obtained. It has been argued that the Christ was an Essene, but this seems hard to believe, as the Essenes were not only secluded from the world, but were certainly vegetarians and total abstainers, while Jesus was neither. On the other hand baptism was not a Jewish rite, and his undergoing it—if He did, indeed, undergo it—marks Him as belonging to some dissenting sect. I say "if He did" because it is perfectly certain that there were forgeries and interpolations introduced into the Gospels in order to square their teaching with the practice of the Church some centuries later. One would look for those forgeries not in the ordinary narrative, which in the adult years bears every mark of truth, but in the passages which support ceremonial or tributes to the Church—such as the allusions to baptism, "Unless a man be born again," to the sacrament, "This is my body, etc.," and the whole story of Ananias and Sapphira, the moral of which is that it is dangerous to hold anything back from the Church.

Physically I picture the Christ as an extremely powerful man. I have known several famous healers and they were all men who looked as if they had redundant health and strength to give to others. His words to the sick woman, "Who has touched me? Much power" (*dunamis* is the word in the original Greek) "has gone out of me," show that His system depended upon His losing what He gave to others. Therefore He was a very strong man. The mere feat of carrying a wooden cross strong enough to bear a man from Jerusalem to Calvary, up a hill, is no light one. It is the details which convince me that the gospel narrative is correct and really represents an actual event. Take the incident during that sad journey of Simon of Cyrene having helped for a time with the cross. Why should anyone invent such a thing, putting an actual name to the person? It is touches of this kind which place the narrative beyond all suspicion of being a pure invention. Again and again in the New Testament one is confronted with incidents which a writer of fiction recognises as being beyond the reach of invention, because the inventor does not put in things which have no direct bearing upon the matter in hand. Take as an example how the maid, seeing Peter outside the door after his escape from prison, ran back to the guests and said that it was his angel (or etheric body) which was

[87]

outside. Such an episode could only have been recorded because it actually occurred.

But these be deep waters. Let me get back to my own humble experiences, these interpolated thoughts being but things which have been found upon the wayside of our journey. On reaching Melbourne we were greeted at the station by a few devoted souls who had waited for two trains before they found us. Covered with the flowers which they had brought we drove to Menzies Hotel, whence we moved a few days later to a flat in the Grand, where we were destined to spend five eventful weeks. We found the atmosphere and general psychic conditions of Melbourne by no means as pleasant or receptive as those of Adelaide, but this of course was very welcome as the greater the darkness the more need of the light. If Spiritualism had been a popular cult in Australia there would have been no object in my visit. I was welcome enough as an individual, but by no means so as an emissary, and both the Churches and the Materialists, in most unnatural combination, had done their best to make the soil stony for me. Their chief agent had been the *Argus,* a solid, stodgy paper, which amply fulfilled the material needs of the public, but was not given to spiritual vision. This paper before my arrival had a very violent and abusive leader which attracted much attention, full of such terms as "black magic," "Shamanism," "witchcraft," "freak religion," "cranky faith," "cruelty," "black evil," "poison," finishing up with the assertion that I represented "a force which we believe to be purely evil." This was from a paper which wholeheartedly supports the liquor interest, and has endless columns of betting and racing news, nor did its principles cause it to refuse substantial sums for the advertising of my lectures. Still, however arrogant or illogical, I hold that a paper has a perfect right to publish and uphold its own view, nor would I say that the subsequent refusal of the *Argus* to print any answer to its tirade was a real breach of the ethics of journalism. Where its conduct became outrageous, however, and where it put itself beyond the pale of all literary decency, was when it reported my first lecture by describing my wife's dress, my own voice, the colour of my spectacles, and not a word of what I said. It capped this by publishing so-called answers to me by Canon Hughes, and by Bishop Phelan—critics whose knowledge of the subject seemed to begin and end with the witch of Endor—while omitting the statements to which these answers applied. Never in any British town have I found such reactionary intolerance as in this great city, for though the *Argus* was the chief offender, the other papers were as timid as rabbits in the matter. My psychic photographs which, as I have said, are the most wonderful collection ever shown in the world, were received in absolute silence by the whole press, though it is notorious that if I had come there with a comic opera or bedroom comedy instead of with the evidence of a series of miracles, I should have had a column. This seems to have been really due to moral cowardice, and not to ignorance, for I saw a private letter afterwards in which a sub-editor remarked that he and the chief leader-writer had both seen the photographs and that they could see no possible answer to them.

There was another and more pleasing side to the local conditions, and that lay in the numbers who had already mastered the principles of Spiritualism, the richer classes as individuals, the poorer as organised churches. They were so numerous that when we received an address of welcome in the auditorium to which only Spiritualists were invited by ticket, the Hall, which holds two thousand, was easily filled. This would mean on the same scale that the Spiritualists of London could fill the Albert Hall several times over—as no doubt they could. Their numbers were in a sense an embarrassment, as I always had the fear that I was addressing the faithful instead of those whom I had come so far to instruct. On the whole, their quality and organisation were disappointing. They had a splendid spiritual paper in their midst, the *Harbinger of Light,* which has run for fifty years, and is most ably edited by Mr. Britton Harvey. When I think of David Gow, Ernest Oaten, John Lewis and Britton Harvey I feel that our cause is indeed well represented by its press. They have also some splendid local workers, like Bloomfield and Tozer, whole-hearted and apostolic. But elsewhere there is the usual tendency to divide and to run into vulgarities and extravagances in which the Spiritual has small share. Discipline is needed, which involves central powers, and that in turn means command of the purse. It would be far better to have no Spiritual churches than some I have seen.

However, I seem to have got to some of my final conclusions at Melbourne before I have begun our actual experience there. We found the place still full of rumours and talk about the recent visit of the Prince of Wales, who seems to have a perfect genius for making himself popular and beloved. May he remain unspoiled and retain the fresh kindliness of his youth. His success is due not to any ordered rule of conduct but to a perfectly natural courtesy which is his essential self and needs no effort. Our waiter at the hotel who had waited upon him remarked: "God never made anything nearer to Nature than that boy. He spoke to me as he might have spoken to the Governor." It was a fine tribute, and characteristic of the humbler classes in this country, who have a vigour of speech and an independence of view which is very refreshing. Once as I passed a public house, a broken old fellow who had been leaning against the wall with a short pipe in his mouth, stepped forward to me and said: "I am all for civil and religious liberty. There is plenty of room for your cult here, sir, and I wish you well against the bigots." I wonder from what heights that old fellow had fallen before he brought up against the public house wall.

One of my first afternoons in Melbourne was spent in seeing the final tie of the Victorian football cup. I have played both Rugby and Soccer, and I have seen the American game at its best, but I consider that the Victorian system has some points which make it the best of all—certainly from the spectacular point of view. There is no off-side, and you get a free kick if you catch the ball. Otherwise you can run as in ordinary Rugby, though there is a law about bouncing the ball as you run, which might, as it seemed to me, be cut out without harming the game. This bouncing rule was put in by Mr. Harrison who drew up the original rules, for the chivalrous reason that he was himself the fastest runner in the Colony, and he did not wish to give himself any advantage. There is not so much man-handling in the Victorian game, and to that extent it is less dramatic, but it is extraordinarily open and fast, with none of the packed scrums which become so weari-some, and with linesmen who throw in the ball the in-stant it goes out. There were several points in which the players seemed better than our best—one was the accurate passing by low drop kicking, very much quicker and faster than a pass by hand. Another was the great accuracy of the place kicking and of the screw kicking when a runner would kick at right angles to his course. There were four long quarters, and yet the men were in such condition that they were going hard at the end. They are all, I understand, semi-profes-sionals. Altogether it was a very fine display, and the crowd was much excited. It was suggestive that the instant the last whistle blew a troop of mounted police cantered over the ground and escorted the referees to the safety of the pavilion. I began at once to endeavor to find out the conditions of local Spiritualism, and had a long conversation with Mr. Tozer, the chairman of the movement, a slow-talking, steady-eyed man, of the type that gets a grip and does not easily let go. After explaining the general situation, which needs some ex-planation as it is full of currents and cross-currents caused by individual schisms and secessions, he told me in his gentle, earnest way some of his own experiences in his home circle which corroborate much which I have heard elsewhere. He has run a rescue circle for the in-struction of the lower spirits who are so material that they can be reached more easily by humanity than by the higher angels. The details he gave me were almost the same as those given by Mr. MacFarlane of Southsea, who had a similar circle of which Mr. Tozer had certainly never heard. A wise spirit control dominates the proceedings. The medium goes into trance. The spirit control then explains what it is about to do, and who the spirit is who is about to be reformed. The next scene is often very violent, the medium having to be held down and using rough language. This comes from some low spirit who has suddenly found this means of expressing himself. At other times the language is not violent but only melancholy, the spirit declaring that he is abandoned and has not a friend in the universe. Some do not realise that they are dead, but only that they wander all alone, under conditions they could not understand, in a cloud of darkness.

Then comes the work of regeneration. They are reasoned with and consoled. Gradually they become more gentle. Finally, they accept the fact that they are spirits, that their condition is their own making, and that by aspiration and repentance they can win their way to the light. When one has found the path and has returned thanks for it, another case is treated. As a rule these errant souls are unknown to fame. Often they are clergymen whose bigotry has hindered development. Occasionally some great sinner of the past may come into view. I have before me a written lament professing to come from Alva, the bigoted governor of the Lowlands. It is gruesome enough. "Picture to yourself the hell I was in. Blood, blood everywhere, corpses on all sides, gashed, maimed, mutilated, quivering with agony and bleeding at every pore! At the same time thousands of voices were raised in bitter reproaches, in curses and execrations! Imagine the appalling spectacle of this multitude of the dead and dying, fresh from the flames, from the sword, the rack, the torture chambers and the gibbet; and the pandemonium of voices shrieking out the most terrible maledictions! Imagine never being able to get away from these sights and sounds, and then tell me, was I not in hell?—a hell of greater torment than that to which I believed all heretics were consigned. Such was the hell of the 'bloody Alva,' from which I have been rescued by what seems to me a great merciful dispensation of Almighty God."

Sometimes in Mr. Tozer's circle the souls of ancient clerics who have slumbered long show their first signs of resuscitation, still bearing their old-world intolerance with them. The spirit control purports to be a well-educated Chinaman, whose presence and air of authority annoy the ecclesiastics greatly. The petrified mind leads to a long period of insensibility which means loss of ground and of time in the journey towards happiness. I was present at the return of one alleged Anglican bishop of the eighteenth century, who spoke with great intolerance. When asked if he had seen the Christ he answered that he had not and that he could not understand it. When asked if he still considered the Christ to be God he threw up his hand and shouted violently, "Stop! That is blasphemy!" The Chinese control said, "He stupid man. Let him wait. He learn better"—and removed him. He was succeeded by a very noisy and bigoted Puritan divine who declared that no one but devils would come to a séance. On being asked whether that meant that he was himself a devil he became so abusive that the Chinaman once more had to intervene. I quote all this as a curious sidelight into some developments of the subject which are familiar enough to students, but not to the general public. It is easy at a distance to sneer at such things and to ask for their evidential value, but they are very impressive to those who view them at closer quarters. As to evidence, I am informed that several of the unfortunates have been identified in this world through the information which they gave of their own careers.

Melbourne is a remarkable city, far more solid and old-established than the European visitor would expect. We spent some days in exploring it. There are few cities which have the same natural advantages, for it is near the sea, with many charming watering places close at hand, while inland it has some beautiful hills for the week-end villas of the citizens. Edinburgh is the nearest analogy which I can recall. Parks and gardens are beautiful, but, as in most British cities, the public statues are more solid than impressive. The best of them, that to Burke and Wills, the heroic explorers, has no name upon it to signify who the two figures are, so that they mean nothing at all to the casual observer, in spite of some excellent bas-reliefs, round the base, which show the triumphant start and the terrible end of that tragic but successful journey which first penetrated the Continent from south to north. Before our departure I appealed in the press to have this omission rectified and it was, I believe, done.

THE WANDERINGS OF A SPIRITUALIST

Mr. Smythe, my agent, had been unfortunate in being unable to secure one of the very few large halls in Melbourne, so we had to confine ourselves to the Play-house which has only seating for about 1,200. Here I opened on October 5th, following my lectures up in the same order as in Adelaide. The press was very shy, but nothing could have exceeded the warmth and receptivity of my hearers. Yet on account of the inadequate reports of the press, with occasional total suppression, no one who was not present could have imagined how packed was the house, or how unanimous the audience.

On October 14th the Spiritualists filled the Auditorium and had a special service of welcome for ourselves. When I went down to it in the tram, the conductor, unaware of my identity, said, when I asked to be put down at the Auditorium, "It's no use, sir; it's jam full an hour ago." "The Pilgrims," as they called us, were in special seats, the seven of us all in a line upon the right of the chair. Many kind things were said, and I replied as best I might. The children will carry the remembrance of that warm-hearted reception through their lives, and they are not likely to forget how they staggered home, laden with the flowers which were literally heaped upon them.

The British Empire League also entertained my wife and myself to lunch, a very select company assembling who packed the room. Sir Joseph Cook, Federal Chancellor of the Exchequer, made a pleasant speech, recalling our adventures upon the Somme, when he had his baptism of fire. In my reply I pulled the leg of my audience with some success, for I wound up by saying,

MELBOURNE, NOVEMBER, 1920.

very solemnly, that I was something greater than Governments and the master of Cabinet Ministers. By the time I had finished my tremendous claims I am convinced that they expected some extravagant occult pretension, whereas I actually wound up with the words, "for I am the man in the street." There was a good deal of amusement caused.

Mr. Thomas Ryan, a very genial and capable member of the State Legislature, took the chair at this function. He had no particular psychic knowledge, but he was deeply impressed by an experience in London in the presence of that remarkable little lady, Miss Scatcherd. Mr. Ryan had said that he wanted some evidence before he could accept psychic philosophy, upon which Miss Scatcherd said: "There is a spirit beside you now. He conveys to me that his name is Roberts. He says he is worried in his mind because the home which you prepared for his widow has not been legally made over to her." All this applied to a matter in Adelaide. In that city, according to Mr. Ryan, a séance was held that night, Mr. Victor Cromer being the medium, at which a message came through from Roberts saying that he was now easy in his mind as he had managed to convey his trouble to Mr. Ryan who could set it right. When these psychic laws are understood the dead as well as the living will be relieved from a load of unnecessary care; but how can these laws be ignored or pooh-poohed in the face of such instances as this which I have quoted? They are so numerous now that it is hardly an exaggeration to say that every circle of human beings which meets can supply one.

Mr. Hughes was good enough to ask me to meet the

members of the Federal Government at lunch, and the experience was an interesting one, for here round one small table were those who were shaping the course of this young giant among the nations. They struck me as a practical hard-worked rough-and-ready lot of men. Mr. Hughes dominated the conversation, which necessarily becomes one-sided as he is very deaf, though his opponents say that he has an extraordinary knack of hearing what he is not meant to hear. He told us a series of anecdotes of his stormy political youth with a great deal of vivacity, the whole company listening in silence. He is a hard, wiry man, with a high-nosed Red Indian face, and a good deal of healthy devilry in his composition—a great force for good during the war.

After lunch he conducted me through the library, and coming to a portrait of Clemenceau he cried: "That's the man I learned to admire in Europe." Then, turning to one of Wilson, he added, "And that's the man I learned to dislike." He added a number of instances of Wilson's ignorance of actual conditions, and of his ungenial coldness of heart. "If he had not been so wrapped in himself, and if he had taken Lodge or some other Republican with him, all could have easily been arranged." I feel that I am not indiscreet in repeating this, for Hughes is not a man who conceals his opinions from the world.

I have been interested in the medium Bailey, who was said to have been exposed in France in 1910. The curious will find the alleged exposure in "Annals of Psychical Science," Vol. IX. Bailey is an apport medium—that is to say, that among his phenomena is the bringing of objects which are said to come from a distance, passing through the walls and being precipitated down upon the table. These objects are of the strangest description — Assyrian tablets (real or forged), tortoises, live birds, snakes, precious stones, etc. In this case, after being searched by the committee, he was able to produce two live birds in the séance room. At the next sitting the committee proposed an obscene and absurd examination of the medium, which he very rightly resented and refused. They then confidently declared that on the first occasion the two live birds were in his intestines, a theory so absurd that it shakes one's confidence in their judgment. They had, however, some more solid grounds for a charge against him, for they produced a married couple who swore that they had sold three such birds with a cage to Bailey some days before. This Bailey denied, pointing out that he could neither speak French, nor had he ever had any French money, which Professor Reichel, who brought him from Australia, corroborated. However, the committee considered the evidence to be final, and the séances came to an end, though Colonel de Rochas, the leading member, wound up the incident by writing: "Are we to conclude from the fraud that we have witnessed that all Bailey's apports may have been fraudulent? I do not think so, and this is also the opinion of the members of the committee, who have had much experience with mediums and are conversant with the literature of the subject."

Reading the alleged exposure, one is struck, as so often in such cases, with its unsatisfactory nature. There is the difficulty of the language and the money.

There is the disappearance of the third bird and the cage. Above all, how did the birds get into the carefully guarded séance room, especially as Bailey was put in a bag during the proceedings? The committee say the bag may not have been efficient, but they also state that Bailey desired the control to be made more effective. Altogether it is a puzzling case. On my applying to Bailey himself for information, he declared roundly that he had been the victim of a theological plot with suborned evidence. The only slight support which I can find for that view is that there was a Rev. Doctor among his accusers. I was told independently that Professor Reichel, before his death in 1918, came also to the conclusion that there had been a plot. But in any case most of us will agree with Mr. Stanford, Bailey's Australian patron, that the committee would have been wise to say nothing, continue the sittings, and use their knowledge to get at some more complete conclusion.

With such a record one had to be on one's guard with Mr. Bailey. I had a sitting in my room at the hotel to which I invited ten guests, but the results were not impressive. We saw so-called spirit hands, which were faintly luminous, but I was not allowed to grasp them, and they were never further from the medium than he could have reached. All this was suspicious but not conclusive. On the other hand, there was an attempt at a materialisation of a head, which took the form of a luminous patch, and seemed to some of the sitters to be further from the cabinet than could be reached. We had an address purporting to come from the control, Dr. Whitcombe, and we also had a message written in bad Italian. On the whole, it was one of those baffling sittings which leave a vague unpleasant impression, and there was a disturbing suggestion of cuffs about those luminous hands.

I have been reading Bailey's record, however, and I cannot doubt that he has been a great apport medium. The results were far above all possible fraud, both in the conditions and in the articles brought into the room by spirit power. For example, I have a detailed account published by Dr. C. W. McCarthy, of Sydney, under the title, "Rigid Tests of the Occult." During these tests Bailey was sealed up in a bag, and in one case was inside a cage of mosquito curtain. The door and windows were secured and the fire-place blocked. The sitters were all personal friends, but they mutually searched each other. The medium was stripped naked before the séance. Under these stringent conditions during a series of six sittings 138 articles were brought into the room, which included eighty-seven ancient coins (mostly of Ptolemy), eight live birds, eighteen precious stones of modest value and varied character, two live turtles, seven inscribed Babylonian tablets, one Egyptian Scarabæus, an Arabic newspaper, a leopard skin, four nests and many other things. It seems to me perfect nonsense to talk about these things being the results of trickery. I may add that at a previous test meeting they had a young live shark about 1½ feet long, which was tangled with wet seaweed and flopped about on the table. Dr. McCarthy gives a photograph of the creature.

My second sitting with Bailey was more successful than the first. On his arrival I and others searched him and satisfied ourselves he carried nothing upon him. I then suddenly switched out all the lights, for it seemed to me that the luminous hands of the first sitting might be the result of phosphorised oil put on before the meeting and only visible in complete darkness, so that it could defy all search. I was wrong, however, for there was no luminosity at all. We then placed Mr. Bailey in the corner of the room, lowered the lights without turning them out, and waited. Almost at once he breathed very heavily, as one in trance, and soon said something in a foreign tongue which was unintelligible to me. One of our friends, Mr. Cochrane, recognised it as Indian, and at once answered, a few sentences being interchanged. In English the voice then said that he was a Hindoo control who was used to bring apports for the medium, and that he would, he hoped, be able to bring one for us. "Here it is," he said a moment later, and the medium's hand was extended with something in it. The light was turned full on and we found it was a very perfect bird's nest, beautifully constructed of some very fine fibre mixed with moss. It stood about two inches high and had no sign of any flattening which would have come with concealment. The size would be nearly three inches across. In it lay a small egg, white, with tiny brown speckles. The medium, or rather the Hindoo control acting through the medium, placed the egg on his palm and broke it, some fine albumen squirting out. There was no trace of yolk. "We are not allowed to interfere with life," said he. "If it had been fertilised we could not have taken it." These words were said before he broke it, so that he was aware of the condition of the egg, which certainly seems remarkable.

"Where did it come from?" I asked.

"From India."

"What bird is it?"

"They call it the jungle sparrow."

The nest remained in my possession, and I spent a morning with Mr. Chubb, of the local museum, to ascertain if it was really the nest of such a bird. It seemed too small for an Indian sparrow, and yet we could not match either nest or egg among the Australian types. Some of Mr. Bailey's other nests and eggs have been actually identified. Surely it is a fair argument that while it is conceivable that such birds might be imported and purchased here, it is really an insult to one's reason to suppose that nests with fresh eggs in them could also be in the market. Therefore I can only support the far more extended experience and elaborate tests of Dr. McCarthy of Sydney, and affirm that I believe Mr. Charles Bailey to be upon occasion a true medium, with a very remarkable gift for apports.

It is only right to state that when I returned to London I took one of Bailey's Assyrian tablets to the British Museum and that it was pronounced to be a forgery. Upon further inquiry it proved that these forgeries are made by certain Jews in a suburb of Bagdad—and, so far as is known, only there. Therefore the matter is not much further advanced. To the transporting agency it is at least possible that the forgery, steeped in recent human magnetism, is more capable of being handled than the original taken from a mound. Bailey has produced at least a hundred of these things, and no Custom House officer has deposed how they could have entered the country. On the other hand, Bailey told me clearly that the tablets had been passed by the British Museum, so that I fear that I cannot acquit him of tampering with truth—and just there lies the great difficulty of deciding upon his case. But one has always to remember that physical mediumship has no connection one way or the other with personal character, any more than the gift of poetry.

To return to this particular séance, it was unequal. We had luminous hands, but they were again within reach of the cabinet in which the medium was seated. We had also a long address from Dr. Whitcombe, the learned control, in which he discoursed like an absolute master upon Assyrian and Roman antiquities and psychic science. It was really an amazing address, and if Bailey were the author of it I should hail him as a master mind. He chatted about the Kings of Babylon as if he had known them all, remarked that the Bible was wrong in calling Belthazar King as he was only Crown Prince, and put in all those easy side allusions which a man uses when he is absolutely full of his subject. Upon his asking for questions, I said: "Please give me some light as to the dematerialisation and subsequent reassembly of an object such as a bird's nest." "It involves," he answered, "some factors which are beyond your human science and which could not be made clear to you. At the same time you may take as a rough analogy the case of water which is turned into steam, and then this steam which is invisible, is conducted elsewhere to be reassembled as visible water." I thought this explanation was exceedingly apt, though

[104]

conquered Canada from the French, removing in successive campaigns the danger from the north and from
the west which threatened our American colonies.
When we had expended our blood and money to that
end, so that the colonies had nothing to fear, they took
the first opportunity to force an unnecessary quarrel
and to leave us. So I have fears for South Africa now
that the German menace has been removed. Australia
is, I think, loyal to the core, and yet self-interest is with
every nation the basis of all policy, and so long as the
British fleet can guard the shores of the great empty
northern territories, a region as big as Britain, Germany, France and Austria put together, they have need
of us. There can be no doubt that if they were alone
in the world in the face of the teeming millions of the
East, they might, like the Siberian travellers, have to
throw a good deal to the wolves in order to save the re-
mainder. Brave and capable as they are, neither their
numbers nor their resources could carry them through
a long struggle if the enemy held the sea. They are
natural shots and soldiers, so that they might be wiser
to spend their money in a strategic railway right across
their northern coast, rather than in direct military
preparations. To concentrate rapidly before the enemy
was firmly established might under some circumstances
be a very vital need.

But so long as the British Empire lasts Australia is
safe, and in twenty years' time her own enlarged population will probably make her safe without help from
anyone. But her empty places are a danger. History
abhors a vacuum and finds someone to fill it up. I have
never yet understood why the Commonwealth has not

made a serious effort to attract to the northern territories those Italians who are flooding the Argentine.
It is great blood and no race is the poorer for it—the
blood of ancient Rome. They are used to semi-tropical
heat and to hard work in bad conditions if there be
only hope ahead. Perhaps the policy of the future may
turn in that direction. If that one weak spot be
guarded then it seems to me that in the whole world
there is no community, save only the United States,
which is so safe from outside attack as Australia. Internal division is another matter, but there Australia is
in some ways stronger than the States. She has no
negro question, and the strife between Capital and
Labour is not likely to be so formidable. I wonder,
by the way, how many people in the United States
realise that this small community lost as many men as
America did in the great war. We were struck also by
the dignified resignation with which this fact was faced,
and by the sense of proportion which was shown in
estimating the sacrifices of various nations.

We like the people here very much more than we had
expected to, for one hears in England exaggerated
stories of their democratic bearing. When democracy
takes the form of equality one can get along with it,
but when it becomes rude and aggressive one would
avoid it. Here one finds a very pleasing good fellowship which no one would object to. Again and again
we have met with little acts of kindness from people
in shops or in the street, which were not personal to
ourselves, but part of their normal good manners. If
you ask the way or any other information, strangers
will take trouble to put you right. They are kindly,

domestic and straight in speech and in dealings. Materialism and want of vision in the broader affairs of life seem to be the national weakness, but that may be only a passing phase, for when a nation has such a gigantic material proposition as this continent to handle it is natural that their thoughts should run on the wool and the wheat and the gold by which it can be accomplished. I am bound to say, however, that I think every patriotic Australian should vote, if not for prohibition, at least for the solution which is most dear to myself, and that is the lowering of the legal standard of alcohol in any drink. We have been shocked and astonished by the number of young men of decent exterior whom we have seen staggering down the street, often quite early in the day. The Biblical test for drunkenness, that it was not yet the third hour, would not apply to them. I hear that bad as it is in the big towns it is worse in the small ones, and worst of all in the northern territories and other waste places where work is particularly needed. It must greatly decrease the national efficiency. A recent vote upon the question in Victoria only carried total abstinence in four districts out of about 200, but a two-third majority was needed to do it. On the other hand a trial of strength in Queensland, generally supposed to be rather a rowdy State, has shown that the temperance men all combined can out-vote the others. Therefore it is certain that reform will not be long delayed.

The other curse of the country, which is a real drag upon its progress, is the eternal horse-racing. It goes on all the year round, though it has its more virulent bouts, as for example during our visit to this town

when the Derby, the Melbourne Cup, and Oaks succeeded each other. They call it sport, but I fear that
in that case I am no sportsman. I would as soon call
the roulette-table a sport. The whole population is unsettled and bent upon winning easy money, which dis-
satisfies them with the money that has to be worked
for. Every shop is closed when the Cup is run, and
you have lift-boys, waiters and maids all backing their
fancies, not with half-crowns but with substantial sums.
The danger to honesty is obvious, and it came under
our own notice that it is not imaginary. Of course
we are by no means blameless in England, but it only
attacks a limited class, while here it seems to the
stranger to be almost universal. In fact it is so bad
that it is sure to get better, for I cannot conceive that
any sane nation will allow it to continue. The book-
makers, however, are a powerful guild, and will fight
tooth and nail. The Catholic Church, I am sorry to
say, uses its considerable influence to prevent drink
reform by legislation, and I fear that it will not support
the anti-gamblers either. I wonder from what hidden
spring, from what ignorant Italian camarilla, this venerable and in some ways admirable Church gets its
secular policy, which must have central direction, since
it is so consistent! When I remember the recent sequence of world events and the part played by that
Church, the attack upon the innocent Dreyfus, the
refusal to support reform in the Congo, and finally
the obvious leaning towards the Central Powers who
were clearly doomed to lose, one would think that it
was ruled by a Council of Lunatics. These matters
bear no relation to faith or dogma, so that one wonders

that the sane Catholics have not risen in protest. No doubt the better class laymen are ahead of the clergy in this as in other religious organisations. I cannot forget how the Duke of Norfolk sent me a cheque for the Congo Reform Movement at the very time when we could not get the Catholic Church to line up with the other sects at a Reform Demonstration at the Albert Hall. In this country also there were many brave and loyal Catholics who took their own line against Cardinal Mannix upon the question of conscription, when that Cardinal did all that one man could do to bring about the defeat of the free nations in the great war. How he could face an American audience afterwards, or how such an audience could tolerate him, is hard to understand.

CHAPTER V

In some ways the Australians are more English than
the English. We have been imperceptibly American-
ised, while our brethren over the sea have kept the old
type. The Australian is less ready to show emotion,
cooler in his bearing, more restrained in applause, more
devoted to personal liberty, keener on sport, and quieter
in expression (as witness the absence of scare lines
in the papers) than our people are. Indeed, they remind me more of the Scotch than the English, and Melbourne on a Sunday, without posts, or Sunday papers,
or any amenity whatever, is like the Edinburgh of my
boyhood. Sydney is more advanced. There are curious anomalies in both towns. Their telephone systems
are so bad that they can only be balanced against each
other, for they are in a class by themselves. One smiles
when one recollects that one used to grumble at the
London lines. On the other hand the tramway services
in both towns are wonderful, and so continuous that
one never hastens one's step to catch a tram since an-

other comes within a minute. The Melbourne trams
have open bogey cars in front, which make a drive a
real pleasure.

One of our pleasant recollections in the early days
of our Melbourne visit was a day in the bush with
Mr. Henry Stead and his wife. My intense admiration for the moral courage and energy of the father
made it easy for me to form a friendship with his son,
who has shown the family qualities by the able way
in which he has founded and conducted an excellent
journal, *Stead's Monthly.* Australia was lucky ever
to get such an immigrant as that, for surely an honest,
fearless and clear-headed publicist is the most valuable
man that a young country, whose future is one long
problem play, could import. We spent our day in the
Dandenong Hills, twenty miles from Melbourne, in a
little hostel built in a bush clearing and run by one
Lucas, of good English cricket stock, his father having
played for Sussex. On the way we passed Madame
Melba's place at Lilydale, and the wonderful woods
with their strange tree-ferns seemed fit cover for such
a singing bird. Coming back in Stead's light American
car we tried a short cut down roads which proved to be
almost impossible. A rather heavier car ahead of us,
with two youths in it, got embedded in the mud, and
we all dismounted to heave it out. There suddenly
appeared on the lonely road an enormous coloured man;
he looked like a cross between negro and black fellow.
He must have lived in some hut in the woods, but the
way his huge form suddenly rose beside us was quite
surprising. He stood in gloomy majesty surveying our
efforts, and repeating a series of sentences which re-

minded one of German exercises. "I have no jack. I had a jack. Some one has taken my jack. This is called a road. It is not a road. There is no road." We finally levered out the Australian car, for which, by the way, neither occupant said a word of thanks, and then gave the black giant a shilling, which he received as a keeper takes his toll. On looking back I am not sure that this slough of despond is not carefully prepared by this negro, who makes a modest income by the tips which he gets from the unfortunates who get bogged in it. No keeper ever darted out to a trap quicker than he did when the car got stuck.

Stead agreed with me that the Australians do not take a big enough view of their own destiny. They—or the labour party, to be more exact—are inclined to buy the ease of the moment at the cost of the greatness of their continental future. They fear immigration lest it induce competition and pull down prices. It is a natural attitude. And yet that little fringe of people on the edge of that huge island can never adequately handle it. It is like an enormous machine with a six horsepower engine to drive it. I have a great sympathy with their desire to keep the British stock as pure as possible. But the land needs the men, and somewhere they must be found. I cannot doubt that they would become loyal subjects of the Empire which had adopted them. I have wondered sometimes whether in Lower California and the warmer States of the Union there may not be human material for Australia. Canada has received no more valuable stock than from the American States, so it might be that another portion of the Union would find the very stamp of man that Queensland and the north require. The American likes a big gamble and a broad life with plenty of elbow-room. Let him bring his cotton seeds over to semi-tropical Australia and see what he can make of it there.

To pass suddenly to other-worldly things, which are my mission. People never seem to realise the plain fact that one positive result must always outweigh a hundred negative ones. It only needs one single case of spirit return to be established, and there is no more to be said. Incidentally, how absurd is the position of those wiseacres who say "nine-tenths of the phenomena are fraud." Can they not see that if they grant us one-tenth, they grant us our whole contention?

These remarks are elicited by a case which occurred in 1883 in Melbourne, and which should have converted the city as surely as if an angel had walked down Collins Street. Yet nearly forty years later I find it as stagnant and material as any city I have ever visited. The facts are these, well substantiated by documentary and official evidence. Mr. Junor Browne, a well-known citizen, whose daughter afterwards married Mr. Alfred Deakin, subsequently Premier, had two sons, Frank and Hugh. Together with a seaman named Murray they went out into the bay in their yacht the *Iolanthe,* and they never returned. The father was fortunately a Spiritualist and upon the second day of their absence, after making all normal inquiries, he asked a sensitive, Mr. George Spriggs, formerly of Cardiff, if he would trace them. Mr. Spriggs collected some of the young men's belongings, so as to get their atmosphere, and then he was

able by psychometry to give an account of their movements, the last which he could see of them being that
they were in trouble upon the yacht and that confusion
seemed to reign aboard her. Two days later, as no
further news was brought in, the Browne family held
a séance, Mr. Spriggs being the medium. He fell
into trance and the two lads, who had been trained in
spiritual knowledge and knew the possibilities, at once
came through. They expressed their contrition to their
mother, who had desired them not to go, and they
then gave a clear account of the capsizing of the yacht,
and how they had met their death, adding that they had
found themselves after death in the exact physical conditions of happiness and brightness which their father's
teaching had led them to expect. They brought with
them the seaman Murray, who also said a few words.
Finally Hugh, speaking through the medium, informed
Mr. Browne that Frank's arm and part of his clothing
had been torn off by a fish.

"A shark?" asked Mr. Browne.

"Well, it was not like any shark I have seen."

Mark the sequel. Some weeks later a large shark
of a rare deep-sea species, unknown to the fishermen,
and quite unlike the ordinary blue shark with which
the Brownes were familiar, was taken at Frankston,
about twenty-seven miles from Melbourne. Inside it
was found the bone of a human arm, and also a watch,
some coins, and other articles which had belonged to
Frank Browne. These facts were all brought out in
the papers at the time, and Mr. Browne put much of
it on record in print before the shark was taken, or
any word of the missing men had come by normal

means. The facts are all set forth in a little book by Mr. Browne himself, called "A Rational Faith." What have fraudulent mediums and all the other decoys to do with such a case as that, and is it not perfectly convincing to any man who is not perverse? Personally, I value it not so much for the evidence of survival, since we have that so complete already, but for the detailed account given by the young men of their new conditions, so completely corroborating what so many young officers, cut off suddenly in the war, have said of their experience. "Mother, if you could see how happy we are, and the beautiful home we are in, you would not weep except for joy. I feel so light in my spiritual body and have no pain, I would not exchange this life for earth life even it were in my power. Poor spirits without number are waiting anxiously to communicate with their friends when an opportunity is offered." The young Brownes had the enormous advantage of the education they had received from their father, so that they instantly understood and appreciated the new conditions.

On October 8th we had a séance with Mrs. Hunter, a pleasant middle-aged woman, with a soft South of England accent. Like so many of our mediums she had little sign of education in her talk. It does not matter in spiritual things, though it is a stumbling block to some inquirers. After all, how much education had the apostles? I have no doubt they were very vulgar provincial people from the average Roman point of view. But they shook the world none the less. Most of our educated people have got their heads so crammed with things that don't matter that they have no room

[117]

for the things that do matter. There was no particular success at our sitting, but I have heard that the medium is capable of better things.

On October 13th I had my first experience of a small town, for I went to Geelong and lectured there. It was an attentive and cultured audience, but the hall was small and the receipts could hardly have covered the expenses. However, it is the press report and the local discussion which really matter. I had little time to inspect Geelong, which is a prosperous port with 35,000 inhabitants. What interested me more was the huge plain of lava which stretches around it and connects it with Melbourne. This plain is a good hundred miles across, and as it is of great depth one can only imagine that there must be monstrous cavities inside the earth to correspond with the huge amount extruded. Here and there one sees stunted green cones which are the remains of the volcanoes which spewed up all this stuff. The lava has disintegrated on the surface to the extent of making good arable soil, but the harder bits remain unbroken, so that the surface is covered with rocks, which are used to build up walls for the fields after the Irish fashion. Every here and there a peak of granite has remained as an island amid the lava, to show what was there before the great out-flow. Eruptions appear to be caused by water pouring in through some crack and reaching the heated inside of the earth where the water is turned to steam, expands, and so gains the force to spread destruction. If this process went on it is clear that the whole sea might continue to pour down the crack until the heat had been all absorbed by the water. I have wondered whether the lava may not be a clever healing process of nature, by which this soft plastic material is sent oozing out in every direction with the idea that it may find the crack and then set hard and stop it up. Wild speculation no doubt, but the guess must always precede the proof.

The Australians are really a very good-natured people. It runs through the whole race, high and low. A very exalted person, the Minister of War, shares our flat in the hotel, his bedroom being imbedded among our rooms. This is General Sir Granville Ryrie, a famous hero of Palestine, covered with wounds and medals—a man, too, of great dignity of bearing. As I was dressing one morning I heard some rather monotonous whistling and, forgetting the very existence of the General, and taking it for granted that it was my eldest boy Denis, I put my head out and said, "Look here, old chap, consider other people's nerves and give up that rotten habit of whistling before breakfast." Imagine my feelings when the deep voice of the General answered, "All right, Sir Arthur, I will!" We laughed together over the incident afterwards, and I told him that he had furnished me with one more example of Australian good humour for my notes.

On October 13th I was at the prosperous 50,000 population town of Bendigo, which everyone, except the people on the spot, believes to have been named after the famous boxer. This must surely be a world record, for so far as my memory serves, neither a Grecian Olympic athletic, nor a Roman Gladiator, nor a Byzantine Charioteer, has ever had a city for a monument. Borrow, who looked upon a good honest pugilist as the pick of humanity, must have rejoiced in it. Is not valour the basis of all character, and where shall we find greater valour than theirs? Alas, that most of them began and ended there! It is when the sage and the saint build on the basis of the fighter that you have the highest to which humanity can attain.

I had a full hall at Bendigo, and it was packed, I am told, by real old-time miners, for, of course, Bendigo is still the centre of the gold mining industry. Mr. Smythe told me that it was quite a sight to see those rows of deeply-lined, bearded faces listening so intently to what I said of that destiny which is theirs as well as mine. I never had a better audience, and it was their sympathy which helped me through, for I was very weary that night. But however weary you may be, when you climb upon the platform to talk about this subject, you may be certain that you will be less weary when you come off. That is my settled conviction after a hundred trials.

On the morning after my lecture I found myself half a mile nearer to dear Old England, for I descended the Unity mine, and they say that the workings extend to that depth. Perhaps I was not at the lowest level, but certainly it was a long journey in the cage, and reminded me of my friend Bang's description of the New York elevator, when he said that the distance to his suburban villa and his town flat was the same, but the one was horizontal and the other perpendicular.

It was a weird experience that peep into the profound depths of the great gold mine. Time was when the quartz veins were on the surface for the poor adventurer to handle. Now they have been followed underground, and only great companies and costly machinery can win it. Always it is the same white quartz vein with the little yellow specks and threads running through it. We were rattled down in pitch darkness until we came to a stop at the end of a long passage dimly lit by an occasional guttering candle. Carrying our own candles, and clad in miner's costume we crept along with bent heads until we came suddenly out into a huge circular hall which might have sprung from Doré's imagination. The place was draped with heavy black shadows, but every here and there was a dim light. Each light showed where a man was squatting toad-like, a heap of broken débris in front of him, turning it over, and throwing aside the pieces with clear traces of gold. These were kept for special treatment, while the rest of the quartz was passed in ordinary course through the mill. These scattered heaps represented the broken stuff after a charge of dynamite had been exploded in the quartz vein. It was strange indeed to see these squatting figures deep in the bowels of the earth, their candles shining upon their earnest faces and piercing eyes, and to reflect that they were striving that the great exchanges of London and New York might be able to balance with bullion their output of paper. This dim troglodyte industry was in truth the centre and mainspring of all industries, without which trade would stop. Many of the men were from Corn-wall, the troll among the nations, where the tools of the miner are still, as for two thousand years, the natural heritage of the man. Dr. Stillwell, the geolo-gist of the company, and I had a long discussion as to where the gold came from, but the only possible conclusion was that nobody knew. We know now that the old alchemists were perfectly right and that one metal may change into another. Is it possible that under some conditions a mineral may change into a metal? Why should quartz always be the matrix? Some Geological Darwin will come along some day and we shall get a great awakening, for at present we are only disguising our own ignorance in this department of knowledge. I had always understood that quartz was one of the old igneous primeval rocks, and yet here I saw it in thin bands, sandwiched in between clays and slates and other water-borne deposits. The books and the strata don't agree.

These smaller towns, like the Metropolis itself, are convulsed with the great controversy between Prohibition and Continuance, no reasonable compromise between the two being suggested. Every wall displays posters, on one side those very prosperous-looking children who demand that some restraint be placed upon their daddy, and on the other hair-raising statements as to the financial results of restricting the publicans. To the great disgust of every decent man they have run the Prince into it, and some remark of his after his return to England has been used by the liquor party. It is dangerous for royalty to be jocose in these days, but this was a particularly cruel example of the exploitation of a harmless little joke. If others felt as I did I expect it cost the liquor interest many a vote.

We had another seance, this time with Mrs. Knight MacLellan, after my return from Bendigo. She is a lady who has grown grey in the service of the cult, and who made a name in London when she was still a child by her mediumistic powers. We had nothing of an evidential character that evening save that one lady who had recently lost her son had his description and an apposite message given. It was the first of several tests which we were able to give this lady, and before we left Melbourne she assured us that she was a changed woman and her sorrow for ever gone.

On October 18th began a very delightful experience, for my wife and I, leaving our party safe in Melbourne, travelled up country to be the guests of the Hon. Agar Wynne and his charming wife at their station of Nerrim-Nerrim in Western Victoria. It is about 140 miles from Melbourne, and as the trains are very slow, the journey was not a pleasant one. But that was soon compensated for in the warmth of the welcome which awaited us. Mr. Agar Wynne was Postmaster-General of the Federal Government, and author of several improvements, one of which, the power of sending long letter-telegrams at low rates during certain hours was a triumph of common sense. For a shilling one could send quite a long communication to the other end of the Continent, but it must go through at the time when the telegraph clerk had nothing else to do.

It was interesting to us to find ourselves upon an old-established station, typical of the real life of Australia, for cities are much the same the world over. Nerrim had been a sheep station for eighty years, but the comfortable verandaed bungalow house, with every convenience within it, was comparatively modern.' What charmed us most, apart from the kindness of our hosts, was a huge marsh or lagoon which extended for many miles immediately behind the house, and which was a bird sanctuary, so that it was crowded with ibises, wild black swans, geese, ducks, herons and all sorts of fowl. We crept out of our bedroom in the dead of the night and stood under the cloud-swept moon listening to the chorus of screams, hoots, croaks and whistles coming out of the vast expanse of reeds. It would make a most wonderful hunting ground for a naturalist who was content to observe and not to slay. The great morass of Nerrim will ever stand out in our memories.

Next day we were driven round the borders of this wonderful marsh, Mr. Wynne, after the Australian fashion, taking no note of roads, and going right across country with alarming results to anyone not used to it. Finally, the swaying and rolling became so terrific that he was himself thrown off the box seat and fell down between the buggy and the front wheel, narrowly escaping a very serious accident. He was able to show us the nests and eggs which filled the reed-beds, and even offered to drive us out into the morass to inspect them, a proposal which was rejected by the unanimous vote of a full buggy. I never knew an answer more decidedly in the negative. As we drove home we passed a great gum tree, and half-way up the trunk was a deep incision where the bark had been stripped in an oval shape some four foot by two. It was where some savage in days of old had cut his shield. Such a mark outside a modern house with every amenity of cultured life is an object lesson of how two systems have overlapped, and how short a time it is since this great continent was washed by a receding wave, ere the great Anglo-Saxon tide came creeping forward.

Apart from the constant charm of the wild life of the marsh there did not seem to be much for the naturalist around Nerrim. Opossums bounded upon the roof at night and snakes were not uncommon. A dangerous tiger-snake was killed on the day of our arrival. I was amazed also at the size of the Australian eels. A returned soldier had taken up fishing as a trade, renting a water for a certain time and putting the contents, so far as he could realise them, upon the market. It struck me that after this wily digger had passed that way there would not be much for the sportsman who followed him. But the eels were enormous. He took a dozen at a time from his cunning eel-pots, and not one under six pounds. I should have said that they were certainly congers had I seen them in England.

I wonder whether all this part of the country has not been swept by a tidal wave at some not very remote period. It is a low coastline with this great lava plain as a hinterland, and I can see nothing to prevent a big wave even now from sweeping the civilisation of Victoria off the planet, should there be any really great disturbance under the Pacific. At any rate, it is my impression that it has actually occurred once already, for I cannot otherwise understand the existence of great shallow lakes of salt water in these inland parts. Are they not the pools left behind by that terrible tide? There are great banks of sand, too, here and there on the top of the lava which I can in no way account for unless they were swept here in some tremendous world-shaking catastrophe which took the beach from St. Kilda and threw it up at Nerrim. God save Australia from such a night as that must have been if my reading of the signs be correct.

One of the sights of Nerrim is the shearing of the sheep by electric machinery. These sheep are merinos, which have been bred as wool producers to such an extent that they can hardly see, and the wool grows thick right down to their hoofs. The large stately creature is a poor little shadow when his wonderful fleece has been taken from him. The electric clips with which the operation is performed, are, I am told, the invention of a brother of Garnet Wolseley, who worked away at the idea, earning the name of being a half-crazy crank, until at last the invention material-ised and did away with the whole slow and clumsy process of the hand-shearer. It is not, however, a pleasant process to watch even for a man, far less a sensitive woman, for the poor creatures get cut about a good deal in the process. The shearer seizes a sheep, fixes him head up between his knees, and then plunges the swiftly-moving clippers into the thick wool which covers the stomach. With wonderful speed he runs it along and the creature is turned out of its covering, and left as bare as a turkey in a poulterer's window, but, alas, its white and tender skin is too often gashed and ripped with vivid lines of crimson by the haste and clumsiness of the shearer. It was worse, they say, in the days of the hand-shearer. I am bound to say, however, that the creature makes no fuss about it, remains perfectly still, and does not appear to suffer any pain. Nature is often kinder than we know, even to her most humble children, and some soothing and healing process seems to be at work.

The shearers appear to be a rough set of men, and spend their whole time moving in gangs from station to station, beginning up in the far north and winding up on the plains of South Australia. They are complete masters of the situation, having a powerful union at their back. They not only demand and receive some two pounds a day in wages, but they work or not by vote, the majority being able to grant a complete holiday. It is impossible to clip a wet sheep, so that after rain there is an interval of forced idleness, which may be prolonged by the vote of the men. They work very rapidly, however, when they are actually at it, and the man who tallies most fleeces, called "the ringer," receives a substantial bonus. When the great shed is in full activity it is a splendid sight with the row of stooping figures, each embracing his sheep, the buzz of the shears, the rush of the messengers who carry the clip to the table, the swift movements of the sorters who separate the perfect from the imperfect wool, and the levering and straining of the packers who compress it all into square bundles as hard as iron with 240 pounds in each. With fine wool at the present price of ninety-six pence a pound it is clear that each of these cubes stands for nearly a hundred pounds.

They are rich men these sheep owners—and I am speaking here of my general inquiry and not at all of Nerrim. On a rough average, with many local exceptions, one may say that an estate bears one sheep to an acre, and that the sheep will show a clear profit of one pound in the year. Thus, after the first initial expense is passed, and when the flock has reached its full, one may easily make an assessment of the owner's income. Estates of 10,000 acres are common, and they run up to 50,000 and 60,000 acres. They can be run so cheaply that the greater part of income is clear profit, for when the land is barb-wired into great enclosures no shepherds are needed, and only a boundary rider or two to see that all is in order. These, with a few hands at lambing time, and two or three odd-job men at the central station, make up the whole staff. It is certainly the short cut to a fortune if one can only get the plant running.

Can a man with a moderate capital get a share of these good things? Certainly he can if he have grit and a reasonable share of that luck which must always be a factor in Nature's processes. Droughts, floods, cyclones, etc., are like the zero at Monte Carlo, which always may turn up to defeat the struggling gamester. I followed several cases where small men had managed to make good. It is reckoned that the man who gets a holding of from 300 to 500 acres is able on an average in three years to pay off all his initial expenses and to have laid the foundations of a career which may lead to fortune. One case was a London baker who knew nothing of the work. He had 300 acres and had laid it out in wheat, cows, sheep and mixed farming. He worked from morning to night, his wife was up at four, and his child of ten was picking up stones behind the furrow. But he was already making his £500 a year. The personal equation was everything. One demobilised soldier was doing well. Another had come to smash. Very often a deal is made between the small

A TYPICAL AUSTRALIAN BACK-COUNTRY SCENE. By H. J. Johnstone, a great painter who died unknown. (Painting in Adelaide National Gallery.)

man and the large holder, by which the latter lets the former a corner of his estate, taking a share, say one-third, of his profits as rent. That is a plan which suits everyone, and the landlord can gradually be bought out by the "cockatoo farmer," as he is styled.

There is a great wool-clip this year, and prices in London are at record figures, so that Australia, which only retains 17 per cent. of her own wool, should have a very large sum to her credit. But she needs it. When one considers that the debt of this small community is heavier now than that of Great Britain before the war, one wonders how she can ever win through. But how can anyone win through? I don't think we have fairly realised the financial problem yet, and I believe that within a very few years there will be an International Council which will be compelled to adopt some such scheme as the one put forward by my friend, Mr. Stilwell, under the name of "The Great Plan." This excellent idea was that every nation should reduce its warlike expenditure to an absolute minimum, that the difference between this minimum and the 1914 pre-war standard should be paid every year to a central fund, and that international bonds be now drawn upon the security of that fund, anticipating not its present amount but what it will represent in fifty years' time. It is, in fact, making the future help the present, exactly as an estate which has some sudden great call upon it might reasonably anticipate or mortgage its own development. I believe that the salvation of the world may depend upon some such plan, and that the Council of the League of Nations is the agency by which it could be made operative.

THE WANDERINGS OF A SPIRITUALIST

Australia has had two plants which have been a perfect curse to her as covering the land and offering every impediment to agriculture. They are the Spinnifex in the West and the Mallee scrub in the East. The latter was considered a hopeless proposition, and the only good which could be extracted from it was that the root made an ideal fire, smouldering long and retaining heat. Suddenly, however, a genius named Lascelles discovered that this hopeless Mallee land was simply unrivalled for wheat, and his schemes have now brought seven million acres under the plough. This could hardly have been done if another genius, unnamed, had not invented a peculiar and ingenious plough, the "stump-jump plough," which can get round obstacles without breaking itself. It is not generally known that Australia really heads the world for the ingenuity and efficiency of her agricultural machinery. There is an inventor and manufacturer, MacKay, of Sunshine, who represents the last word in automatic reapers, etc. He exports them, a shipload at a time, to the United States, which, if one considers the tariff which they have to surmount, is proof in itself of the supremacy of the article. With this wealth of machinery the real power of Australia in the world is greater than her population would indicate, for a five-million nation, which, by artificial aid, does the work normally done by ten million people, becomes a ten-million nation so far as economic and financial strength is concerned.

On the other hand, Australia has her hindrances as well as her helps. Certainly the rabbits have done her no good, though the evil is for the moment under control. An efficient rabbiter gets a pound a day, and he is a wise insurance upon any estate, for the creatures, if they get the upper-hand, can do thousands of pounds' worth of damage. This damage takes two shapes. First, they eat off all the grass and leave nothing at all for the sheep. Secondly, they burrow under walls, etc., and leave the whole place an untidy ruin. Little did the man who introduced the creature into Australia dream how the imprecations of a continent would descend upon him.

Alas! that we could not linger at Nerrim; but duty was calling at Melbourne. Besides, the days of the Melbourne Cup were at hand, and not only was Mr. Wynne a great pillar of the turf, but Mr. Osborne, owner of one of the most likely horses in the race, was one of the house-party. To Melbourne therefore we went. We shall always, however, be able in our dreams to revisit that broad verandah, the low hospitable façade, the lovely lawn with its profusion of scented shrubs, the grove of towering gum trees, where the opossums lurked, and above all the great marsh where with dark clouds drifting across the moon we had stolen out at night to hear the crying of innumerable birds. That to us will always be the real Australia.

CHAPTER VI

The Melbourne Cup.—Psychic healing.—M. J. Bloomfield.—
My own experience.—Direct healing.—Chaos and Ritual.
—Government House Ball.—The Rescue Circle again.—
Sitting with Mrs. Harris.—A good test case.—Australian
botany.—The land of myrtles.—English cricket team.—
Great final meeting in Melbourne.

It was the week of weeks in Melbourne when we
returned from Nerrim, and everything connected with
my mission was out of the question. When the whole
world is living vividly here and now there is no room
for the hereafter. Personally, I fear I was out of
sympathy with it all, though we went to the Derby,
where the whole male and a good part of the female
population of Melbourne seemed to be assembled, rein-
forced by contingents from every State in the Federation. A fine handsome body of people they are when
you see them *en masse,* strong, solid and capable, if
perhaps a little lacking in those finer and more spiritual
graces which come with a more matured society. The
great supply of animal food must have its effect upon
the mind as well as the body of a nation. Lord Forster
appeared at the races, and probably, as an all round
sportsman, took a genuine interest, but the fate of the
Governor who did not take an interest would be a
rather weary one—like that kind-hearted Roman Em-
peror, Claudius, if I remember right, who had to
attend the gladiatorial shows, but did his business there

so as to distract his attention from the arena. We managed to get out of attending the famous Melbourne Cup, and thereby found the St. Kilda Beach deserted for once, and I was able to spend a quiet day with my wife watching the children bathe and preparing for the more strenuous times ahead.

One psychic subject which has puzzled me more than any other, is that of magnetic healing. All my instincts as a doctor, and all the traditional teaching of the profession, cry out against unexplained effects, and the opening which their acceptance must give to the quack. The man who has paid a thousand pounds for his special knowledge has a natural distaste when he sees a man who does not know the subclavian artery from the pineal gland, effecting or claiming to effect cures on some quite unconventional line. And yet . . . and yet!

The ancients knew a great deal which we have forgotten, especially about the relation of one body to another. What did Hippocrates mean when he said, "The affections suffered by the body the soul sees with shut eyes"? I will show you exactly what he means. My friend, M. J. Bloomfield, as unselfish a worker for truth as the world can show, tried for nearly two years to develop the medical powers of a clairvoyant. Suddenly the result was attained, without warning. He was walking with a friend in Collins Street laughing over some joke. In an instant the laugh was struck from his lips. A man and woman were walking in front, their backs towards Bloomfield. To his amazement he saw the woman's inner anatomy mapped out before him, and especially marked a rounded mass near the liver which he felt intuitively should not be there. His companion rallied him on his sudden gravity, and still more upon the cause of it, when it was explained. Bloomfield was so certain, however, that the vision was for a purpose, that he accosted the couple, and learned that the woman was actually about to be operated on for cancer. He reassured them, saying that the object seemed clearly defined and not to have widespread roots as a cancer might have. He was asked to be present at the operation, pointed out the exact place where he had seen the growth, and saw it extracted. It was, as he had said, innocuous. With this example in one's mind the words of Hippocrates begin to assume a very definite meaning. I believe that the surgeon was so struck by the incident that he was most anxious that Bloomfield should aid him permanently in his diagnoses.

I will now give my own experience with Mr. Bloomfield. Denis had been suffering from certain pains, so I took him round as a test case. Bloomfield, without asking the boy any questions, gazed at him for a couple of minutes. He then said that the pains were in the stomach and head, pointing out the exact places. The cause, he said, was some slight stricture in the intestine and he proceeded to tell me several facts of Denis's early history which were quite correct, and entirely beyond his normal knowledge. I have never in all my experience of medicine known so accurate a diagnosis.

Another lady, whom I knew, consulted him for what she called a "medical reading." Without examining her in any way he said: "What a peculiar throat you have! It is all pouched inside." She admitted that this was so, and that doctors in London had commented upon it. By his clairvoyant gift he could see as much as they with their laryngoscopes.

Mr. Bloomfield has never accepted any fees for his remarkable gifts. Last year he gave 3,000 consultations. I have heard of mediums with similar powers in England, but I had never before been in actual contact with one. With all my professional prejudices I am bound to admit that they have powers, just as Braid and Esdaile, the pioneers of hypnotism, had powers, which must sooner or later be acknowledged.

There are, as I understand it, at least two quite different forms of psychic healing. In such cases as those quoted the result may be due only to subtle powers of the human organism which some have developed and others have not. The clairvoyance and the instinctive knowledge may both belong to the individual. In the other cases, however, there are the direct action and advice of a wise spirit control, a deceased physician usually, who has added to his worldly stock of knowledge. He can, of course, only act through a medium— and just there, alas, is the dangerous opening for fraud and quackery. But if anyone wishes to study the operation at its best let him read a tiny book called "One Thing I Know," which records the cure of the writer, the sister of an Anglican canon, when she had practically been given up by doctors of this world after fifteen years of bed, but was rescued by the ministrations of Dr. Beale, a physician on the other side. Dr. Beale received promotion to a higher sphere in the course of the treatment, which was completed by his assistant and successor. It is a very interesting and convincing narrative.

We were invited to another spiritual meeting at the Auditorium. Individuality runs riot sometimes in our movement. On this occasion a concert had been mixed up with a religious service and the effect was not good, though the musical part of the proceedings disclosed one young violinist, Master Hames, who should, I think, make a name in the world. I have always been against ritual, and yet now that I see the effect of being without it I begin to understand that some form of it, however elastic, is necessary. The clairvoyance was good, if genuine, but it offends me to see it turned off and on like a turn at a music hall. It is either nonsense or the holy of holies and mystery of mysteries. Perhaps it was just this conflict between the priest with his ritual and the medium without any, which split the early Christian Church, and ended in the complete victory of the ritual, which meant the extinction not only of the medium but of the living, visible, spiritual forces which he represented. Flowers, music, incense, architecture, all tried to fill the gap, but the soul of the thing had gone out of it. It must, I suppose, have been about the end of the third century that the process was completed, and the living thing had set into a petrifaction. That would be the time no doubt when, as already mentioned, special correctors were appointed to make the gospel texts square with the elaborate machinery of the Church. Only now does the central fire begin to glow once more through the ashes which have been heaped above it.

We attended the great annual ball at the Government House, where the Governor-General and his wife were supported by the Governors of the various States, the vice-regal party performing their own stately quadrille with a dense hedge of spectators around them. There were few chaperons, and nearly everyone ended by dancing, so that it was a cheerful and festive scene. My friend Major Wood had played with the Governor-General in the same Hampshire eleven, and it was singular to think that after many years they should meet again like this.

Social gaieties are somewhat out of key with my present train of thought, and I was more in my element next evening at a meeting of the Rescue Circle under Mr. Tozer. Mr. Love was the medium and it was certainly a very remarkable and consistent performance. Even those who might imagine that the different characters depicted were in fact various strands of Mr. Love's subconscious self, each dramatising its own peculiarities, must admit that it was a very absorbing exhibition. The circle sits round with prayer and hymns while Mr. Love falls into a trance state. He is then controlled by the Chinaman Quong, who is a person of such standing and wisdom in the other world, that other lower spirits have to obey him. The light is dim, but even so the characteristics of this Chinaman get across very clearly, the rolling head, the sidelong, humorous glance, the sly smile, the hands crossed and buried in what should be the voluminous folds of a mandarin's gown. He greets the company in somewhat laboured English and says he has many who would be the better for our ministrations. "Send them along, please!" says Mr. Tozer. The medium suddenly sits straight and his whole face changes into an austere harshness. "What is this ribald nonsense?" he cries. "Who are you, friend?" says Tozer. "My name is Mathew Barret. I testified in my life to the Lamb and to Him crucified." I ask again: "What is this ribald nonsense?" "It is not nonsense, friend. We are here to help you and to teach you that you are held down and punished for your narrow ideas, and that you cannot progress until they are more charitable." "What I preached in life I still believe." "Tell us, friend, did you find it on the other side as you had preached?" "What do you mean?" "Well, did you, for example, see Christ?" There was an embarrassed silence. "No, I did not." "Have you seen the devil?" "No, I have not." "Then, bethink you, friend, that there may be truth in what we teach." "It is against all that I have preached." A moment later the China-man was back with his rolling head and his wise smile. "He good man—stupid man. He learn in time. Plenty time before him."

We had a wonderful succession of "revenants." One was a very dignified Anglican, who always referred to the Control as "this yellow person." Another was an Australian soldier. "I never thought I'd take my or-ders from a 'Chink,' " said he, "but he says 'hist!' and by gum you've got to 'hist' and no bloomin' error." Yet another said he had gone down in the *Monmouth*. "Can you tell me anything of the action?" I asked. "We never had a chance. It was just hell." There was a world of feeling in his voice. He was greatly amused at their "sky-pilot," as he called the chaplain, and at his confusion when he found the other world quite different to what he had depicted. A terrifying Ghurkha came along, who still thought he was in action and charged about the circle, upsetting the medium's chair, and only yielding to a mixture of force and persuasion. There were many others, most of whom returned thanks for the benefit derived from previous meetings. "You've helped us quite a lot," they said. Between each the old Chinese sage made comments upon the various cases, a kindly, wise old soul, with just a touch of mischievous humour running through him. We had an exhibition of the useless apostolic gift of tongues during the evening, for two of the ladies present broke out into what I was informed was the Maori language, keeping up a long and loud conversation. I was not able to check it, but it was certainly a coherent language of some sort. In all this there was nothing which one could take hold of and quote as absolutely and finally evidential, and yet the total effect was most convincing. I have been in touch with some Rescue Circles, however, where the identity of the "patients," as we may call them, was absolutely traced.

As I am on the subject of psychic experiences I may as well carry on, so that the reader who is out of sympathy may make a single skip of the lot. Mrs. Susanna Harris, the American voice-medium, who is well known in London, had arrived here shortly after ourselves, and gave us a sitting. Mrs. Harris's powers have been much discussed, for while on the one hand she passed a most difficult test in London, where, with her mouth full of coloured water, she produced the same voice effects as on other occasions, she had no success in Norway when she was examined by their Psychic Research Committee; but I know how often these intellectuals ruin their own effects by their mental attitude, which acts like those anti-ferments which prevent a chemical effervescence. We must always get back to the principle, however, that one positive result is more important than a hundred negative ones—just as one successful demonstration in chemistry makes up for any number of failures. We cannot command spirit action, and we can only commiserate with, not blame, the medium who does not receive it when it is most desired. Personally I have sat four times with Mrs. Harris and I have not the faintest doubt that on each of these occasions I got true psychic results, though I cannot answer for what happens in Norway or elsewhere.

Shortly after her arrival in Melbourne she gave us a séance in our private room at the hotel, no one being present save at my invitation. There were about twelve guests, some of whom had no psychic experience, and I do not think there was one of them who did not depart convinced that they had been in touch with preternatural forces. There were two controls, Harmony, with a high girlish treble voice, and a male control with a strong decisive bass. I sat next to Mrs. Harris, holding her hand in mine, and I can swear to it that again and again she spoke to me while the other voices were conversing with the audience. Harmony is a charming little creature, witty, friendly and innocent. I am quite ready to consider the opinion expressed by the Theosophists that such controls as Harmony with Mrs. Harris, Bella with Mrs. Brittain, Feda with Mrs.

Leonard, and others are in reality nature-spirits who have never lived in the flesh but take an intelligent interest in our affairs and are anxious to help us. The male control, however, who always broke in with some final clinching remark in a deep voice, seemed altogether human.

Whilst these two controls formed, and were the chorus of the play, the real drama rested with the spirit voices, the same here as I have heard them under Mrs. Wriedt, Mrs. Johnson or Mr. Powell in England, intense, low, vibrating with emotion and with anxiety to get through. Nearly everyone in the circle had communications which satisfied them. One lady who had mourned her husband very deeply had the inexpressible satisfaction of hearing his voice thanking her for putting flowers before his photograph, a fact which no one else could know. A voice claiming to be "Moore-Usborne Moore," came in front of me. I said, "Well, Admiral, we never met but we corresponded in life." He said, "Yes, and we disagreed," which was true. Then there came a voice which claimed to be Mr. J. Morse, the eminent pioneer of Spiritualism. I said, "Mr. Morse, if that is you, you can tell me where we met last." He answered, "Was it not in 'Light' office in London?" I said, "No, surely it was when you took the chair for me at that great meeting at Sheffield." He answered, "Well, we lose some of our memory in passing." As a matter of fact he was perfectly right, for after the sitting both my wife and I remembered that I had exchanged a word or two with him as I was coming out of *Light* office at least a year after the Sheffield meeting. This was a good test as telepathy was excluded. General Sir Alfred Turner also came and said that he remembered our conversations on earth. When I asked him whether he had found the conditions beyond the grave as happy as he expected he answered, "infinitely more so." Altogether I should think that not less than twenty spirits manifested during this remarkable séance. The result may have been the better because Mrs. Harris had been laid up in bed for a week beforehand, and so we had her full force. I fancy that like most mediums, she habitually overworks her wonderful powers. Such séances have been going on now for seventy years, with innumerable witnesses of credit who will testify, as I have done here, that all fraud or mistake was out of the question. And still the men of no experience shake their heads. I wonder how long they will succeed in standing between the world and the consolation which God has sent us.

There is one thing very clear about mediumship and that is that it bears no relation to physical form. Mrs. Harris is a very large lady, tall and Junoesque, a figure which would catch the eye in any assembly. She has, I believe, a dash of the mystic Red Indian blood in her, which may be connected with her powers. Bailey, on the other hand, is a little, ginger-coloured man, while Campbell of Sydney, who is said to have apport powers which equal Bailey, is a stout man, rather like the late Corney Grain. Every shape and every quality of vessel may hold the psychic essence.

I spend such spare time as I have in the Melbourne Botanical Gardens, which is, I think, absolutely the most beautiful place that I have ever seen. I do not know what genius laid them out, but the effect is a succession of the most lovely vistas, where flowers, shrubs, large trees and stretches of water, are combined in an extraordinary harmony. Green swards slope down to many tinted groves, and they in turn droop over still ponds mottled with lovely water plants. It is an instructive as well as a beautiful place, for every tree has its visiting card attached and one soon comes to know them. Australia is preeminently the Land of the Myrtles, for a large proportion of its vegetation comes under this one order, which includes the gum trees, of which there are 170 varieties. They all shed their bark instead of their leaves, and have a generally untidy, not to say indecent appearance, as they stand with their covering in tatters and their white under-bark shining through the rents. There is not the same variety of species in Australia as in England, and it greatly helps a superficial botanist like myself, for when you have learned the ti-tree, the wild fig tree and the gum trees, you will be on terms with nature wherever you go. New Zealand, however, offers quite a fresh lot of problems.

The Melbourne Cricket Club has made me an honorary member, so Denis and I went down there, where we met the giant bowler, Hugh Trumble, who left so redoubtable a name in England. As the Chela may look at the Yogi so did Denis, with adoring eyes, gaze upon Trumble, which so touched his kind heart that he produced a cricket ball, used in some famous match, which he gave to the boy—a treasure which will be reverently brought back to England. I fancy Denis slept with it that night, as he certainly did in his pads and gloves the first time that he owned them.

We saw the English team play Victoria, and it was pleasant to see the well-known faces once more. The luck was all one way, for Armstrong was on the sick list, and Armstrong is the mainstay of Victorian cricket. Rain came at a critical moment also, and gave Woolley and Rhodes a wicket which was impossible for a batsman. However, it was all good practice for the more exacting games of the future. It should be a fine eleven which contains a genius like Hobbs, backed by such men as the bustling bulldog, Hendren, a great out-field as well as a grand bat, or the wily, dangerous Hearne, or Douglas, cricketer, boxer, above all warrior, a worthy leader of Englishmen. Hearne I remember as little more than a boy, when he promised to carry on the glories of that remarkable family, of which George and Alec were my own playmates. He has ended by proving himself the greatest of them all.

My long interval of enforced rest came at last to an end, when the race fever had spent itself, and I was able to have my last great meeting at the Town Hall. It really was a great meeting, as the photograph of it will show. I spoke for over two hours, ending up by showing a selection of the photographs. I dealt faithfully with the treatment given to me by the *Argus*. I take the extract from the published account. "On this, the last time in my life that I shall address a Melbourne audience, I wish to thank the people for the courtesy with which we have been received. It would, however, be hypocritical upon my part if I were to thank the Press. A week before I entered Melbourne

AT MELBOURNE TOWN HALL, NOVEMBER 12TH, 1920.

the *Argus* declared that I was an emissary of the devil (laughter). I care nothing for that. I am out for a fight and can take any knocks that come. But the *Argus* refused to publish a word I said. I came 12,000 miles to give you a message of hope and comfort, and I appeal to you to say whether three or four gentlemen sitting in a board-room have a right to say to the people of Melbournè, 'You shall not listen to that man nor read one word of what he has to say.' (Cries of 'Shame!') You, I am sure, resent being spoon-fed in such a manner." The audience showed in the most hearty fashion that they did resent it, and they cheered loudly when I pointed out that my remarks did not arise, as anyone could see by looking round, from any feeling on my part that my mission had failed to gain popular support. It was a great evening, and I have never addressed a more sympathetic audience. The difficulty always is for my wife and myself to escape from our kind well-wishers, and it is touching and heartening to hear the sincere "God bless you!" which they shower upon us as we pass.

This then was the climax of our mission in Melbourne. It was marred by the long but unavoidable delay in the middle, but it began well and ended splendidly. On November 13th we left the beautiful town behind us, and embarked upon what we felt would be a much more adventurous period at Sydney, for all we had heard showed that both our friends and our enemies were more active in the great seaport of New South Wales.

CHAPTER VII

Great reception at Sydney.—Importance of Sydney.—
Journalistic luncheon.—A psychic epidemic.—Gregory.
—Barracking.—Town Hall reception.—Regulation of
Spiritualism.—An ether apport.—Surfing at Manly.—
A challenge.—Bigoted opponents.—A disgruntled pho-
tographer.—Outing in the Harbour.—Dr. Mildred
Creed.—Leon Gellert.—Norman Lindsay.—Bishop Lead-
beater.—Our relations with Theosophy.—Incongruities
of H. P. B.—Of D. D. Home.

WE had a wonderful reception at Sydney. I have a
great shrinking from such deputations as they catch
you at the moment when you are exhausted and unkempt after a long journey, and when you need all
your energies to collect your baggage and belongings
so as to make your way to your hotel. But on this
occasion it was so hearty, and the crowd of faces
beamed such good wishes upon us that it was quite a
pick-me-up to all of us. "God bless you!" and "Thank
God you have come!" reached us from all sides. My
wife, covered with flowers, was hustled off in one direction, while I was borne away in another, and each of
the children was the centre of a separate group. Major
Wood had gone off to see to the luggage, and Jakeman
was herself embedded somewhere in the crowd, so at
last I had to shout, "Where's that little girl? Where's
that little boy?" until we reassembled and were able,
laden with bouquets, to reach our carriage. The evening paper spread itself over the scene.

[146]

THE WANDERINGS OF A SPIRITUALIST

"When Sir Conan Doyle, his wife and their three children arrived from Melbourne by the express this morning, an assembly of Spiritualists accorded them a splendid greeting. Men swung their hats high and cheered, women danced in their excitement, and many of their number rushed the party with rare bouquets. The excitement was at its highest, and Sir Conan being literally carried along the platform by the pressing crowds, when a digger arrived on the outskirts. 'Who's that?' he asked of nobody in particular. Almost immediately an urchin replied, 'The bloke that wrote "Sherlock Holmes."' When asked if the latter gentleman was really and irretrievably dead the author of his being remarked, 'Well, you can say that a coroner has never sat upon him.'"

It was a grand start, and we felt at once in a larger and more vigorous world, where, if we had fiercer foes, we at least had warm and well-organised friends. Better friends than those of Melbourne do not exist, but there was a method and cohesion about Sydney which impressed us from the first day to the last. There seemed, also, to be fewer of those schisms which are the bane of our movement. If Wells's dictum that organisation is death has truth in it, then we are very much alive.

We had rooms in Petty's Hotel, which is an old-world hostel with a very quiet, soothing atmosphere. There I was at once engaged with the usual succession of journalists with a long list of questions which ranged from the destiny of the human soul to the chances of the test match. What with the constant visitors, the unpacking of our trunks, and the settling down of the children, we were a very weary band before evening.

I had no idea that Sydney was so great a place. The population is now very nearly a million, which represents more than one-sixth of the whole vast Continent. It seems a weak point of the Australian system that 41 per cent. of the whole population dwell in the six capital cities. The vital statistics of Sydney are extraordinarily good, for the death rate is now only twelve per thousand per annum. Our standard in such matters is continually rising, for I can remember the days when twenty per thousand was reckoned to be a very good result. In every civic amenity Sydney stands very high. Her Botanical Gardens are not so supremely good as those of Melbourne, but her Zoo is among the very best in the world. The animals seem to be confined by trenches rather than by bars, so that they have the appearance of being at large. It was only after Jakeman had done a level hundred with a child under each arm that she realised that a bear, which she saw approaching, was not really in a state of freedom.

As to the natural situation of Sydney, especially its harbour, it is so world-renowned that it is hardly necessary to allude to it. I can well imagine that a Sydney man would grow homesick elsewhere, for he could never find the same surroundings. The splendid landlocked bay with its numerous side estuaries and its narrow entrance is a grand playground for a sea-loving race. On a Saturday it is covered with every kind of craft, from canoe to hundred-tonner. The fact that the water swarms with sharks seems to present no fears to these strong-nerved people, and I have found myself horrified as I watched little craft, manned by boys, heeling over in a fresh breeze until the water was up to their gunwales. At very long intervals some one gets eaten, but the fun goes on all the same.

The people of Sydney have their residences (bungalows with verandas) all round this beautiful bay, forming dozens of little townlets. The system of ferry steamers becomes as important as the trams, and is extraordinarily cheap and convenient. To Manly, for example, which lies some eight miles out, and is a favourite watering place, the fare is fivepence for adults and twopence for children. So frequent are the boats that you never worry about catching them, for if one is gone another will presently start. Thus, the whole life of Sydney seems to converge into the Circular Quay, from which as many as half a dozen of these busy little steamers may be seen casting off simultaneously for one or another of the oversea suburbs. Now and then, in a real cyclone, the service gets suspended, but it is a rare event, and there is a supplementary, but roundabout, service of trams.

The journalists of New South Wales gave a lunch to my wife and myself, which was a very pleasant function. One leading journalist announced, amid laughter, that he had actually consulted me professionally in my doctoring days, and had lived to tell the tale, which contradicts the base insinuation of some orator who remarked once that though I was known to have practised, no *living* patient of mine had ever yet been seen.

Nothing could have been more successful than my first lecture, which filled the Town Hall. There were evidently a few people who had come with intent to make a scene, but I had my audience so entirely with me, that it was impossible to cause real trouble. One fanatic near the door cried out, "Anti-Christ!" several times, and was then bundled out. Another, when I described how my son had come back to me, cried out that it was the devil, but on my saying with a laugh that such a remark showed the queer workings of some people's minds, the people cheered loudly in assent. Altogether it was a great success, which was repeated in the second, and culminated in the third, when, with a hot summer day, and the English cricketers making their début, I still broke the record for a Town Hall matinée. The rush was more than the officials could cope with, and I had to stand for ten long minutes looking at the audience before it was settled enough for me to begin. Some Spiritualists in the audience struck up "Lead, Kindly Light!" which gave the right note to the assemblage. Mr. Smythe, with all his experience, was amazed at our results. "This is no longer a mere success," he cried. "It is a triumph. It is an epidemic!" Surely, it will leave some permanent good behind it and turn the public mind from religious shadows to realities.

We spent one restful day seeing our cricketers play New South Wales. After a promising start they were beaten owing to a phenomenal first-wicket stand in the second innings by Macartney and Collins, both batsmen topping the hundred. Gregory seemed a dangerous bowler, making the ball rise shoulder high even on that Bulli wicket, where midstump is as much as an ordinary bowler can attain. He is a tiger of a man,

putting every ounce of his strength and inch of his
great height into every ball, with none of the artistic
finesse of a Spofforth, but very effective all the same.
We have no one of the same class, and that will win
Australia the rubber unless I am—as I hope I am—a
false prophet. I was not much impressed either by
the manners or by the knowledge of the game shown
by the barrackers. Every now and then, out of the
mass of people who darken the grass slopes round
the ground, you hear a raucous voice giving advice to
the captain, or, perhaps, conjuring a fast bowler to
bowl at the wicket when the man is keeping a perfect
length outside the off stump and trying to serve his
three slips. When Mailey went on, because he was
slow and seemed easy, they began to jeer, and, yet, you
had only to watch the batsman to see that the ball was
doing a lot and kept him guessing. One wonders why
the neighbors of these bawlers tolerate it. In England such men would soon be made to feel that they
were ill-mannered nuisances. I am bound to testify,
however, that they seem quite impartial, and that the
English team had no special cause for complaint. I
may also add that, apart from this cricketing peculiarity, which is common to all the States, the Sydney
crowd is said to be one of the most good-humoured
and orderly in the world. My own observation confirms this, and I should say that there was a good deal
less drunkenness than in Melbourne, but, perhaps the
races gave me an exaggerated impression of the latter.

On Sunday, 28th, the Spiritualists gave the pilgrims
(as they called us) a reception at the Town Hall.
There was not a seat vacant, and the sight of these

3,500 well-dressed, intelligent people must have taught the press that the movement is not to be despised. There are at least 10,000 professed Spiritualists in Sydney, and even as a political force they demand consideration. The seven of us were placed in the front of the platform, and the service was very dignified and impressive. When the great audience sang, "God hold you safely till we meet once more," it was almost overpowering, for it is a beautiful tune, and was sung with real feeling. In my remarks I covered a good deal of ground, but very particularly I warned them against all worldly use of this great knowledge, whether it be fortune telling, prophecies about races and stocks, or any other prostitution of our subject. I also exhorted them when they found fraud to expose it at once, as their British brethren do, and never to trifle with truth. When I had finished, the whole 3,500 people stood up, and everyone waved a handkerchief, producing a really wonderful scene. We can never forget it.

Once more I must take refuge behind the local *Observer.* "The scene as Sir Arthur rose will be long remembered by those who were privileged to witness it. A sea of waving handkerchiefs confronted the speaker, acclaiming silently and reverently the deep esteem in which he was held by all present. Never has Sir Arthur's earnestness in his mission been more apparent than on this occasion as he proceeded with a heart to heart talk with the Spiritualists present, offering friendly criticisms, sound advice, and encouragement to the adherents of the great movement.

" 'He had got,' he said, 'so much into the habit of lecturing that he was going to lecture the Spiritualists.'

With a flash of humour Sir Arthur added: 'It does none of us any harm to be lectured occasionally. I am a married man myself' (laughter). 'I would say to the Spiritualists, "For Heaven's sake keep this thing high and unspotted. Don't let it drop into the regions of fortune telling and other things which leave such an ugly impression on the public mind, and which we find it so difficult to justify. Keep it in its most religious and purest aspect." ' " At the same time, I expressed my view that there was no reason at all why a medium should not receive moderate payment for work done, since it is impossible, otherwise, that he can live.

Every solid Spiritualist would, I am sure, agree with me that our whole subject needs regulating, and is in an unsatisfactory condition. We cannot approve of the sensation mongers who run from medium to medium (or possibly pretended medium) with no object but excitement or curiosity. The trouble is that you have to recognise a thing before you can regulate it, and the public has not properly recognised us. Let them frankly do so, and take us into counsel, and then we shall get things on a solid basis. Personally, I would be ready to go so far as to agree that an inquirer should take out a formal permit to consult a medium, showing that it was done for some definite object, if in return we could get State recognition for those mediums who were recommended as genuine by valid spiritual authorities. My friends will think this a reactionary proposition, but none the less I feel the need of regulation almost as much as I do that of recognition.

One event which occurred to me at Sydney I shall

always regard as an instance of that fostering care of which I have been conscious ever since we set forth upon our journey. I had been overtired, had slept badly and had a large meeting in the evening, so that it was imperative that I should have a nap in the afternoon. My brain was racing, however, and I could get no rest or prospect of any. The second floor window was slightly open behind me, and outside was a broad open space, shimmering in the heat of a summer day. Suddenly, as I lay there, I was aware of a very distinct pungent smell of ether, coming in waves from outside. With each fresh wave I felt my over-excited nerves calming down as the sea does when oil is poured upon it. Within a few minutes I was in a deep sleep, and woke all ready for my evening's work. I looked out of the window and tried to picture where the ether could have come from, then I returned thanks for one more benefit received. I do not suppose that I am alone in such interpositions, but I think that our minds are so centred on this tiny mud patch, that we are deaf and blind to all that impinges on us from beyond.

Having finished in Sydney, and my New Zealand date having not yet arrived, we shifted our quarters to Manly, upon the seacoast, about eight miles from the town. Here we all devoted ourselves to surf-bathing, spending a good deal of our day in the water, as is the custom of the place. It is a real romp with Nature, for the great Pacific rollers come sweeping in and break over you, rolling you over on the sand if they catch you unawares. It was a golden patch in our restless lives. There were surf boards, and I am told that there were men competent to ride them, but I saw none of Jack London's Sun Gods riding in erect upon the crest of the great rollers. Alas, poor Jack London! What right had such a man to die, he who had more vim and passion, and knowledge of varied life than the very best of us? Apart from all his splendid exuberance and exaggeration he had very real roots of grand literature within him. I remember, particularly, the little episodes of bygone days in "The Jacket." The man who wrote those could do anything. Those whom the American public love die young. Frank Norris, Harold Frederic, Stephen Crane, the author of "David Harum," and now Jack London—but the greatest of these was Jack London.

There is a grand beach at Manly, and the thundering rollers carry in some flotsam from the great ocean. One morning the place was covered with beautiful blue jelly-fish, like little Roman lamps with tendrils hanging down. I picked up one of these pretty things, and was just marvelling at its complete construction when I discovered that it was even more complete than I supposed, for it gave me a violent sting. For a day or two I had reason to remember my little blue castaway, with his up-to-date fittings for keeping the stranger at a distance.

I was baited at Sydney by a person of the name of Simpson, representing Christianity, though I was never clear what particular branch of religion he represented, and he was disowned by some leaders of Christian Thought. I believe he was president of the Christian Evidence Society. His opposition, though vigorous, and occasionally personal, was perfectly legitimate, but his well-advertised meeting at the Town Hall (though no charge was made for admission) was not a success. His constant demand was that I should meet him in debate, which was, of course, out of the question, since no debate is possible between a man who considers a text to be final, and one who cannot take this view. My whole energies, so much needed for my obvious work, would have been frittered away in barren controversies had I allowed my hand to be forced. I had learned my lesson, however, at the M'Cabe debate in London, when I saw clearly that nothing could come from such proceedings. On the other hand, I conceived the idea of what would be a real test, and I issued it as a challenge in the public press. "It is clear," I said, "that one single case of spirit return proves our whole contention. Therefore, let the question be concentrated upon one, or, if necessary, upon three cases. These I would undertake to prove, producing my witnesses in the usual way. My opponent would act the part of hostile counsel, cross-examining and criticising my facts. The case would be decided by a majority vote of a jury of twelve, chosen from men of standing, who pledged themselves as open-minded on the question. Such a test could obviously only take place in a room of limited dimensions, so that no money would be involved and truth only be at stake. That is all that I seek. If such a test can be arranged I am ready for it, either before I leave, or after I return from New Zealand." This challenge was not taken up by my opponents.

Mr. Simpson had a long tirade in the Sydney papers about the evil religious effects of my mission, which caused me to write a reply in which I defined our position in a way which may be instructive to others. I said :—

"The tenets which we Spiritualists preach and which I uphold upon the platform are that any man who is deriving spirituality from his creed, be that creed what it may, is learning the lesson of life. For this reason we would not attack your creed, however repulsive it might seem to us, so long as you and your colleagues might be getting any benefit from it. We desire to go our own way, saying what we know to be true, and claiming from others the same liberty of conscience and of expression which we freely grant to them.

"You, on the other hand, go out of your way to attack us, to call us evil names, and to pretend that those loved ones who return to us are in truth devils, and that our phenomena, though they are obviously of the same sort as those which are associated with early Christianity, are diabolical in their nature. This absurd view is put forward without a shadow of proof, and entirely upon the supposed meaning of certain ancient texts which refer in reality to a very different matter, but which are strained and twisted to suit your purpose.

"It is men like you and your colleagues who, by your parody of Christianity and your constant exhibition of those very qualities which Christ denounced in the Pharisees, have driven many reasonable people away from religion and left the churches half empty. Your predecessors, who took the same narrow view of the literal interpretation of the Bible, were guilty of the murder of many thousands of defenceless old women who were burned in deference to the text, 'Suffer no witch to live.' Undeterred by this terrible result of the literal reading, you still advocate it, although you must be well aware that polygamy, slavery and murder can all be justified by such a course.

"In conclusion, let me give you the advice to reconsider your position, to be more charitable to your neighbours, and to devote your redundant energies to combating the utter materialism which is all round you, instead of railing so bitterly at those who are proving immortality and the need for good living in a way which meets their spiritual wants, even though it is foreign to yours."

A photographer, named Mark Blow, also caused me annoyance by announcing that my photographs were fakes, and that he was prepared to give £25 to any charity if he could not reproduce them. I at once offered the same sum if he could do so, and I met him by appointment at the office of the evening paper, the editor being present to see fair play. I placed my money on the table, but Mr. Blow did not cover it. I then produced a packet of plates from my pocket and suggested that we go straight across to Mr. Blow's studio and produce the photographs. He replied by asking me a long string of questions as to the conditions under which the Crewe photographs were produced, noting down all my answers. I then renewed my proposition. He answered that it was absurd to expect him to produce a spirit photograph since he did not believe in such foolish things. I answered that I did not ask him to produce a spirit photograph, but to fulfil his promise which was to produce a similar result upon the plate under similar conditions. He held out that they should be his own conditions. I pointed out that any school boy could make a half-exposed impression upon a plate, and that the whole test lay in the conditions. As he refused to submit to test conditions the matter fell through, as all such foolish challenges fall through. It was equally foolish on my part to have taken any notice of it.

I had a conversation with Mr. Maskell, the capable Secretary of the Sydney Spiritualists, in which he described how he came out originally from Leicester to Australia. He had at that time developed some power of clairvoyance, but it was very intermittent. He had hesitated in his mind whether he should emigrate to Australia, and sat one night debating it within himself, while his little son sat at the table cutting patterns out of paper. Maskell said to his spirit guides, mentally, "If it is good that I go abroad give me the vision of a star. If not, let it be a circle." He waited for half an hour or so, but no vision came, and he was rising in disappointment when the little boy turned round and said, "Daddy, here is a star for you," handing over one which he had just cut. He has had no reason to regret the subsequent decision.

We had a very quiet, comfortable, and healthy ten days at the Pacific Hotel at Manly, which was broken only by an excursion which the Sydney Spiritualists had organised for us in a special steamer, with the intention of showing us the glories of the harbour. Our party assembled on Manly Pier, and the steamer was still far away when we saw the fluttering handkerchiefs which announced that they had sighted us. It was a long programme, including a picnic lunch, but it all went off with great success and good feeling. It was fairly rough within the harbour, and some of the party were seasick, but the general good spirits rose above such trifles, and we spent the day in goodly fellowship. On Sunday I was asked to speak to his congregation by Mr. Sanders, a very intelligent young Congregational minister of Manly, far above the level of Australasian or, indeed, British clerics. It was a novel experience for me to be in a Nonconformist pulpit, but I found an excellent audience, and I hope that they in turn found something comforting and new.

One of the most interesting men whom I met in Australia was Dr. Creed, of the New South Wales Parliament, an elderly medical man who has held high posts in the Government. He is blessed with that supreme gift, a mind which takes a keen interest in everything which he meets in life. His researches vary from the cure of diabetes and of alcoholism (both of which he thinks that he has attained) down to the study of Australian Aborigines and of the palæontology of his country. I was interested to find the very high opinion which he has of the brains of the black fellows, and he asserts that their results at the school which is devoted to their education are as high as with the white Australians. They train into excellent telegraphic operators and other employments needing quick intelligence. The increasing brain power of the human race seems to be in the direction of originating rather than of merely accomplishing. Many can do the latter, but only the very highest can do the former. Dr. Creed is clear upon the fact that no very ancient remains of any sort are to be found anywhere in

Australia, which would seem to be against the view of a Lemurian civilisation, unless the main seat of it lay to the north where the scattered islands represent the mountain tops of the ancient continent. Dr. Creed was one of the very few public men who had the intelligence or the courage to admit the strength of the spiritual position, and he assured me that he would help in any way.

Another man whom I was fortunate to meet was Leon Gellert, a very young poet, who promises to be the rising man in Australia in this, the supreme branch of literature. He served in the war, and his verses from the front attain a very high level. His volume of war poems represents the most notable literary achievement of recent years, and its value is enhanced by being illustrated by Norman Lindsay, whom I look upon as one of the greatest artists of our time. I have seen three pictures of his, "The Goths," "Who Comes?" and "The Crucifixion of Venus," each of which, in widely different ways, seemed very remarkable. Indeed, it is the versatility of the man that is his charm, and now that he is turning more and more from the material to the spiritual it is impossible to say how high a level he may attain. Another Australian whose works I have greatly admired is Henry Lawson, whose sketches of bush life in "Joe Wilson" and other of his studies, remind one of a subdued Bret Harte. He is a considerable poet also, and his war poem, "England Yet," could hardly be matched.

Yet another interesting figure whom I met in Sydney was Bishop Leadbeater, formerly a close colleague of Mrs. Besant in the Theosophical movement, and now a prelate of the so-called Liberal Catholic Church, which aims at preserving the traditions and forms of the old Roman Church, but supplementing them with all modern spiritual knowledge. I fear I am utterly out of sympathy with elaborate forms, which always in the end seem to me to take the place of facts, and to become a husk without a kernel, but none the less I can see a definite mission for such a church as appealing to a certain class of mind. Leadbeater, who has suffered from unjust aspersion in the past, is a venerable and striking figure. His claims to clairvoyant and other occult powers are very definite, and so far as I had the opportunity of observing him, he certainly lives the ascetic life, which the maintenance of such power demands. His books, especially the little one upon the Astral Plane, seem to me among the best of the sort.

But the whole subject of Theosophy is to me a perpetual puzzle. I asked for proofs and Spiritualism has given them to me. But why should I abandon one faith in order to embrace another one? I have done with faith. It is a golden mist in which human beings wander in devious tracks with many a collision. I need the white clear light of knowledge. For that we build from below, brick upon brick, never getting beyond the provable fact. There is the building which will last. But these others seem to build from above downwards, beginning by the assumption that there is supreme human wisdom at the apex. It may be so. But it is a dangerous habit of thought which has led the race astray before, and may again. Yet, I am struck by the fact that this ancient wisdom does describe the etheric body, the astral world, and the general scheme which we have proved for ourselves. But when the high priestess of the cult wrote of this she said so much that was against all our own spiritual experience, that we feel she was in touch with something very different from our angels of light. Her followers appreciate that now, and are more charitable than she, but what is the worth of her occult knowledge if she so completely misread that which lies nearest to us, and how can we hope that she is more correct when she speaks of that which is at a distance?

I was deeply attracted by the subject once, but Madame Blavatsky's personality and record repelled me. I have read the defence, and yet Hodgson and the Coulombs seem to me to hold the field. Could any conspiracy be so broad that it included numerous forged letters, trap doors cut in floors, and actually corroborative accounts in the books of a flower seller in the bazaar? On the other hand, there is ample evidence of real psychic powers, and of the permanent esteem of men like Sinnett and Olcott whom none could fail to respect. It is the attitude of these honourable men which commends and upholds her, but sometimes it seems hard to justify it. As an example, in the latter years of her life she wrote a book, "The Caves and Jungles of Hindustan," in which she describes the fearsome adventures which she and Olcott had in certain expeditions, falling down precipices and other such escapes. Olcott, like the honest gentleman he was, writes in his diary that there is not a word of truth in this, and that it is pure fiction. And yet, after this very damaging admission, in the same page he winds up, "Ah, if the world ever comes to know who was the mighty entity, who laboured sixty years under that quivering mask of flesh, it will repent its cruel treatment of H. P. B., and be amazed at the depth of its ignorance." These are the things which make it so difficult to understand either her or the cult with which she was associated. Had she never lived these men and women would, as it seems to me, have been the natural leaders of the Spiritualist movement, and instead of living in the intellectual enjoyment of far-off systems they would have concentrated upon the all-important work of teaching poor suffering humanity what is the meaning of the dark shadow which looms upon their path. Even now I see no reason why they should not come back to those who need them, and help them forward upon their rocky road.

Of course, we Spiritualists are ourselves vulnerable upon the subject of the lives of some of our mediums, but we carefully dissociate those lives from the powers which use the physical frame of the medium for their own purposes, just as the religious and inspired poetry of a Verlaine may be held separate from his dissipated life. Whilst upon this subject I may say that whilst in Australia I had some interesting letters from a solicitor named Rymer. All students of Spiritualism will remember that when Daniel Home first came to England in the early fifties he received great kindness from the Rymer family, who then lived at Ealing. Old Rymer treated him entirely as one of the family. This Bendigo Rymer was the grandson of Home's benefactor, and he had no love for the great medium because he considered that he had acted with ingratitude towards his people. The actual letters of his father, which he permitted me to read, bore out this statement, and I put it on record because I have said much in praise of Home, and the balance should be held true. These letters, dating from about '57, show that one of the sons of old Rymer was sent to travel upon the Continent to study art, and that Home was his companion. They were as close as brothers, but when they reached Florence, and Home became a personage in society there, he drifted away from Rymer, whose letters are those of a splendid young man. Home's health was already indifferent, and while he was laid up in his hotel he seems to have been fairly kidnapped by a strong-minded society lady of title, an Englishwoman living apart from her husband. For weeks he lived at her villa, though the state of his health would suggest that it was rather as patient than lover. What was more culpable was that he answered the letters of his comrade very rudely and showed no sense of gratitude for all that the family had done for him. I have read the actual letters and confess that I was chilled and disappointed. Home was an artist as well as a medium, the most unstable combination possible, full of emotions, flying quickly to extremes, capable of heroisms and self-denials, but also of vanities and ill-humour. On this occasion the latter side of his character was too apparent. To counteract the effect produced upon one's mind one should read in Home's Life the letter of the Bavarian captain whom he rescued upon the field of battle, or of the many unfortunates whom he aided with unobtrusive charity. It cannot, however, be too often repeated—since it is never grasped by our critics—that the actual character of a man is as much separate from his mediumistic powers, as it would be from his musical powers. Both are inborn gifts beyond the control of their possessor. The medium is the telegraph instrument and the telegraph boy united in one, but the real power is that which transmits the message, which he only receives and delivers. The remark applies to the Fox sisters as much as it does to Home.

Talking about Home, it is astonishing how the adverse judgment of the Vice-Chancellor Gifford, a materialist, absolutely ignorant of psychic matters, has influenced the minds of men. The very materialists who quote it, would not attach the slightest importance to the opinion of an orthodox judge upon the views of Hume, Payne, or any free-thinker. It is like quoting a Roman tribune against a Christian. The real facts of the case are perfectly clear to anyone who reads the documents with care. The best proof of how blameless Home was in the matter is that of all the men of honour with whom he was on intimate terms—men like Robert Chambers, Carter Hall, Lord Seaton, Lord Adare and others—not one relaxed in their friendship after the trial. This was in 1866, but in 1868 we find these young noblemen on Christian-name terms with the man who would have been outside the pale of society had the accusations of his enemies been true.

Whilst we were in Sydney, a peculiar ship, now called the *Marella,* was brought into the harbour as part of the German ship surrender. It is commonly reported that this vessel, of very grandiose construction, was built to conduct the Kaiser upon a triumphal progress round the world after he had won his war. It is, however, only of 8,000 tons, and, personally, I cannot believe that this would have had room for his swollen head, had he indeed been the victor. All the fittings, even to the carpet holders, are of German silver. The saloon is of pure marble, eighty by fifty, with beautiful hand-painted landscapes. The smoke-room is the reproduction of one in Potsdam Palace. There is a great swimming bath which can be warmed. Altogether a very notable ship, and an index, not only of the danger escaped, but of the danger to come, in the form of the superexcellence of German design and manufacture.

Our post-bag is very full, and it takes Major Wood and myself all our time to keep up with the letters. Many of them are so wonderful that I wish I had preserved them all, but it would have meant adding another trunk to our baggage. There are a few samples which have been rescued. Many people seemed to think that I was myself a wandering medium, and I got this sort of missive:

"DEAR SIR,—*I am very anxious to ask you a question, trusting you will answer me. What I wish to know I have been corresponding with a gentleman for nearly three years. From this letter can you tell me if I will marry him. I want you to answer this as I am keeping it strictly private and would dearly love you to answer this message if possible, and if I will do quite right if I marry him. Trusting to hear from you soon. Yours faithfully——.*

P.S.—I thoroughly believe in Spirit-ualism."

[167]

Here is another.

> "HONORED SIR,—*Just a few lines in limited time to ask you if you tell the future. If so, what is your charges? Please excuse no stamped and ad. envelope —out of stamps and in haste to catch mail. Please excuse."*

On the other hand, I had many which were splendidly instructive and helpful. I was particularly struck by one series of spirit messages which were received in automatic writing by a man living in the Bush in North Queensland, and thrown upon his own resources. They were descriptive of life in the beyond, and were in parts extremely corroborative of the Vale Owen messages, though they had been taken long prior to that date. Some of the points of resemblance were so marked and so unusual that they seem clearly to come from a common inspiration. As an example, this script spoke of the creative power of thought in the beyond, but added the detail that when the object to be created was large and important a band of thinkers was required, just as a band of workers would be here. This exactly corresponds to the teaching of Vale Owen's guide.

CHAPTER VIII

Dangerous fog.—The six photographers.—Comic advertisements.—Beauties of Auckland.—A Christian clergyman. —Shadows in our American relations.—The Gallipoli Stone.—Stevenson and the Germans.—Position of De Rougemont.—Mr. Clement Wragge.—Atlantean theories. —A strange psychic.—Wellington the windy.—A literary Oasis.—A Maori Séance.—Presentation.

My voyage to New Zealand in the *Maheno* was pleasant and uneventful, giving me four days in which to arrange my papers and look over the many manuscripts which mediums, or, more often, would-be mediums, had discharged at me as I passed. Dr. Bean, my Theosophic friend, who had been somewhat perturbed by my view that his people were really the officers of our movement who had deserted their army, formed an officers' corps, and so taken the money and brains and leadership away from the struggling masses, was waiting on the Sydney Quay, and gave me twelve books upon his subject to mend my wicked ways, so that I was equipped for a voyage round the world. I needed something, since I had left my wife and family behind me in Manly, feeling that the rapid journey through New Zealand would be too severe for them. In Mr. Carlyle Smythe, however, I had an admirable "cobber," to use the pal phrase of the Australian soldier.

Mr. Smythe had only one defect as a comrade, and

that was his conversation in a fog. It was of a distinctly depressing character, as I had occasion to learn when we ran into very thick weather among the rocky islands which make navigation so difficult to the north of Auckland. Between the screams of the siren I would hear a still small voice in the bunk above me.

"We are now somewhere near the Three Kings. It is an isolated group of rocks celebrated for the wreck of the *Elingamite,* which went ashore on just such a morning as this." (Whoo-ee! remarked the foghorn). "They were nearly starved, but kept themselves alive by fish which were caught by improvised lines made from the ladies' stay laces. Many of them died."

I lay digesting this and staring at the fog which crawled all round the port hole. Presently he was off again.

"You can't anchor here, and there is no use stopping her, for the currents run hard and she would drift on to one of the ledges which would rip the side out of her." (Whoo-ee! repeated the foghorn). "The islands are perpendicular with deep water up to the rocks, so you never know they are there until you hit them, and then, of course, there is no reef to hold you up." (Whoo-ee!) "Close by here is the place where the *Wairarapa* went down with all hands a few years ago. It was just such a day as this when she struck the Great Barrier——"

It was about this time that I decided to go on deck. Captain Brown had made me free of the bridge, so I climbed up and joined him there, peering out into the slow-drifting scud.

I spent the morning there, and learned something

of the anxieties of a sailor's life. Captain Brown had in his keeping, not only his own career and reputation, but what was far more to him, the lives of more than three hundred people. We had lost all our bearings, for we had drifted in the fog during those hours when it was too thick to move. Now the scud was coming in clouds, the horizon lifting to a couple of miles, and then sinking to a few hundred yards. On each side of us and ahead were known to be rocky islands or promontories. Yet we must push on to our destination. It was fine to see this typical British sailor working his ship as a huntsman might take his horse over diffi-cult country, now speeding ahead when he saw an opening, now waiting for a fogbank to get ahead, now pushing in between two clouds. For hours we worked along with the circle of oily lead-coloured sea around us, and then the grey veil, rising and falling, drifting and waving, with danger lurking always in its shadow. There are strange results when one stares intently over such a sea, for after a time one feels that it all slopes upwards, and that one is standing deep in a saucer with the rim far above one. Once in the rifts we saw a great ship feeling her way southwards, in the same difficulties as ourselves. She was the *Niagara,* from Vancouver to Auckland. Then, as suddenly as the raising of a drop-curtain, up came the fog, and there ahead of us was the narrow path which led to safety. The *Niagara* was into it first, which seemed to matter little, but really mattered a good deal, for her big business occupied the Port Authorities all the evening, while our little business was not even allowed to come alongside until such an hour that we could

not get ashore, to the disappointment of all, and very
especially of me, for I knew that some of our faithful
had been waiting for twelve hours upon the quay to
give me a welcoming hand. It was breakfast time on
the very morning that I was advertised to lecture before
we at last reached our hotel.

Here I received that counter-demonstration which
always helped to keep my head within the limits of
my hat. This was a peremptory demand from six
gentlemen, who modestly described themselves as the
leading photographers of the city, to see the negatives
of the photographs which I was to throw upon the
screen. I was assured at the same time by other photographers that they had no sympathy with such a
demand, and that the others were self-advertising busy-
bodies who had no mandate at all for such a request.
My experience at Sydney had shown me that such
challenges came from people who had no knowledge
of psychic conditions, and who did not realise that it
is the circumstances under which a photograph is taken,
and the witnesses who guarantee such circumstances,
which are the real factors that matter, and not the negative which may be so easily misunderstood by those who
have not studied the processes by which such things
are produced. I therefore refused to allow my photographs to pass into ignorant hands, explaining at the
same time that I had no negatives, since the photographs in most cases were not mine at all, so that the
negatives would, naturally, be with Dr. Crawford, Dr.
Geley, Lady Glenconnor, the representatives of Sir
William Crookes, or whoever else had originally taken
the photograph. Their challenge thereupon appeared

in the Press with a long tirade of abuse attached to it, founded upon the absurd theory that all the photos had been taken by me, and that there was no proof of their truth save in my word. One gets used to being indirectly called a liar, and I can answer arguments with self-restraint which once I would have met with the toe of my boot. However, a little breeze of this sort does no harm, but rather puts ginger into one's work, and my audience were very soon convinced of the absurdity of the position of the six dissenting photographers who had judged that which they had not seen.

Auckland is the port of call of the American steamers, and had some of that air of activity and progress which America brings with her. The spirit of enterprise, however, took curious shapes, as in the case of one man who was a local miller, and pushed his trade by long advertisements at the head of the newspapers, which began with abuse of me and my ways, and ended by a recommendation to eat desiccated corn, or whatever his particular commodity may have been. The result was a comic jumble which was too funny to be offensive, though Auckland should discourage such pleasantries, as they naturally mar the beautiful impression which her fair city and surroundings make upon the visitor. I hope I was the only victim, and that every stranger within her gates is not held up to ridicule for the purpose of calling attention to Mr. Blank's desiccated corn.

I seemed destined to have strange people mixed up with my affairs in Auckland, for there was a conjuror in the town, who, after the fashion of that rather blatant fraternity, was offering £1,000 that he could do anything I could do. As I could do nothing, it seemed easy money. In any case, the argument that because you can imitate a thing therefore the thing does not exist, is one which it takes the ingenuity of Mr. Maskelyne to explain. There was also an ex-Spiritualist medium (so-called) who covered the papers with his advertisements, so that my little announcement was quite overshadowed. He was to lecture the night after me in the Town Hall, with most terrifying revelations. I was fascinated by his paragraphs, and should have liked greatly to be present, but that was the date of my exodus. Among other remarkable advertisements was one "What has become of 'Pelorus Jack'? Was he a lost soul?" Now, "Pelorus Jack" was a white dolphin, who at one time used to pilot vessels into a New Zealand harbour, gambolling under the bows, so that the question really did raise curiosity. However, I learned afterwards that my successor did not reap the harvest which his ingenuity deserved, and that the audience was scanty and derisive. What the real psychic meaning of "Pelorus Jack" may have been was not recorded by the press.

From the hour I landed upon the quay at Auckland until I waved my last farewell my visit was made pleasant, and every wish anticipated by the Rev. Jasper Calder, a clergyman who has a future before him, though whether it will be in the Church of England or not, time and the Bishop will decide. Whatever he may do, he will remain to me and to many more the nearest approach we are likely to see to the ideal Christian—much as he will dislike my saying so. After all, if enemies are given full play, why should not

friends redress the balance? I will always carry away
the remembrance of him, alert as a boy, rushing about
to serve anyone, mixing on equal terms with scally-
wags on the pier, reclaiming criminals whom he called
his brothers, winning a prize for breaking-in a buck-
jumper, which he did in order that he might gain the
respect of the stockmen; a fiery man of God in the
pulpit, but with a mind too broad for special dispen-
sations, he was like one of those wonderfully virile
creatures of Charles Reade. The clergy of Australasia
are stagnant and narrow, but on the other hand, I
have found men like the Dean of Sydney, Strong of
Melbourne, Sanders of Manly, Calder of Auckland,
and others whom it is worth crossing this world to
meet.

Of my psychic work at Auckland there is little to be
said, save that I began my New Zealand tour under
the most splendid auspices. Even Sydney had not
furnished greater or more sympathetic audiences than
those which crowded the great Town Hall upon two
successive nights. I could not possibly have had a
better reception, or got my message across more suc-
cessfully. All the newspaper ragging and offensive
advertisements had produced (as is natural among a
generous people) a more kindly feeling for the
stranger, and I had a reception I can never forget.

This town is very wonderfully situated, and I have
never seen a more magnificent view than that from
Mount Eden, an extinct volcano about 900 feet high,
at the back of it. The only one which I could class
with it is that from Arthur's Seat, also an extinct
volcano about 900 feet high, as one looks on Edinburgh

[175]

and its environs. Edinburgh, however, is for ever shrouded in smoke, while here the air is crystal clear, and I could clearly see Great Barrier Island, which is a good eighty miles to the north. Below lay the most marvellous medley of light blue water and light green land mottled with darker foliage. We could see not only the whole vista of the wonderful winding harbour, and the seas upon the east of the island, but we could look across and see the firths which connected with the seas of the west. Only a seven-mile canal is needed to link the two up, and to save at least two hundred miles of dangerous navigation amid those rock-strewn waters from which we had so happily emerged. Of course it will be done, and when it is done it should easily pay its way, for what ship coming from Australia—or going to it—but would gladly pay the fees? The real difficulty lies not in cutting the canal, but in dredging the western opening, where shifting sandbanks and ocean currents combine to make a dangerous approach. I see in my mind's eye two great breakwaters, stretching like nippers into the Pacific at that point, while, between the points of the nippers, the dredgers will for ever be at work. It will be difficult, but it is needed and it will be done.

The Australian Davis Cup quartette—Norman Brooks, Patterson, O'Hara Wood and another—had come across in the *Maheno* with us and were now at the Grand Hotel. There also was the American team, including the formidable Tilden, now world's champion. The general feeling of Australasia is not as cordial as one would wish to the United States for the moment. I have met several men back from that country who rather bitterly resent the anti-British agitation which plays such a prominent part in the American press. This continual nagging is, I am sorry to say, wearing down the stolid patience of the Britisher more than I can ever remember, and it is a subject on which I have always been sensitive as I have been a life-long advocate of Anglo-American friendship, leading in the fullness of time to some loose form of Anglo-American Union. At present it almost looks as if these racial traitors who make the artificial dissensions were succeeding for a time in their work of driving a wedge between the two great sections of the English-speaking peoples. My fear is that when some world crisis comes, and everything depends upon us all pulling together, the English-speakers may neutralise each other. There lies the deadly danger. It is for us on both sides to endeavour to avoid it.

Everyone who is in touch with the sentiment of the British officers in Flanders knows that they found men of their own heart in the brave, unassuming American officers who were their comrades, and often their pupils. It is some of the stay-at-home Americans who appear to have such a false perspective, and who fail to realise that even British Dominions, such as Canada and Australia, lost nearly as many men as the United States in the war, while Britain herself laid down ten lives for every one spent by America. This is not America's fault, but when we see apparent forgetfulness of it on the part of a section of the American people when our wounds are still fresh, it cannot be wondered at that we feel sore. We do not advertise, and as a result there are few who know that we lost more men and made larger captures during the last two years of the war than our gallant ally of France. When we hear that others won the war we smile—but it is a bitter smile.

Strange, indeed, are some of the episodes of psychic experience. There came to me at my hotel in Auckland two middle-aged hard-working women, who had come down a hundred miles from the back country to my lecture. One had lost her boy at Gallipoli. She gave me a long post-mortem account from him as to the circumstances of his own death, including the military operations which led up to it. I read it afterwards, and it was certainly a very coherent account of the events both before and after the shell struck him. Having handed me the pamphlet the country woman then, with quivering fingers, produced from her bosom a little silver box. Out of this she took an object, wrapped in white silk. It was a small cube of what looked to me like sandstone, about an inch each way. She told me it was an apport, that it had been thrown down on her table while she and her family, including, as I understood, the friend then present, were holding a séance. A message came with it to say that it was from the boy's grave at Gallipoli. What are we to say to that? Was it fraud? Then why were they playing tricks upon themselves? If it was, indeed, an apport, it is surely one of the most remarkable for distance and for purpose recorded of any private circle.

A gentleman named Moors was staying at the same hotel in Auckland, and we formed an acquaintance. I find that he was closely connected with Stevenson, and had actually written a very excellent book upon his comradeship with him at Samoa. Stevenson dabbled in the politics of Samoa, and always with the best motives and on the right side, but he was of so frank and impetuous a nature that he was not trusted with any inside knowledge. Of the German rule Mr. Moors says that for the first twelve years Dr. Solf was as good as he could be, and did fair justice to all. Then he went on a visit to Berlin, and returned "bitten by the military bug," with his whole nature changed, and began to "imponieren" in true Prussian fashion. It is surely extraordinary how all the scattered atoms of a race can share the diseases of the central organism from which they sprang. I verily believe that if a German had been alone on a desert island in 1914 he would have begun to dance and brandish a club. How many cases are on record of the strange changes and wild deeds of individuals?

Mr. Moors told me that he dropped into a developing circle of Spiritualists at Sydney, none of whom could have known him. One of them said, "Above your head I see a man, an artist, long hair, brown eyes, and I get the name of Stephens." If he was indeed unknown, this would seem fairly evidential.

I was struck by one remark of Mr. Moors, which was that he had not only seen the natives ride turtles in the South Sea lagoons, but that he had actually done so himself, and that it was by no means difficult. This was the feat which was supposed to be so absurd when De Rougemont claimed to have done it. There are, of course, some gross errors which are probably pure misuse of words in that writer's narrative, but he places the critic in a dilemma which has never been fairly

[179]

faced. Either he is a liar, in which case he is, beyond all doubt, the most realistic writer of adventure since Defoe, or else he speaks the truth, in which case he is a great explorer. I see no possible avoidance of this dilemma, so that which ever way you look at it the man deserves credit which he has never received.

We set off, four of us, to visit Mr. Clement Wragge, who is the most remarkable personality in Auckland—dreamer, mystic, and yet very practical adviser on all matters of ocean and of air.

On arriving at the charming bungalow, buried among all sorts of broad-leaved shrubs and trees, I was confronted by a tall, thin figure, clad in black, with a face like a sadder and thinner Bernard Shaw, dim, dreamy eyes, heavily pouched, with a blue turban surmounting all. On repeating my desire he led me apart into his study. I had been warned that with his active brain and copious knowledge I would never be able to hold him to the point, so, in the dialogue which followed, I perpetually headed him off as he turned down bye paths, until the conversation almost took the form of a game.

"Mr. Wragge, you are, I know, one of the greatest authorities upon winds and currents."

"Well, that is one of my pursuits. When I was young I ran the Ben Nevis Observatory in Scotland and——"

"It was only a small matter I wished to ask you. You'll excuse my directness as I have so little time."

"Certainly. What is it?"

"If the Maoris came, originally, from Hawaii, what

[180]

prevailing winds would their canoes meet in the 2,000 miles which they crossed to reach New Zealand?"

The dim eyes lit up with the joy of the problem, and the nervous fingers unrolled a chart of the Pacific. He flourished a pair of compasses.

"Here is Hawaii. They would start with a north-westerly trade wind. That would be a fair wind. I may say that the whole affair took place far further back than is usually supposed. We have to get back to astronomy for our fixed date. Don't imagine that the obliquity of the ecliptic was always 23 degrees."

"The Maoris had a fair wind then?"

The compasses stabbed at the map.

"Only down to this point. Then they would come on the Doldrums—the calm patch of the equator. They could paddle their canoes across that. Of course, the remains at Easter Island prove——"

"But they could not paddle all the way."

"No; they would run into the south-easterly trades. Then they made their way to Rarotonga in Tahiti. It was from here that they made for New Zealand."

"But how could they know New Zealand was there?"

"Ah, yes, how did they know?"

"Had they compasses?"

"They steered by the stars. We have a poem of theirs which numbers the star-gazer as one of the crew. We have a chart, also, cut in the rocks at Hawaii, which seems to be the plot of a voyage. Here is a slide of it." He fished out a photo of lines and scratches upon a rock.

"Of course," said he, "the root of the matter is that missionaries from Atlantis permeated the Pacific, coming across Central America, and left their traces everywhere."

Ah, Atlantis! I am a bit of an Atlantean myself, so off we went at scratch and both enjoyed ourselves greatly until time had come to rejoin the party and meet Mr. Wragge's wife, a charming Brahmin lady from India, who was one of the most gracious personalities I have met in my wanderings. The blue-turbaned, eager man, half western science, half eastern mystic, and his dark-eyed wife amid their profusion of flowers will linger in my memory. Mrs. Wragge was eager that I go and lecture in India. Well, who knows?

I was so busy listening to Mr. Wragge's Atlantean theories that I had no chance of laying before him my own contribution to the subject, which is, I think, both original and valid. If the huge bulk of Atlantis sank beneath the ocean, then, assuredly, it raised such a tidal wave as has never been known in the world's history. This tidal wave, since all sea water connects, would be felt equally all over the world, as the wave of Krakatoa was in 1883 felt in Europe. The wave must have rushed over all flat coasts and drowned every living thing, as narrated in the biblical narrative. Therefore, since this catastrophe was, according to Plato's account, not very much more than 10,000 years ago, there should exist ample evidence of a wholesale destruction of life, especially in the flatter lands of the globe. Is there such evidence? Think of Darwin's account of how the pampas of South America are in places one huge grave-yard. Think, also, of the mammoth remains which strew the Tundras of Siberia, and which are so numerous that some of the arctic islands are really covered with bones. There is ample evidence of some great flood which would exactly correspond with the effect produced by the sinking of Atlantis. The tragedy broadens as one thinks of it. Everyone everywhere must have been drowned save only the hill-dwellers. The object of the catastrophe was, according to some occult information, to remove the Atlantean race and make room for the Aryan, even as the Lemurian had been removed to make room for the Atlantean. How long has the Aryan race to run? The answer may depend upon themselves. The great war is a warning bell perhaps.

I had a talk with a curious type of psychic while I was in Auckland. He claimed to be a psychologist who did not need to be put *en rapport* with his object by any material starting point. A piece of clothing is, as a rule, to a psychometrist what it would be to a bloodhound, the starting point of a chase which runs down the victim. Thus Van Bourg, when he discovered by crystal gazing the body of Mr. Foxhall (I quote the name from memory) floating in the Thames, began by covering the table with the missing man's garments. This is the usual procedure which will become more familiar as the public learn the full utility of a psychic.

This gentleman, Mr. Pearman, was a builder by trade, a heavy, rather uneducated man with the misty eye of a seer. He told me that if he desired to turn his powers upon anything he had only to sit in a dim room and concentrate his thought upon the matter, without any material nexus. For example, a murder had been done in Western Australia. The police asked his help. Using his power, he saw the man, a stranger, and yet he *knew* that it was the man, descending the Swan River in a boat. He saw him mix with the dockmen of Fremantle. Then he saw him return to Perth. Finally, he saw him take train on the Transcontinental Railway. The police at once acted, and intercepted the man, who was duly convicted and hanged. This was one of several cases which this man told me, and his stories carried conviction with them. All this, although psychic, has, of course, nothing to do with Spiritualism, but is an extension of the normal, though undefined, powers of the human mind and soul.

The reader will be relieved to hear that I did not visit Rotorua. An itinerant lecturer upon an unpopular cause has enough hot water without seeking out a geyser. My travels would make but an indifferent guide book, but I am bound to put it upon record that Wellington is a very singular city plastered upon the side of a very steep hill. It is said that the plan of the city was entirely drawn up in England under the impression that the site was a flat one, and that it was duly carried out on the perpendicular instead of the horizontal. It is a town of fine buildings, however, in a splendid winding estuary ringed with hills. It is, of course, the capital, and the centre of all officialdom in New Zealand, but Auckland, in the north, is already the greater city.

I had the opportunity of spending the day after my arrival with Dr. Morrice, who married the daughter of the late Premier, Sir R. Seddon, whom I had known in years gone by. Their summer house was down the Bay, and so I had a long drive which gave me an admirable chance of seeing the wonderful panorama. It was blowing a full gale, and the road is so exposed that even motors are sometimes upset by the force of the wind. On this occasion nothing more serious befell us than the loss of Mr. Smythe's hat, which disappeared with such velocity that no one was able to say what had become of it. It simply was, and then it was not. The yellow of the foreshore, the green of the shallows, the blue mottled with purple of the deep, all fretted with lines of foam, made an exhilarating sight. The whole excursion was a brief but very pleasant break in our round of work. Another pleasant experience was that I met Dr. Purdey, who had once played cricket with me, when we were very young, at Edinburgh University. *Eheu fugaces!* I had also the pleasure of meeting Mr. Massey, the Premier, a bluff, strong, downright man who impresses one with his force and sincerity.

I had the privilege when I was at Wellington of seeing the first edition of "Robinson Crusoe," which came out originally in three volumes. I had no idea that the three-decker dated back to 1719. It had a delightful map of the island which would charm any boy, and must have been drawn up under the personal guidance of Defoe himself. I wonder that map has not been taken as an integral part of the book, and reproduced in every edition, for it is a fascinating and a helpful document.

I saw this rare book in the Turnbull Library, which, under the loving care of Mr. Anderson (himself no mean poet), is a fine little collection of books got together by a Wellington man of business. In a raw

young land such a literary oasis is like a Gothic Cathedral in the midst of a suburb of modern villas. Anyone can come in to consult the books, and if I were a
Wellingtonian I would certainly spend a good deal of
time there. I handled with fitting reverence a first
edition of "Lyrical Ballads," where, in 1798, Coleridge
and Wordsworth made their entry hand in hand into
poetical literature. I saw an original Hakluyt, the book
which has sent so many brave hearts a-roving. There,
too, was a precious Kelmscott "Chaucer," a Plutarch
and Montaigne, out of which Shakespeare might have
done his cribbing; Capt. Cook's manuscript "Diary,"
written in the stiff hand of a very methodical man; a
copy of Swinburne's "Poems and Ballads," which is
one of twenty from a recalled edition, and many other
very rare and worthy volumes carefully housed and
clad. I spent a mellow hour among them.

I have been looking up all the old books upon the
Maoris which I could find, with the special intent of
clearing up their history, but while doing so I found
in one rather rare volume, "Old New Zealand," an
account of a Maori séance, which seems to have been
in the early forties, and, therefore, older than the
Hydesville knockings. I only wish every honest
materialist could read it and compare it with the experiences which we have, ourselves, independently
reported. Surely they cannot persist in holding that
such identical results are obtained by coincidence, or
that fraud would work in exactly the same fashion
in two different hemispheres.

A popular young chief had been killed in battle.
The white man was invited to join the solemn circle

who hoped to regain touch with him. The séance was in the dark of a large hut, lit only by the ruddy glow of a low fire. The white man, a complete unbeliever, gives his evidence in grudging fashion, but cannot get past the facts. The voice came, a strange melancholy sound, like the wind blowing into a hollow vessel. "Salutation! Salutation to you all! To you, my tribe! Family, I salute you! Friends, I salute you!" When the power waned the voice cried, "Speak to me, the family! Speak to me!" In the published dialogue between Dr. Hodgson after his death and Professor Hyslop, Hodgson cries, "Speak, Hyslop!" when the power seemed to wane. For some reason it would appear either by vibrations or by concentrating attention to help the communicator. "It is well with me," said the chief. "This place is a good place." He was with the dead of the tribe and described them, and offered to take messages to them. The incredulous white man asked where a book had been concealed which only the dead man knew about. The place was named and the book found. The white man himself did not know, so there was no telepathy. Finally, with a "Farewell!" which came from high in the air, the spirit passed back to immaterial conditions.

This is, I think, a very remarkable narrative. If you take it as literally true, which I most certainly do, since our experience corroborates it, it gives us some points for reflection. One is that the process is one known in all the ages, as our Biblical reading has already told us. A second is that a young barbarian chief with no advantages of religion finds the next world a very pleasant place, just as our dead do, and that they love to come back and salute those whom they have left, showing a keen memory of their earth life. Finally, we must face the conclusion that the mere power of communication has no elevating effect in itself, otherwise these tribes could not have continued to be ferocious savages. It has to be united with the Christ message from beyond before it will really help us upon the upward path.

Before I left Wellington the Spiritualists made me a graceful presentation of a travelling rug, and I was able to assure them that if they found the rug I would find the travelling. It is made of the beautiful woollen material in which New Zealand is supreme. The presentation was made by Mrs. Stables, the President of the New Zealand Association, an energetic lady to whom the Cause owes much. A greenstone penholder was given to me for my wife, and a little charm for my small daughter, the whole proceedings being marked with great cordiality and good feeling. The faithful are strong in Wellington, but are much divided among themselves, which, I hope, may be alleviated as a consequence of my visit. Nothing could have been more successful than my two meetings. The Press was splendidly sympathetic, and I left by a night boat in high heart for my campaign in the South Island.

CHAPTER IX

The Anglican Colony.—Psychic dangers.—The learned dog.
—Absurd newspaper controversy.—A backward commu-
nity.—The Maori tongue.—Their origin.—Their treat-
ment by the Empire.—A fiasco.—The Pa of Kaiopoi.—
Dr. Thacker.—Sir Joseph Kinsey.—A generous collector.
—Scott and Amundsen.—Dunedin.—A genuine medium.
—Evidence.—The shipping strike.—Sir Oliver.—Fare-
well.

I AM afraid that the average Britisher looks upon New
Zealand as one solid island. If he had to cross Cook's
Strait to get from the northern to the southern half,
he would never forget his lesson in geography, for
it can be as nasty a bit of water as is to be found in
the world, with ocean waves, mountain winds and
marine currents all combining into a horrible chaos.
Twelve good hours separate Wellington in the north
from Lyttleton, which is the port of Christchurch in
the south. A very short railway joins the two latter
places. My luck held good, and I had an excellent passage, dining in Wellington and breakfasting in Christchurch. It is a fine city, the centre of the famous Canterbury grazing country. Four shiploads of people
calling themselves the Canterbury Pilgrims arrived here
in 1852, built a cathedral, were practically ruled over by
Bishop Selwyn, and tried the successful experiment of
establishing a community which should be as Anglican
as New England is Nonconformist. The distinctive

character has now largely disappeared, but a splendid and very English city remains as a memorial of their efforts. When you are on the green, sloping banks of the river Avon, with the low, artistic bridges, it would not be hard to imagine that you were in the Backs at Cambridge.

At Christchurch I came across one of those little bits of psychic evidence which may be taken as certainly true, and which can be regarded, therefore, as pieces which have to be fitted into the jig-saw puzzle in order to make the completed whole, at that far-off date when a completed whole is within the reach of man's brain. It concerns Mr. Michie, a local Spiritualist of wide experience. On one occasion some years ago, he practised a short cut to psychic power, acquired through a certain method of breathing and of action, which amounts, in my opinion, to something in the nature of self-hypnotisation. I will not give details, as I think all such exercises are dangerous save for very experienced students of these matters, who know the risk and are prepared to take it. The result upon Mr. Michie, through some disregard upon his part of the conditions which he was directed to observe, was disastrous. He fell into an insidious illness with certain psychic symptoms, and within a few months was reduced to skin and bone. Mr. Michie's wife is mediumistic and liable to be controlled. One day an entity came to her and spoke through her to her husband, claiming to be the spirit of one, Gordon Stanley. He said: "I can sympathise with your case, because my own death was brought about in exactly the same way. I will help you, however, to fight against it and to recover." The spirit then gave an account of his own life, described himself as a clerk in Cole's Book Arcade in Melbourne, and said that his widow was living at an address in Melbourne, which was duly given. Mr. Michie at once wrote to this address and received this reply, the original of which I have seen:

> "*Park Street,*
> "*Melbourne.*
>
> "DEAR SIR,—*I have just received your strange— I must say, your very strange letter. Yes, I am Mrs. Stanley. My husband did die two years ago from consumption. He was a clerk in Cole's Arcade. I must say your letter gave me a great shock. But I cannot doubt after what you have said, for I know you are a complete stranger to me.*"

Shortly afterwards Mr. Stanley returned again through the medium, said that his widow was going to marry again, and that it was with his full approbation. The incident may be taken by our enemies as illustrating the danger of psychic research, and we admit that there are forms of it which should be approached with caution, but I do not think that mankind will ever be warned off by putting a danger label upon it, so long as they think there is real knowledge to be gained. How could the motor-car or the aeroplane have been developed if hundreds had not been ready to give their lives to pay the price? Here the price has been far less, and the goal far higher, but if in gaining it a man were assured that he would lose his health, his reason, or his life, it is none the less his duty to go forward if he clearly sees that there is something to be won. To meet death in conquering death is to die in victory—the ideal death.

Whilst I was at Auckland Mr. Poynton, a stipendiary magistrate there, told me of a dog in Christchurch which had a power of thought comparable, not merely to a human being, but even, as I understood him, to a clairvoyant, as it would bark out the number of coins in your pocket and other such questions. The alternative to clairvoyance was that he was a very quick and accurate thought-reader, but in some cases the power seemed to go beyond this. Mr. Poynton, who had studied the subject, mentioned four learned beasts in history: a marvellous horse in Shakespeare's time, which was burned with its master in Florence; the Boston skipper's dog; Hans, the Russian horse, and Darkie of Christchurch. He investigated the latter himself, as one of a committee of three. On the first occasion they got no results. On the second, ninety per cent. of the questions were right, and they included sums of addition, subtraction, etc. "It was uncanny," he wrote.

I called, therefore, upon Mrs. McGibbon, the owner, who allowed me to see the dog. He was a dark, vivacious fox terrier, sixteen years old, blind and deaf, which obviously impaired his powers. In spite of his blindness he dashed at me the moment he was allowed into the room, pawing at me and trembling all over with excitement. He was, in fact, so excited that he was of little use for demonstration, as when once he began to bark he could not be induced to stop. Occasionally he steadied down, and gave us a touch of his

THE PEOPLE OF TURI'S CANOE, AFTER A VOYAGE OF GREAT HARDSHIP,
AT LAST SIGHT THE SHORES OF NEW ZEALAND.

From a painting in the Auckland Art Gallery by C. F. Goldie and L. J. Steele.

true quality. When a half-crown was placed before him and he was asked how many sixpences were in it, he gave five barks, and four for a florin, but when a shilling was substituted he gave twelve, which looked as if he had pennies in his mind. On the whole the performance was a failure, but as he had raised by exhibiting his gifts, £138 for war charities, I took my hat off to him all the same. I will not imitate those psychic researchers who imagine that because they do not get a result, therefore, everyone else who has reported it is a cheat or a fool. On the contrary, I have no doubt that the dog had these powers, though age and excitement had now impaired them.

The creature's powers were first discovered when the son of the house remarked one day: "I will give you a biscuit if you bark three times." He at once did it. "Now, six times." He did so. "Now, take three off." He barked three times once again. Since then they have hardly found any problem he could not tackle. When asked how many males in the room he always included himself in the number, but omitted himself when asked how many human beings. One wonders how many other dogs have human brains without the humans being clever enough to detect it.

I had an amusing controversy in Christchurch with one of the local papers, *The Press,* which represents the clerical interest, and, also, the clerical intolerance of a cathedral city. It issued an article upon me and my beliefs, severe, but quite within the limits of legitimate criticism, quoting against me Professor Hyslop, "who," it said, "is Professor of Logic at Columbia, etc." To this I made the mild and obvious retort in the course of my lecture that as Professor Hyslop was dead, *The Press* went even further than I in saying that he *is* Professor at Columbia. Instead of accepting this correction, *The Press* made the tactical error of standing by their assertion, and aggravated it by head-lines which challenged me, and quoted my statement as "typical of the inaccuracy of a Spiritualist." As I rather pride myself on my accuracy, which has seldom been challenged, I answered shortly but politely, as follows:

"Sir,—*I am surprised that the news of the death of Professor Hyslop has not reached New Zealand, and even more surprised that it could be imagined that I would make such a statement on a matter so intimately connected with the subject upon which I lecture without being sure of my fact. I am reported as saying 'some years,' but, if so, it was a slip of the tongue for 'some time.' The Professor died either late last year or early in the present one.*"

I should have thought that my answer was conclusive, and would have elicited some sort of apology; but instead of this, *The Press* called loudly upon me in a leading article to apologise, though for what I know not, save that they asserted I had said "some years," whereas I claim that I actually said "some time." This drew the following rather more severe letter from me:

"Sir,—*I am collecting New Zealand curiosities, so I will take your leading article home with me. To get the full humour of it one has to remember*
[194]

the sequence of events. In a leading article you remarked that Professor Hyslop IS Professor of Logic. I answered with mild irony that he certainly is not, as he had been dead 'some years' or 'some time'—which of the two is perfectly immaterial, since I presume that in either case you would agree that he has ceased to be Professor of Logic. To this you were rash enough to reply with a challenging article with large head-lines, declaring that I had blundered, and that this was typical of the inaccuracy of Spiritualists. I wrote a gentle remonstrance to show that I had not blundered, and that my assertion was essentially true, since the man was dead. This you now tacitly admit, but instead of expressing regret you ask for an apology from me. I have engaged in much newspaper controversy, but I can truly say that I can recall no such instance of effrontery as this."

This led to another leader and considerable abuse. The controversy was, however, by no means one-sided, in spite of the shadow of the Cathedral. Mr. Peter Trolove is a man of wit as well as knowledge, and wields a pretty pen. A strong man, also, is Dr. John Guthrie, whose letter contains words so kindly that I must quote them:

"Sir Arthur Conan Doyle stands above it all, not only as a courteous gentleman, but as a fair controversialist throughout. He is, anyhow, a chivalrous and magnanimous personality, whether or not his beliefs have any truth. Fancy quoting authori-

*ties against a man who has spent great part of his
life studying the subject, and who knows the authorities better than all his opponents put together—a
man who has deliberately used his great gifts in an
honest attempt to get at truth. I do think that
Christchurch has some need to apologise for its con-
troversialists—much more need than our distinguished visitor has to apologise for what we all know
to be his honest convictions."*

I have never met Dr. John Guthrie in the flesh, but
I would thank him here, should this ever meet his eye,
for this kindly protest.

It will be gathered that I succeeded at Christchurch
in performing the feat of waking up a Cathedral City,
and all the ex-sleepers were protesting loudly against
such a disturbing inrush from the outer world. Glanc-
ing at the head lines I see that Bishop Brodie declared
it to be "A blasphemy nurtured in fraud," the Dean of
Christchurch writes it down as "Spiritism, the abroga-
tion of Reason," the Rev. John Patterson calls it "an
ancient delusion," the Rev. Mr. North says it is "a
foolish Paganism," and the Rev. Mr. Ready opines
that it is "a gospel of uncertainty and conjecture."
Such are the clerical leaders of thought in Christchurch
in the year 1920. I think of what the wise old Chinese
Control said of similar types at the Melbourne Rescue
Circle. "He good man but foolish man. He learn
better. Never rise till he learn better. Plenty time
yet." Who loses except themselves?

The enormous number of letters which I get upon
psychic subjects—which I do my best to answer—give

[196]

me some curious sidelights, for they are often confidential, and would not bear publication. Some of them are from devout, but narrow Christians, who narrate psychic and prophetic gifts which they possess, and at the same time almost resent them on the ground that they are condemned by the Bible. As if the whole Bible was not psychic and prophetic! One very long letter detailed a whole succession of previsions of the most exact character, and wound up by the conviction that we were on the edge of some great discovery. This was illustrated by a simile which seemed very happy. "Have you noticed a tree covered in spider webs during a fog? Well, it was only through the law of the fog that we saw them. They were there all the time, but only when the moisture came could we see them." It was a good illustration. Many amazing experiences are detailed to me in every town I visit, and though I have no time to verify them and go into details, none the less they fit so accurately with the various types of psychic cases with which I am familiar that I cannot doubt that such occurrences are really very common. It is the injudicious levity with which they are met which prevents their being published by those who experience them.

As an amateur philologist of a superficial type, I am greatly interested in studying the Maori language, and trying to learn whence these wonderful savages came before their twenty-two terrible canoes came down upon the unhappy land which would have been safer had as many shiploads of tigers been discharged upon its beach. The world is very old, and these folk have wandered from afar, and by many devious paths. Surely there are Celtic traces both in their appearance, their character and their language. An old Maori woman smoking her pipe is the very image of an old Celtic woman occupied the same way. Their word for water is *wei,* and England is full of Wye and Way river names, dating from the days before the Germans arrived. Strangest of all is their name for the supreme God. A name never mentioned and taboo among them, is Io. "J" is, of course, interchangeable with "I," so that we get the first two letters of Jove and an approximation of Jehovah. Papa is parent. Altogether there is good evidence that they are from the same root as some European races, preferably the Celts. But on the top of this comes a whole series of Japanese combinations of letters, Rangi, Muru, Tiki, and so forth, so that many of the place names seem pure Japanese. What are we to make of such a mixture? Is it possible that one Celtic branch, far away in the mists of time, wandered east while their racial brethren wandered west, so that part reached far Corea while the others reached Ireland? Then, after getting a tincture of Japanese terms and word endings, they continued their migration, taking to the seas, and finally subduing the darker races who inhabited the Polynesian Islands, so making their way to New Zealand. This wild imagining would at least cover the observed facts. It is impossible to look at some of the Maori faces without realising that they are of European stock.

I must interpolate a paragraph here to say that I was pleased, after writing the above, to find that in my blind gropings I had come upon the main conclusions which have been put forward with very full knowledge by the well-known authority, Dr. McMillan Brown. He has worked out the very fact which I surmised, that the Maoris are practically of the same stock as Europeans, that they had wandered Japanwards, and had finally taken to the sea. There are two points of interest which show the date of their exodus was a very ancient one. The first is that they have not the use of the bow. The second is that they have no knowledge of metals. Such knowledge once possessed would never have been lost, so it is safe to say that they left Asia a thousand years (as a minimum) before Christ, for at that date the use of bronze, at any rate, was widespread. What adventures and vicissitudes this remarkable race, so ignorant in some directions and so advanced in others, must have endured during those long centuries. If you look at the wonderful ornaments of their old war canoes, which carry a hundred men, and can traverse the whole Pacific, it seems almost incredible that human patience and ingenuity could construct the whole fabric with instruments of stone. They valued them greatly when once they were made, and the actual names of the twenty-two original invading canoes are still recorded.

In the public gallery of Auckland they have a duplicate of one of these enormous canoes. It is 87 feet in length and the thwarts are broad enough to hold three or four men. When it was filled with its hundred warriors, with the chief standing in the centre to give time to the rowers, it must, as it dashed through the waves, have been a truly terrific object. I should think that it represented the supreme achievement of neolithic man.   There are a series of wonderful pictures of Maori life in the same gallery by Goldie and Steele. Of these I reproduce, by permission, one which represents the starving crew of one canoe sighting the distant shore.   The engraving only gives a faint indication of the effect of the vividly-coloured original.

Reference has been made to the patient industry of the Maori race.   A supreme example of this is that every man had his tikki, or image of a little idol made of greenstone, which was hung round his neck.   Now, this New Zealand greenstone is one of the hardest objects in nature, and yet it is worn down without metals into these quaint figures.   On an average it took ten years to make one, and it was rubbed down from a chunk of stone into an image by the constant friction of a woman's foot.

It is said that the Tahungas, or priests, have much hereditary knowledge of an occult sort.   Their oracles were famous, and I have already quoted an example of their séances.   A student of Maori lore told me the following interesting story.   He was a student of Maori words, and on one occasion a Maori chief let slip an unusual word, let us say "buru," and then seemed confused and refused to answer when the Englishman asked the meaning.   The latter took it to a friend, a Tohunga, who seemed much surprised and disturbed, and said it was a word of which a paheka or white man should know nothing.   Not to be beaten, my informant took it to an old and wise chief who owed him a return for some favours.   This chief was also much exercised in mind when he heard the word, and walked up and down in agitation.   Finally he said,

"Friend, we are both Christians. You remember the chapter in the Bible where Jacob wrestled with an angel. Well, this word 'buru' represents that for which they were wrestling." He would say no more and there it had perforce to be left.

The British Empire may be proud of their treatment of the Maoris. Like the Jews, they object to a census, but their number cannot be more than 50,000 in a population of over a million. There is no question, therefore, of our being constrained to treat them well. Yet they own vast tracts of the best land in the country, and so unquestioned are their rights that when they forbade a railway to pass down the centre of the North Island, the traffic had to go by sea from Auckland until, at last, after many years, it was shown to the chiefs that their financial interests would be greatly aided by letting the railway through. These financial interests are very large, and many Maoris are wealthy men, buying expensive motor cars and other luxuries. Some of the more educated take part in legislative work, and are distinguished for their eloquence. The half-castes make a particularly fine breed, especially in their youth, for they tend as they grow older to revert to the pure Maori type. New Zealand has no national sin upon its conscience as regards the natives, which is more, I fear, than can be said whole-heartedly for Australia, and even less for Tasmania. Our people never descended to the level of the old Congo, but they have something on their conscience none the less.

On December 18th there was some arrangement by which I should meet the Maoris and see the historic Pa of Kaiopoi. The affair, however, was, I am sorry

to say, a fiasco. As we approached the building, which
was the village school room, there emerged an old lady
—a very old lady—who uttered a series of shrill cries,
which I was told meant welcome, though they sounded
more like the other thing. I can only trust that my
informants were right. Inside was a very fine assemblage of atmospheric air, and of nothing else. The
explanation was that there had been a wedding the
night before, and that the whole community had been
—well, tired. Presently a large man in tweeds of
the reach-me-down variety appeared upon the scene,
and several furtive figures, including a row of children, materialised in corners of the big empty room.
The visitors, who were more numerous than the
visited, sat on a long bench and waited developments
which refused to develop. My dreams of the dignified
and befeathered savage were drifting away. Finally,
the large man, with his hands in his pockets, and looking hard at a corner of the rafters, made a speech of
welcome, punctuated by long stops and gaps. He then,
at our request, repeated it in Maori, and the children
were asked to give a Maori shout, which they sternly
refused to do. I then made a few feeble bleats, uncer-
tain whether to address my remarks to the level of the
large man or to that of the row of children. I ended
by handing over some books for their library, and we
then escaped from this rather depressing scene.

But it was a very different matter with the Pa. I
found it intensely interesting. You could still trace
quite clearly the main lines of the battle which de-
stroyed it. It lay on about five acres of ground, with
deep swamp all round save for one frontage of some

hundreds of yards. That was all which really needed defence. The North Island natives, who were of a sterner breed than those of the South, came down under the famous Rauparaha (these Maori names are sad snags in a story) and besieged the place. One can see the saps and follow his tactics, which ended by piling brushwood against the palings—please observe the root "pa" in palings—with the result that he carried the place. Massacre Hill stands close by, and so many of the defenders were eaten that their gnawed bones covered the ground within the memory of living men. Such things may have been done by the father of the elderly gentleman who passes you in his motor car with his race glasses slung across his chest. The siege of Kaiopoi was about 1831. Even on a fine sunlit day I was conscious of that heavy atmosphere within the enclosure which impresses itself upon me when I am on the scene of ancient violence. So frightful an episode within so limited a space, where for months the garrison saw its horrible fate drawing nearer day by day, must surely have left some etheric record even to our blunt senses.

I was indebted to Dr. Thacker, the mayor, for much kind attention whilst in Christchurch. He is a giant man, but a crippled giant, alas, for he still bears the traces of an injury received in a historic football match, which left his and my old University of Edinburgh at the top of the tree in Scotland. He showed me some curious, if ghastly, relics of his practice. One of these was a tumour of the exact size and shape of a boxing glove, thumb and all, which he cut out of the back of a boxer who had lost a glove fight and taken it greatly to heart. Always on many converging lines we come back to the influence of mind over matter.

Another most pleasant friendship which I made in Christchurch was with Sir Joseph Kinsey, who has acted as father to several successive British Arctic expeditions. Scott and Shackleton have both owed much to him, their constant agent, adviser and friend. Scott's dying hand traced a letter to him, so unselfish and so noble that it alone would put Scott high in the gallery of British worthies. Of all modern men of action Scott seems to me the most lofty. To me he was only an acquaintance, but Kinsey, who knew him well as a friend, and Lady Kinsey, who had all Arctic exploration at her finger ends, were of the same opinion.

Sir Joseph discussed the action of Amundsen in making for the pole. When it was known that Amundsen was heading south instead of pursuing his advertised intentions, Kinsey smelled danger and warned Scott, who, speaking from his own noble loyalty, said, "He would never do so dishonourable a thing. My plans are published and are known to all the world." However, when he reached the ice, and when Pennell located the "Fram," he had to write and admit that Kinsey was right. It was a sad blow, that forestalling, though he took it like the man that he was. None the less, it must have preyed upon the spirits of all his party and weakened their resistance in that cruel return journey. On the other hand Amundsen's expedition, which was conducted on rather less than a sixth of the cost of the British, was a triumph of organisation, and he had the good luck or deep wisdom to strike a route which was clear of those great blizzards which overwhelmed Scott. The scurvy was surely a slur upon our medical preparations. According to Stefansson, who knows more of the matter than any living man, lime juice is useless, vegetables are of secondary importance, but fresh animal food, be it seal, penguin, or what you will, is the final preventive.

Sir Joseph is a passionate and discriminating collector, and has but one fault in collecting, which is a wide generosity. You have but to visit him often enough and express sufficient interest to absorb all his treasures. Perhaps my protests were half-hearted, but I emerged from his house with a didrachm of Alexander, a tetradrachm of some Armenian monarch, a sheet of rare Arctic stamps for Denis, a lump of native greenstone, and a small nugget of gold. No wonder when I signed some books for him I entered the date as that of "The Sacking of Woomeroo," that being the name of his dwelling. The mayor, in the same spirit of hospitality, pressed upon me a huge bone of the extinct Moa, but as I had never failed to impress upon my wife the extreme importance of cutting down our luggage, I could not face the scandal of appearing with this monstrous impedimentum.

Leaving Christchurch in the journalistic uproar to which allusion has been made, our engagements took us on to Dunedin, which is reached by rail in a rather tiring day's journey. A New Zealand train is excellent while it is running, but it has a way of starting with an epileptic leap, and stopping with a bang, which becomes wearisome after a while. On the other hand this particular journey is beguiled by the fact that the line runs high for two hours round the curve of the hills with the Pacific below, so that a succession of marvellous views opens out before you as you round each spur. There can be few more beautiful lines.

Dunedin was founded in 1848 by a group of Scotsmen, and it is modelled so closely upon Edinburgh that the familiar street names all reappear, and even Portobello has its duplicate outside the town. The climate, also, I should judge to be about the same. The prevailing tone of the community is still Scottish, which should mean that they are sympathetic with my mission, for nowhere is Spiritualism more firmly established now than in Scotland, especially in Glasgow, where a succession of great mediums and of earnest workers have built up a considerable organisation. I soon found that it was so, for nowhere had I more private assurances of support, nor a better public reception, the theatre being filled at each lecture. In the intervals kind friends put their motors at my disposal and I had some splendid drives over the hills, which look down upon the winding estuary at the head of which the town is situated.

At the house of Mr. Reynolds, of Dunedin, I met one of the most powerful clairvoyants and trance mediums whom I have tested. Her name is Mrs. Roberts, and though her worldly circumstances are modest, she has never accepted any money for her wonderful psychic gifts. For this I honour her, but, as I told her, we all sell the gifts which God has given us, and I cannot see why, and within reason, psychic gifts should not also be placed within the reach of the public, instead of being confined to a favoured few. How can the bulk of the people ever get into touch with a good medium if they are debarred from doing so in the ordinary way of business?

Mrs. Roberts is a stout, kindly woman, with a motherly manner, and a sensitive, expressive face. When in touch with my conditions she at once gave the names of several relatives and friends who have passed over, without any slurring or mistakes. She then cried, "I see an elderly lady here—she is a beautifully high spirit—her name is Selina." This rather unusual name belonged to my wife's mother, who died nearly two years ago. Then, suddenly, becoming slightly convulsed, as a medium does when her mechanism is controlled by another, she cried with an indescribable intensity of feeling, "Thank God! Thank God to get in touch again! Jean! Jean! Give my dear love to Jean!" Both names, therefore, had been got correctly, that of the mother and the daughter. Is it not an affront to reason to explain away such results by wild theories of telepathy, or by anything save the perfectly plain and obvious fact that spirit communion is indeed true, and that I was really in touch with that dead lady who was, even upon earth, a beautifully high and unselfish spirit. I had a number of other communications through Mrs. Roberts that night, and at a second interview two days later, not one of which erred so far as names were concerned. Among others was one who professed to be Dr. Russell Wallace. I should be honoured, indeed, to think that it was so, but I was unable to hit on anything which would be evidential. I asked him if his further experience had taught him anything more about reincarnation, which he disputed in his lifetime. He answered that he now accepted it, though I am not clear whether he meant for all cases. I thanked him for any spiritual help I had from him. His answer was "Me! Don't thank me! You would be surprised if you knew who your real helpers are." He added, "By your work I rise. We are co-workers!" I prayed that it be so, for few men have lived for whom I have greater respect; wise and brave, and mellow and good. His biography was a favourite book of mine long before I understood the full significance of Spiritualism, which was to him an evolution of the spirit on parallel lines to that evolution of the body which he did so much to establish.

Now that my work in New Zealand was drawing to a close a very grave problem presented itself to Mr. Smythe and myself, and that was how we were to get back to our families in Australia. A strike had broken out, which at first seemed a small matter, but it was accentuated by the approach of Christmas and the fact that many of the men were rather looking for an excuse for a holiday. Every day things became blacker. Once before Mr. Smythe had been held up for four months by a similar cause, and, indeed, it has become a very serious consideration for all who visit New Zealand. We made a forced march for the north amid constant rumours that far from reaching Australia we could not even get to the North Island, as the twelve-hour ferry boats were involved in the strike. I had every trust in my luck, or, as I should prefer to say, in my helpers, and we got the *Maori* on the last ferry trip which she was sure to take. Up to the last moment the firemen wavered, and we had no stewards on board, but none the less, to our inexpressible relief we got off. There was no food on the ship and no one to serve it, so we went into a small hostel at Lyttleton before we started, to see what we could pick up. There was a man seated opposite to me who assumed the air of laboured courtesy and extreme dignity, which is one phase of alcoholism.

" 'Scuse me, sir!" said he, looking at me with a glassy stare, "but you bear most 'straordinary resemblance Olver Lodge."

I said something amiable.

"Yes, sir—'straordinary! Have you ever seen Olver Lodge, sir?"

"Yes, I have."

"Well, did you perceive resemblance?"

"Sir Oliver, as I remember him, was a tall man with a grey beard."

He shook his head at me sadly.

"No, sir—I heard him at Wellington last week No beard. A moustache, sir, same as your own."

"You're sure it was Sir Oliver?"

A slow smile came over his face.

"Blesh my soul—Conan Doyle—that's the name. Yes, sir, you bear truly remarkable resemblance Conan Doyle."

I did not say anything further so I daresay he has not discovered yet the true cause of the resemblance.

All the nerve-wracking fears of being held up which we endured at Lyttleton were repeated at Wellington, where we had taken our passages in the little steamer *Paloona.* In any case we had to wait for a day, which

I spent in clearing up my New Zealand affairs while Mr. Smythe interviewed the authorities and paid no less than £141 war tax upon the receipts of our lectures —a heavy impost upon a fortnight's work. Next morning, with our affairs and papers all in order, we boarded our little craft.

Up to the last moment we had no certainty of starting. Not only was the strike in the air, but it was Christmas Eve, and it was natural enough that the men should prefer their own homes to the stokehold of the *Paloona*. Agents with offers of increased pay were scouring the docks. Finally our complement was completed, and it was a glad moment when the hawsers were thrown off, and after the usual uncomfortable preliminaries we found ourselves steaming in a sharp wind down the very turbulent waters of Cook's Strait.

The place is full of Cook's memory. Everywhere the great man has left his traces. We passed Cook's Island where the *Endeavour* actually struck and had to be careened and patched. What a nerve the fellow had! So coolly and deliberately did he do his work that even now his charting holds good, I understand, in many long stretches of coast. Tacking and wearing, he poked and pried into every estuary, naming capes, defining bays, plotting out positions, and yet all the while at the mercy of the winds, with a possible lee shore always before him, with no comrade within hail, and with swarms of cannibals eyeing his little ship from the beach. After I have seen his work I shall feel full of reverence every time I pass that fine statue which adorns the mall side of the great Admiralty building.

THE WANDERINGS OF A SPIRITUALIST

And now we are out in the open sea, with Melbourne, Sydney and love in front of our prow. Behind the sun sets in a slur of scarlet above the olive green hills, while the heavy night fog, crawling up the valleys, turns each of them into a glacier. A bright star twinkles above. Below a light shines out from the gloom. Farewell, New Zealand! I shall never see you again, but perhaps some memory of my visit may remain—or not, as God pleases.

Anyhow, my own memory will remain. Every man looks on his own country as God's own country if it be a free land, but the New Zealander has more reason than most. It is a lovely place, and contains within its moderate limits the agricultural plains of England, the lakes and hills of Scotland, the glaciers of Switzerland, and the fiords of Norway, with a fine hearty people, who do not treat the British newcomer with ignorant contempt or hostility. There are so many interests and so many openings that it is hard to think that a man will not find a career in New Zealand. Canada, Australia and South Africa seem to me to be closely balanced so far as their attractions for the emigrant goes, but when one considers that New Zealand has neither the winter of Canada, the droughts of Australia, nor the racial problems of Africa, it does surely stand supreme, though it demands, as all of them do, both labour and capital from the newcomer.

CHAPTER X

THE voyage back from New Zealand to Melbourne was pleasant and uneventful, though the boat was small and there was a sea rough enough to upset many of the passengers. We were fortunate in our Captain, Doorby, who, I found, was a literary confrère with two books to his credit, one of them a record of the relief ship *Morning,* in which he had served at the time of Scott's first expedition, the other a little book, "The Handmaiden of the Navy," which gave some of his adventures and experiences in the merchant service during the great war. He had been torpedoed once, and had lost, on another occasion, nearly all his crew with plague, so that he had much that was interesting to talk about. Mr. Blake, of the *Strand Magazine,* was also on board. A Unitarian Minister, Mr. Hale, was also a valuable companion, and we had much discussion over the origins of Christianity, which was the more interesting to me as I had taken advantage of the voyage to re-read the Acts and Paul's Epistles. There are no documents which can be read so often and yet reveal something new, the more so when you have that occult clue which is needful before Paul can be understood. It is necessary also to know something of Mythra worship and the other philosophies which Paul had learned, and woven into his Christianity. I have stated elsewhere my belief that all expressions about redemption by blood, the blood of the lamb, etc., are founded upon the parallel of the blood of the bull which was shed by the Mythra-worshippers, and in which they were actually baptised. Enlarging upon this, Mr. Hale pointed out on the authority, if I remember right, of Pfleiderer's "Christian Origins," that in the Mythra service something is placed over the candidate, a hide probably, which is called "putting on Mythra," and corresponds with Paul's expression about "putting on Christ." Paul, with his tremendous energy and earnestness, fixed Christianity upon the world, but I wonder what Peter and those who had actually heard Christ's words thought about it all. We have had Paul's views about Christ, but we do not know Christ's views about Paul. He had been, as we are told by himself, a Jewish Pharisee of the strictest type in his youth at Jerusalem, but was a Roman citizen, had lived long at Tarsus, which was the centre of Mithraism, and was clearly famous for his learning, since Festus twitted him with it. The simple tenets of the carpenter and the fishermen would take strange involved forms in such a brain as that. His epistles are presumably older than the gospels, which may, in their simplicity, represent a protest against his confused theology.

THE WANDERINGS OF A SPIRITUALIST

It was an enjoyable voyage in the little *Paloona,* and rested me after the whirlwind campaign of New Zealand.   In large liners one loses in romance what one gains in comfort.   On a small ship one feels nearer to Nature, to the water and even to the stars.   On clear nights we had magnificent displays of the Southern heaven.   I profited by the astronomical knowledge of Mr. Smythe.   Here first I was introduced to Alpha Centauri, which is the nearest fixed star, and, therefore, the cobber to the sun.   It is true that it is distant 3½ years of light travel, and light travels at about 182,000 miles a second, but when one considers that it takes centuries for average starlight to reach us, we may consider Alpha as snuggling close up to us for companionship in the lonely wastes of space.   The diamond belt of Orion looks homely enough with the bright solitaire Sirius sparkling beside it, but there are the Magellanic clouds, the scattered wisps torn from the Milky Way, and there is the strange black space called the Coalsack, where one seems to look right past all created things into a bottomless void. What would not Galileo and all the old untravelled astronomers have given to have one glimpse of this wondrous Southern display?

Captain Doorby, finding that he had time in hand, ran the ship into a small deserted bay upon the coast, and, after anchoring, ordered out all the boats for the sake of practice.   It was very well done, and yet what I saw convinced me that it should be a Board of Trade regulation, if it is not one already, that once, at least, near the beginning of every long voyage, this should be compulsory.   It is only when you come to launch them that you really realise which of the davits is rusted up, and which block is tangled, or which boat is without a plug. I was much impressed by this idea as I watched the difficulties which were encountered even in that secluded anchorage.

The end of my journey was uneventful, but my joy at being reunited with my family was clouded by the news of the death of my mother. She was eighty-three years of age, and had for some years been almost totally blind, so that her change was altogether a release, but it was sad to think that we should never see the kind face and gracious presence again in its old material form. Denis summed up our feelings when he cried, "What a reception Grannie must have had!" There was never anyone who had so broad and sympathetic a heart, a world-mother mourning over everything which was weak or oppressed, and thinking nothing of her own time and comfort in her efforts to help the sufferers. Even when blind and infirm she would plot and plan for the benefit of others, thinking out their needs, and bringing about surprising results by her intervention. For my own psychic work she had, I fear, neither sympathy nor understanding, but she had an innate faith and spirituality which were so natural to her that she could not conceive the needs of others in that direction. She understands now.

Whilst in the Blue Mountains I was forced to reconsider my plans on account of the strike which has paralysed all coastal trade. If I should be able to reach Tasmania I might be unable to return, and it would, indeed, be a tragic situation if my family were ready to start for England in the *Naldera,* and I was unable to join them. I felt, therefore, that I was not justified in going to Tasmania, even if I were able, which is very doubtful. It was sad, as it spoiled the absolute completeness of my tour, but on the other hand I felt sure that I should find plenty of work to do on the mainland, without taking so serious a risk.

It is a terrible thing to see this young country, which needs every hour of time and every ounce of energy for its speedy development, frittering itself away in these absurd conflicts, which never give any result to compare with the loss. One feels that in the stern contests of nations one will arise which has economic discipline, and that none other could stand against it. If the training of reorganised Germany should take this shape she will conquer and she will deserve to conquer. It is a monstrous abuse that Compulsory Arbitration Courts should be established, as is the case in Australia, and that Unions should either strike against their decisions, or should anticipate their decisions, as in the case of these stewards, by forcing a strike. In such a case I hold that the secretary and every other official of the Union should be prosecuted and heavily fined, if not imprisoned. It is the only way by which the community can be saved from a tyranny which is quite as real as that of any autocrat. What would be said, for example, of a king who cut off the islands of Tasmania and New Zealand from communication with the outer world, deranging the whole Christmas arrangements of countless families who had hoped to reunite? Yet this is what has been done by a handful of stewards with some trivial griev-ance. A fireman who objects to the cooking can hold up a great vessel. There is nothing but chaos in front of a nation unless it insists upon being master in its own house, and forbids either employed or employer to do that which is for the common scathe. The time seems to be coming when Britons, the world over, will have to fight for liberty against licence just as hard as ever they fought for her against tyranny. This I say with full sympathy for the Labour Party, which I have often been tempted to join, but have always been repelled by their attempt to bully the rest of the State instead of using those means which would certainly ensure their legitimate success, even if it took some years to accomplish. There are many anomalies and injustices, and it is only a people's party which can set them right. Hereditary honours are an injustice, lands owned by feudal or royal gift are an injustice, increased private wealth through the growth of towns is an injustice, coal royalties are an injustice, the expense of the law is a glaring injustice, the support of any single religion by the State is an injustice, our divorce laws are an injustice—with such a list a real honest Labour Party would be a sure winner if it could persuade us all that it would not commit injustices itself, and bolster up labour artificially at the expense of everyone else. It is not organised labour which moves me, for it can take care of itself, but it is the indigent governesses with thirty pounds a year, the broken people, the people with tiny pensions, the struggling widows with children—when I think of all these and then of the man who owns a county I feel that there is something deeply, deeply wrong which nothing but some great strong new force can set right.

[217]

THE WANDERINGS OF A SPIRITUALIST

One finds in the Blue Mountains that opportunity of getting alone with real Nature, which is so healing and soothing a thing. The wild scrub flows up the hillsides to the very grounds of the hotels, and in a very few minutes one may find oneself in the wilderness of ferns and gum trees unchanged from immemorial ages. It is a very real danger to the young or to those who have no sense of direction, for many people have wandered off and never come back alive —in fact there is a specially enrolled body of searchers who hunt for the missing visitor. I have never in all my travels seen anything more spacious and wonderful than the view from the different sandstone bluffs, looking down into the huge gullies beneath, a thousand feet deep, where the great gum trees look like rows of cabbages. I suppose that in water lies the force which, in the course of ages, has worn down the soft, sandy rock and formed these colossal clefts, but the effects are so enormous that one is inclined to think some great earth convulsion must also have been concerned in their production. Some of the cliffs have a sheer drop of over one thousand feet, which is said to be unequalled in the world.

These mountains are so precipitous and tortuous, presenting such a maze to the explorer, that for many years they were a formidable barrier to the extension of the young Colony. There were only about forty miles of arable land from the coast to the great Hawkesbury River, which winds round the base of the mountains. Then came this rocky labyrinth. At last, in 1812, four brave and persevering men—Blaxland, Evans, Wentworth and Lawson—took the matter in hand, and after many adventures, blazed a trail across, by which all the splendid hinterland was opened up, including the gold fields, which found their centre in the new town of Bathurst. When one reflects that all the gold had to be brought across this wilderness, with unexplored woodlands fringing the road, it is no wonder that a race of bushrangers sprang into existence, and the marvel is that the police should ever have been able to hunt them down. So fresh is all this very vital history in the development of a nation, that one can still see upon the trees the marks of the explorers' axes, as they endeavoured to find a straight trail among the countless winding gullies. At Mount York, the highest view-point, a monument has been erected to them, at the place from which they got the first glimpse of the promised land beyond.

We had been told that in the tropical weather now prevailing, it was quite vain for us to go to Queensland, for no one would come to listen to lectures. My own belief was, however, that this subject has stirred people very deeply, and that they will suffer any inconvenience to learn about it. Mr. Smythe was of opinion, at first, that my audiences were drawn from those who came from curiosity because they had read my writings, but when he found that the second and the third meetings were as full as the first, he was forced to admit that the credit of success lay with the matter rather than with the man. In any case I reflected that my presence in Brisbane would certainly bring about the usual Press controversy, with a free ventilation of the subject, so we determined to go. Mr. Smythe, for once, did not accompany us, but the very capable lady who assists him, Miss Sternberg, looked after all arrangements.

It was a very wearisome train journey of twenty-eight hours; tropically hot, rather dusty, with a change in the middle, and the usual stuffiness of a sleeper, which was superior to the ordinary American one, but below the British standard. How the Americans, with their nice sense of decency, can stand the awful accommodation their railway companies give them, or at any rate, used to give them, is incomprehensible, but public opinion in all matters asserts itself far less directly in America than in Britain. Australia is half-way between, and, certainly, I have seen abuses there in the management of trains, posts, telegrams and telephones, which would have evoked loud protests at home. I think that there is more initiative at home. For example, when the railway strike threatened to throttle the country, the public rose to the occasion and improvised methods which met the difficulty. I have not heard of anything of the kind in the numerous strikes with which this community is harassed. Any individual action arouses attention. I remember the amusement of the Hon. Agar Wynne when, on arriving late at Melbourne, in the absence of porters, I got a trolley, placed my own luggage on it, and wheeled it to a cab. Yet we thought nothing of that when labour was short in London.

The country north of Sydney is exactly like the Blue Mountains, on a lesser scale—riven ranges of sand-stone covered with gum trees. I cannot understand those who say there is nothing worth seeing in Australia, for I know no big city which has glorious scenery so near it as Sydney. After crossing the Queensland border, one comes to the Darling Downs, unsurpassed for cattle and wheat. Our first impressions of the new State were that it was the most naturally rich of any Australian Colony, and the longer we were in it, the more did we realise that this was indeed so. It is so enormous, however, that it is certain, sooner or later, to be divided into a South, Middle, and North, each of which will be a large and flourishing community. We observed from the railway all sorts of new vegetable life, and I was especially interested to notice that our English yellow mullein was lining the track, making its way gradually up country.

Even Sydney did not provide a warmer and more personal welcome than that which we both received when we at last reached Brisbane. At Toowoomba, and other stations on the way, small deputations of Spiritualists had met the train, but at Brisbane the platform was crowded. My wife was covered with flowers, and we were soon made to realise that we had been misinformed in the south, when we were told that the movement was confined to a small circle.

We were tired, but my wife rose splendidly to the occasion. The local paper says: "Carefully concealing all feelings of fatigue and tiredness after the long and wearisome train journey from Sydney, Lady Doyle charmed the large gathering of Spiritualists assembled at the Central Railway Station on Saturday night, to meet her and her husband. In vivacious fashion, Lady Doyle responded to the many enthusiastic greetings, and she was obviously delighted with the floral gifts

[221]

presented to her on her arrival. To a press representative, Lady Doyle expressed her admiration of the Australian scenery, and she referred enthusiastically to the Darling Downs district and to the Toowoomba Range. During her husband's absence in New Zealand, Lady Doyle and her children spent a holiday in the Blue Mountains (New South Wales), and were delighted with the innumerable gorgeous beauty spots there."

After a short experience, when we were far from comfortable, we found our way to the Bellevue Hotel, where a kindly old Irish proprietress, Mrs. Finegan, gave us greater attention and luxury than we had found anywhere up to then on the Australian continent.

The usual press discussion was in full swing. The more bigoted clergy in Brisbane, as elsewhere, were very vituperative, but so unreasonable and behind their own congregations in knowledge and intelligence, that they must have alienated many who heard them. Father Lane, for example, preaching in the cathedral, declared that the whole subject was "an abomination to the Lord." He does not seem to have asked himself why the Lord gave us these powers if they are an abomination. He also declared that we denied our moral responsibility to God in this life, a responsibility which must have weighed rather lightly upon Father Lane when he made so false a statement. The Rev. L. H. Jaggers, not to be outdone in absurdity by Father Lane, described all our fellow-mortals of India, China and Japan as "demoniacal races." Dr. Cosh put forward the Presbyterian sentiment that I was Anti-Christ and a serious menace to the spiritual life of Australia. Really, when I see the want of all truth and charity shown by these gentlemen, it does begin to convince me of the reality of diabolical interference in the affairs of mankind, for I cannot understand why, otherwise, such efforts should be made to obscure, by falsehood and abuse, the great revelation and comfort which God has sent us. The opposition culminated in an open letter from Dr. Cosh in the *Mail,* demanding that I should define my exact views as to the Trinity, the Atonement, and other such mysteries. I answered by pointing out that all the religious troubles of the past had come from the attempt to give exact definitions of things which were entirely beyond the human power of thought, and that I refused to be led along so dangerous a path. One Baptist clergyman, named Rowe, had the courage to say that he was on my side, but with that exception I fear that I had a solid phalanx against me.

On the other hand, the general public were amazingly friendly. It was the more wonderful as it was tropical weather, even for Brisbane. In that awful heat the great theatre could not hold the people, and they stood in the upper galleries, packed tightly, for an hour and a half without a movement or a murmur. It was a really wonderful sight. Twice the house was packed this way, so (as the Tasmanian venture was now hopeless, owing to the shipping strike) I determined to remain in our very comfortable quarters at the Bellevue Hotel, and give one more lecture, covering fresh ground. The subject opens up so that I am sure I could lecture for a week without repeating myself. On this occasion the house was crowded once more.

THE WANDERINGS OF A SPIRITUALIST

The theatrical manager said, "Well, if it was comic opera in the season, it could not have succeeded better!" I was rather exhausted at the end, for I spoke, as usual, with no chairman, and gave them a full ninety minutes, but it was nearing the end of my work, and the prospect of the quiet time ahead of us helped me on.

I met a kinsman, Dr. A. A. Doyle, who is a distinguished skin specialist, in Brisbane. He knew little of psychic matters, but he had met with a remarkable experience. His son, a splendid young fellow, died at the front. At that moment his father woke to find the young soldier stooping over him, his face quite close. He at once woke his wife and told her that their son, he feared, was dead. But here comes a fine point. He said to the wife, "Eric has had a return of the acne of the face, for which I treated him years ago. I saw the spots." The next post brought a letter, written before Eric's death, asking that some special ointment should be sent, as his acne had returned. This is a very instructive case, as showing that even an abnormal thing is reproduced at first upon the etheric body. But what has a materialist to say to the whole story? He can only evade it, or fall back upon his usual theory, that every one who reports such occurrences is either a fool or a liar.

We had a pleasant Sunday among the birds of Queensland. Mr. Chisholm, an enthusiastic bird-lover, took us round to see two very large aviaries, since the haunt of the wild birds was beyond our reach. Birds in captivity have always saddened me, but here I found them housed in such great structures, with every comfort included, and every natural enemy excluded, that

LAYING FOUNDATION STONE OF SPIRITUALIST CHURCH AT BRISBANE.

really one could not pity them. One golden pheasant amused us, for he is a very conceited bird when all is well with him, and likes to occupy the very centre of the stage, with the spot light upon him, and a chorus of drab hens admiring him from the rear. We had caught him, however, when he was moulting, and he was so conscious of his bedraggled glories that he dodged about behind a barrel, and scuttled under cover every time we tried to put him out. A fearful thing happened one day, for a careless maid left the door ajar, and in the morning seventy of the inmates were gone. It must have been a cruel blow to Mr. Baldwin, who is devoted to his collection. However, he very wisely left the door open, after securing the remaining birds, and no less than thirty-four of the refugees returned. The fate of the others was probably tragic, for they were far from the mountains which are their home.

Mr. Farmer Whyte, the very progressive editor of the *Daily Mail,* who is miles ahead of most journalists in psychic knowledge, took us for an interesting drive through the dense woods of One Tree Hill. Here we were courteously met by two of the original owners, one of them an iguana, a great, heavy lizard, which bolted up a tree, and the other a kangaroo, who stood among the brushwood, his ears rotating with emotion, while he gazed upon our halted car. From the summit of the hill one has a wonderful view of the ranges stretching away to the horizon in all directions, while at one's feet lies the very widespread city. As nearly every dwelling house is a bungalow, with its own little ground, the Australian cities take up great space, which is nullified by their very excellent tram services. A beautiful river, the Brisbane, rather wider than the Thames, winds through the town, and has sufficient depth to allow ocean steamers to come within cab-drive of the hotels.

About this time I had the usual experience which every visitor to the States or to the Dominions is liable to, in that his own utterances in his letters home get into print, and boomerang back upon him. My own feelings, both to the Australian people and their country, have been so uniformly whole-hearted that I should have thought no mischief could be made, but at the same time, I have always written freely that which I was prepared to stand by. In this case, the extract, from a private letter, removed from all modifying context, came through as follows:

"Sir Conan Doyle, quoted in the *International Psychic Gazette,* in referring to his 'ups and downs' in Australia, says: 'Amid the "downs" is the Press boycott, caused partly by ignorance and want of proportion, partly by moral cowardice and fear of finding out later that they had backed the wrong horse, or had given the wrong horse fair play. They are very backward, and far behind countries like Iceland and Denmark in the knowledge of what has been done in Spiritualism. They are dear folk, these Australians, but, Lord, they want Spirituality, and dynamiting out of their grooves! The Presbyterians actually prayed that I might not reach the country. This is rather near murder, if they thought their rotten prayers would avail. The result was an excellent voyage, but it is the spiritual deadness of this place which gets on my nerves.' "

[226]

THE WANDERINGS OF A SPIRITUALIST

This was copied into every paper in Australia, but it was soon recognised that "this place" was not Australia, but Melbourne, from which the letter was dated. I have already recorded how I was treated by the leading paper in that city, and my general experience there was faithfully reflected in my remarks. Therefore, I had nothing to withdraw. My more extended experience taught me that the general level of intelligence and of spirituality in the Australasian towns is as high as in the average towns of Great Britain, though none are so far advanced as towns like Manchester or Glasgow, nor are there the same number of professional and educated men who have come forward and given testimony. The thirst for information was great, however, and that proved an open mind, which must now lead to a considerable extension of knowledge within the churches as well as without.

My remarks had been caused by the action of the *Argus,* but the *Age,* the other leading Melbourne paper, seemed to think that its honour was also touched, and had a very severe leading article upon my delinquencies, and my alleged views, which was, as usual, a wild travesty of my real ones. It began this article by the assertion that, apparently, I still thought that Australia was inhabited by the aborigines, before I ventured to bring forward such theories. Such a remark, applied to a subject which has won the assent in varying degrees of everyone who has seriously examined it, and which has its foundation resting upon the labours of some of the greatest minds in the world, did not help me to recover my respect for the mentality and breadth of view of the journals of Melbourne. I answered, pointing out that David Syme, the very distinguished founder of the paper, by no means shared this contempt to Spiritualism, as is shown by two long letters included in his published Life.

This attitude, and that of so many other objectors, is absolutely unintelligible to me. They must know that this cult is spreading and that many capable minds have examined and endorsed it. They must know, also, that the views we proclaim, the continuance of happy life and the practical abolition of death are, if true, the grandest advance that the human race has ever made. And yet, so often, instead of saying, "Well, here is some one who is supposed to know something about the matter. Let us see if this grand claim can possibly be established by evidence and argument," they break into insults and revilings as if something offensive had been laid before them. This attitude can only arise from the sluggish conservatism of the human brain, which runs easily in certain well-worn grooves, and is horrified by the idea that something may come to cause mental exertion and readjustment.

I am bound to add that the general public went out of their way to show that their Press did not represent their views. The following passage is typical of many: "The criticism which you have so justly resented is, I am sure, not in keeping with the views of the majority of the Australian people. In my own small sphere many of my friends have been stirred deeply by your theories, and the inspiration in some cases has been so marked that the fact should afford you satisfaction. We are not all spiritually defunct. Many are quite satisfied that you are giving your best for humanity, and believe that there is a tremendous revelation coming to this weary old world."

The Spiritualists of Brisbane, greatly daring, have planned out a church which is to cost £10,000, trusting to those who work with us on the other side to see the enterprise through. The possible fallacy lies in the chance that those on the other side do not desire to see this immense movement become a separate sect, but are in favour of the peaceful penetration of all creeds by our new knowledge. It is on record that early in the movement Senator Talmadge asked two different spirit controls, in different States of the Union, what the ultimate goal of this spiritual outburst might be, and received exactly the same answer from each, namely, that it was to prove immortality and to unify the Churches. The first half has been done, so far as survival implies immortality, and the second may well come to pass, by giving such a large common platform to each Church that they will learn to disregard the smaller differences.

Be this as it may, one could not but admire the faith and energy of Mr. Reinhold and the others who were determined to have a temple of their own. I laid the foundation stone at three in the afternoon under so tropical a sun that I felt as if the ceremony was going to have its immemorial accompaniment of a human sacrifice and even of a whole-burned offering. The crowd made matters worse, but a friendly bystander with an umbrella saved me from heat apoplexy. I felt the occasion was a solemn one, for it was certainly the first Spiritual Church in the whole of Queensland, and I doubt if we have many anywhere in Australia, for among our apostolic gifts poverty is conspicuous. It has always amazed me how Theosophists and Christian Scientists get their fine halls and libraries, while we, with our zeal and our knowledge, have some bare schoolroom or worse as our only meeting place. It reflects little credit upon the rich people who accept the comforts we bring, but share none of the burdens we bear. There is a kink in their souls.

I spoke at some length, and the people listened with patience in spite of the great heat. It was an occasion when I could, with propriety, lay emphasis upon the restraint and charity with which such a church should be run. The Brisbane paper reports me as follows: "I would emphasise three things. Mind your own business; go on quietly in your own way; you know the truth and do not need to quarrel with other people. There are many roads to salvation. The second point I would urge is that you should live up to your knowledge. We know for certain that we live on after death, that everything we do in this world influences what comes after; therefore, we can afford to be unselfish and friendly to other religions. Some Spiritualists run down the Bible, whereas it is from cover to cover a spiritual book. I would like to see the Bible read in every Spiritualistic Church with particular attention paid to the passages dealing with occultism. The third point I would emphasise is that you should have nothing to do with fortune-telling or anything of that kind. All fortune-telling is really a feeling out in the dark. If good things are going to happen to you be content to wait for them, and if evil is to come nothing is to be gained by attempting to anticipate it. My sympathies are with the police in their attitude to fortune-tellers, whose black magic is far removed from the services of our mediums in striving to bring comfort to those whose loved ones have gone before. If these three things are lived up to, this church will be a source of great brightness and happiness."

Our work was pleasantly broken by an invitation to lunch with Sir Matthew Nathan, at Government House. Sir Matthew impresses one as a man of character, and as he is a financial authority he is in a position to help by his advice in restoring the credit of Queensland. The matter in dispute, which has been called repudiation, does not, as it seems to me, deserve so harsh a term, as it is one of those cases where there are two sides to the question, so equally balanced that it is difficult for an outsider to pronounce a judgment. On the one hand the great squatters who hold millions of acres in the State had received the land on considerable leases which charged them with a very low rent—almost a nominal one— on condition of their taking up and developing the country. On the other hand, the Government say these leases were granted under very different circumstances, the lessees have already done very well out of them, the war has made it imperative that the State raise funds, and the assets upon which the funds can be raised are all in the hands of these lessees, who should consent to a revision of their agreements. So stands the quarrel, so far as I could understand it, and the

State has actually imposed the increased rates. Hence the cry that they have repudiated their own contract. The result of the squatters' grievance was that Mr. Theodore, the Premier, was unable to raise money in the London market, and returned home with the alternative of getting a voluntary loan in the Colony, or of raising a compulsory loan from those who had the money. The latter has an ugly sound, and yet the need is great, and if some may be compelled to serve with their bodies I do not see why some may not also be compelled to serve with their purses. The assets of the Colony compare very favourably, I believe, with others, for while these others have sold their lands, the Government of Queensland has still the ownership of the main tracts of the gloriously fertile country. Therefore, with an issue at 6½ per cent., without tax, one would think that they should have no difficulty in getting any reasonable sum. I was cinemaed in the act of applying for a small share in the issue, but I think the advertisement would have been of more value to the loan, had they captured some one of greater financial stability.

The more one examines this alleged "repudiation" the less reason appears in the charge, and as it has assuredly injured Queensland's credit, it is well that an impartial traveller should touch upon it. The squatters are the richer folk and in a position to influence the public opinion of the world, and in their anxiety to exploit their own grievance they seem to have had little regard for the reputation of their country. It is like a man burning down his house in the hope of roasting some other inmate of whom he disapproves. A conservative paper (the *Producer's Review,* January 10th, 1921) says: "No living man can say how much Queensland has been damaged by the foolish partisan statements that have been uttered and published." The article proceeds to show in very convincing style, with chapter and verse, that the Government has always been well within its rights, and that a Conservative Government on a previous occasion did the same thing, framing a Bill on identical lines.

On January 12th my kinsman, Dr. Doyle, with his charming wife, took us out into the bush for a billy tea—that is, to drink tea which is prepared as the bushmen prepare it in their tin cans. It was certainly excellent, and we enjoyed the drive and the whole experience, though uninvited guests of the mosquito tribe made things rather lively for us. I prayed that my face would be spared, as I did not wish to turn up at my lecture as if I had been having a round with Dr. Cosh, and I react in a most whole-hearted way to any attentions from an insect. The result was certainly remarkable, be it coincidence or not, for though my hands were like boxing-gloves, and my neck all swollen, there was not a mark upon my face. I fancy that the hardened inhabitants hardly realise what new chums endure after they are bitten by these pests. It means to me not only disfigurement, but often a sleepless night. My wife and the children seem to escape more lightly. I found many objects of interest in the bush—among others a spider's web so strong that full-sized dragon flies were enmeshed in it. I could not see the creature itself, but it must have been as big as a tarantula. Our host was a large landowner as well as a specialist, and he talked seriously of leaving the country, so embittered was he by the land-policy of the Government. At the same time, the fact that he could sell his estate at a fair price seemed to imply that others took a less grave view of the situation. Many of the richer classes think that Labour is adopting a policy of deliberate petty irritation in order to drive them out of the country, but perhaps they are oversensitive.

So full was our life in Brisbane that there was hardly a day that we had not some memorable experience, even when I had to lecture in the evening. Often we were going fourteen and fifteen hours a day, and a tropical day at that. On January 14th we were taken to see the largest bee-farm in Australia, run by Mr. H. L. Jones. Ever since I consigned Mr. Sherlock Holmes to a bee farm for his old age, I have been supposed to know something of the subject, but really I am so ignorant that when a woman wrote to me and said she would be a suitable housekeeper to the retired detective because she could "segregate the queen," I did not know what she meant. On this occasion I saw the operation and many other wonderful things which make me appreciate Maeterlinck's prose-poem upon the subject. There is little poetry about Mr. Jones, however, and he is severely practical. He has numbers of little boxes with a store of bee-food compressed into one end of them. Into each he thrusts a queen with eight attendants to look after her. The food is enough to last two months, so he simply puts on a postage stamp and sends it off to any one in California or South Africa who is starting an apiary. Several hives were opened for our inspection with the precaution of blowing in some smoke to pacify the bees. We were told that this sudden inrush of smoke gives the bees the idea that some great cataclysm has occurred, and their first action is to lay in a store of honey, each of them, as a man might seize provisions in an earthquake so as to be ready for whatever the future might bring. He showed us that the queen, fed with some special food by the workers, can lay twice her own weight of eggs in a day, and that if we could find something similar for hens we could hope for an unbroken stream of eggs. Clever as the bee is it is clearly an instinctive hereditary cleverness, for man has been able to make many improvements in its methods, making artificial comb which is better than the original, in that it has cells for more workers and fewer drones. Altogether it was a wonderful demonstration, which could be viewed with comfort under a veil with one's hands in one's pockets, for though we were assured they would not sting if they knew we would not hurt them, a misunderstanding was possible. One lady spectator seemed to have a sudden ambition to break the standing jump record, and we found that she had received two stings, but Mr. Jones and his assistants covered their hands with the creatures and were quite immune. A half-wild wallaby appeared during our visit, and after some coyness yielded to the fascination which my wife exercises over all animals, and fed out of her hand. We were assured that this had never before occurred in the case of any visitor.

We found in Brisbane, as in every other town, that the question of domestic service, the most important of all questions to a householder, was very acute. Ladies who occupied leading positions in the town assured us that it was impossible to keep maids, and that they were compelled now to give it up in despair, and to do all their own house work with such casual daily assistance as they could get. A pound a week is a common wage for very inefficient service. It is a serious matter and no solution is in sight. English maids are, I am sorry to say, looked upon as the worst of all, for to all the other faults they add constant criticism of their employers, whom they pronounce to be "no ladies" because they are forced to do many things which are not done at home. Inefficiency plus snobbishness is a dreadful mixture. Altogether the lot of the Australian lady is not an easy one, and we admired the brave spirit with which they rose above their troubles.

This servant question bears very directly upon the Imperial puzzle of the northern territory. A white man may live and even work there, but a white woman cannot possibly run a household unless domestic labour is plentiful. In that climate it simply means absolute breakdown in a year. Therefore it is a mad policy which at present excludes so rigorously the Chinese, Indians or others who alone can make white households possible. White labour assumes a dog in the manger policy, for it will not, or cannot, do the work itself, and yet it shuts out those who could do it. It is an impossible position and must be changed. How severe and unreasonable are the coloured immigrant laws is shown by the fact that the experienced and popular Commander of the *Naldera*, Captain Lewellin, was fined at Sydney a large sum of money because three Goa Indians deserted from his ship. There is a great demand for Indian camel drivers in the north, and this no doubt was the reason for the desertion, but what a *reductio ad absurdum* of the law which comes between the demand and the supply, besides punishing an innocent victim.

As usual a large number of psychic confidences reached us, some of which were very interesting. One lady is a clairaudient, and on the occasion of her mother falling ill she heard the words "Wednesday— the fifteenth." Death seemed a matter of hours, and the date far distant, but the patient, to the surprise of the doctors, still lingered. Then came the audible message "She will tell you where she is going." The mother had lain for two days helpless and comatose. Suddenly she opened her eyes and said in a clear strong voice, "I have seen the mansions in my father's house. My husband and children await me there. I could not have imagined anything so exquisitely lovely." Then she breathed her last, the date being the 15th.

We were entertained to dinner on the last evening by the Hon. John Fihilly, acting Premier of the Colony, and his wife. He is an Irish labour leader with a remarkable resemblance to Dan O'Connell in his younger days. I was pleased to see that the toast of the King was given though it was not called for at a private dinner. Fihilly is a member of the Government, and I tackled him upon the question of British emigrants being enticed out by specious promises on the part of Colonial Agents in London, only to find that no work awaited them. Some deplorable cases had come within my own observation, one, an old Lancashire Fusilier, having walked the streets for six months. He assured me that the arrangements were now in perfect order, and that emigrants were held back in the old country until they could be sure that there was a place for them. There are so many out of work in Australia that one feels some sympathy with those labour men who are against fresh arrivals.

And there lies the great problem which we have not, with all our experience, managed to master. On the one side illimitable land calling for work. On the other innumerable workers calling for land. And yet the two cannot be joined. I remember how it jarred me when I saw Edmonton, in Western Canada, filled with out-of-workers while the great land lay uninhabited. The same strange paradox meets one here. It is just the connecting link that is missing, and that link lies in wise prevision. The helpless newcomer can do nothing if he and his family are dumped down upon a hundred acres of gum trees. Put yourself in their position. How can they hope with their feeble hands to clear the ground? All this early work must be done for them by the State, the owner repaying after he has made good. Let the emigrant move straight on to a cleared farm, with a shack-house already prepared, and clear instructions as to the best crops, and how to get them. Then it seems to me that emigration would bring no want of employment in its train. But the State must blaze the trail and the

CURIOUS PHOTOGRAPHIC EFFECT REFERRED TO IN THE TEXT.
Taken by the Official Photographer, Brisbane. "Absolutely mystifying" is his description.

public follow after. Such arrangements may even now exist, but if so they need expansion and improvement, for they do not seem to work.

Before leaving Brisbane my attention was drawn to the fact that the State photographer, when he took the scene of the opening of the loan, had produced to all appearance a psychic effect. The Brisbane papers recorded it as follows:—

" 'It is a remarkable result, and I cannot offer any opinion as to what caused it. It is absolutely mystifying.' Such was the declaration made yesterday by the Government photographer, Mr. W. Mobsby, in regard to the unique effect associated with a photograph he took on Thursday last of Sir A. Conan Doyle. Mr. Mobsby, who has been connected with photography since boyhood, explained that he was instructed to take an official photograph of the function at which Sir A. Conan Doyle handed over his subscription to the State Loan organiser. When he arrived, the entrance to the building was thronged by a large crowd, and he had to mount a stepladder, which was being used by the *Daily Mail* photographer, in order to get a good view of the proceedings. Mr. Mobsby took only one picture, just at the moment Sir A. Conan Doyle was mounting the steps at the Government Tourist Bureau to meet the Acting Premier, Mr. J. Fihilly. Mr. Mobsby developed the film himself, and was amazed to find that while all the other figures in the picture were distinct the form of Sir A. Conan Doyle appeared enveloped in mist and could only be dimly seen. The photograph was taken on an ordinary film with a No. 3a Kodak, and careful examination does not in any way indicate the cause of the sensational result." I have had so many personal proofs of the intervention of supernormal agencies during the time that I have been engaged upon this task that I am prepared to accept the appearance of this aura as being an assurance of the presence of those great forces for whom I act as a humble interpreter. At the same time, the sceptic is very welcome to explain it as a flawed film and a coincidence.

We returned from Brisbane to Sydney in the Orient Liner *Orsova*, which is a delightful alternative to the stuffy train. The sea has always been a nursing mother to me, and I suppose I have spent a clear two years of my life upon the waves. We had a restful Sunday aboard the boat, disturbed only by the Sunday service, which left its usual effect upon my mind. The Psalms were set to some unhappy tune, very different from the grand Gregorian rhythm, so that with its sudden rise to a higher level it sounded more like the neighing of horses than the singing of mortals. The words must surely offend anyone who considers what it is that he is saying—a mixture of most unmanly wailing and spiteful threats. How such literature has been perpetuated three thousand years, and how it can ever have been sacred, is very strange. Altogether from first to last there was nothing, save only the Lord's Prayer, which could have any spiritual effect. These old observances are like an iron ball tied to the leg of humanity, for ever hampering spiritual progress. If now, after the warning of the great war, we have not the mental energy and the moral courage to get back to realities, we shall deserve what is coming to us.

On January 17th we were back, tired but contented, in the Medlow Bath Hotel in the heart of the Blue Mountains—an establishment which I can heartily recommend to any who desire a change from the summer heats of Sydney.

CHAPTER XI

WE recuperated after our Brisbane tour by spending the next week at Medlow Bath, that little earthly paradise, which is the most restful spot we have found in our wanderings. It was built originally by Mr. Mark Foy, a successful draper of Sydney, and he is certainly a man of taste, for he has adorned it with a collection of prints and of paintings—hundreds of each—which would attract attention in any city, but which on a mountain top amid the wildest scenery give one the idea of an Arabian Nights palace. There was a passage some hundreds of yards long, which one has to traverse on the way to each meal, and there was a certain series of French prints, representing events of Byzantine history, which I found it difficult to pass, so that I was often a late comer. A very fair library is among the other attractions of this remarkable place.

Before leaving we spent one long day at the famous Jenolan Caves, which are distant about forty-five miles. As the said miles are very up-and-down, and as the cave exploration involves several hours of climbing, it makes a fairly hard day's work. We started all seven in a motor, as depicted by the wayside photographers, but Baby got sick and had to be left with Jakeman at the halfway house, where we picked her up, quite recovered, on our return. It was as well, for the walk would have been quite beyond her, and yet having once started there is no return, so we should have ended by carrying her through all the subterranean labyrinths. The road is a remarkably good one, and represents a considerable engineering feat. It passes at last through an enormous archway of rock which marks the entrance to the cave formations. These caves are hollowed out of what was once a coral reef in a tropical sea, but is now sixty miles inland with a mountain upon the top of it—such changes this old world has seen. If the world were formed only that man might play his drama upon it, then mankind must be in the very earliest days of his history, for who would build so elaborate a stage if the play were to be so short and insignificant?

The caves are truly prodigious. They were discovered first in the pursuit of some poor devil of a bushranger who must have been hard put to it before he took up his residence in this damp and dreary retreat. A brave man, Wilson, did most of the actual exploring, lowering himself by a thin rope into noisome abysses of unknown depth and charting out the whole of this devil's warren. It is so vast that many weeks would be needed to go through it, and it is usual at one visit to take only a single sample. On this occasion it was the River Cave, so named because after many wanderings you come on a river about twenty feet across and forty-five feet deep which has to be navigated for some distance in a punt. The stalactite effects, though very wonderful, are not, I think, superior to those which I have seen in Derbyshire, and the caves have none of that historical glamour which is needed in order to link some large natural object to our own comprehension. I can remember in Derbyshire how my imagination and sympathy were stirred by a Roman lady's brooch which had been found among the rubble. Either a wild beast or a bandit knew best how it got there. Jenolan has few visible links with the past, but one of them is a tremendous one. It is the complete, though fractured, skeleton of a very large man—seven foot four said the guide, but he may have put it on a little—who was found partly imbedded in the lime. Many ages ago he seems to have fallen through the roof of the cavern, and the bones of a wallaby hard by give some indication that he was hunting at the time, and that his quarry shared his fate. He was of the Black fellow type, with a low-class cranium. It is remarkable the proportion of very tall men who are dug up in ancient tombs. Again and again the bogs of Ireland have yielded skeletons of seven and eight feet. Some years ago a Scythian chief was dug up on the Southern Steppes of Russia who was eight feet six. What a figure of a man with his winged helmet and his battle axe! All over the world one comes upon these giants of old, and one wonders whether they represented some race, further back still, who were all gigantic. The Babylonian tradition in our Bible says: "And there were giants in those days." The big primeval kangaroo has grown down to the smaller modern one, the wombat, which was an animal as big as a tapir, is now as small as a badger, the great saurians have become little lizards, and so it would seem not unreasonable to suppose that man may have run to great size at some unexplored period in his evolution.

We all emerged rather exhausted from the bowels of the earth, dazed with the endless succession of strange gypsum formations which we had seen, minarets, thrones, shawls, coronets, some of them so made that one could imagine that the old kobolds had employed their leisure hours in fashioning their freakish outlines. It was a memorable drive home in the evening. Once as a bird flew above my head, the slanting ray of the declining sun struck it and turned it suddenly to a vivid scarlet and green. It was the first of many parrots. Once also a couple of kangaroos bounded across the road, amid wild cries of delight from the children. Once, too, a long snake writhed across and was caught by one of the wheels of the motor. Rabbits, I am sorry to say, abounded. If they would confine themselves to these primeval woods, Australia would be content.

This was the last of our pleasant Australian excursions, and we left Medlow Bath refreshed not only by its charming atmosphere, but by feeling that we had gained new friends. We made our way on January 26th to Sydney, where all business had to be settled up and preparations made for our homeward voyage.

Whilst in Sydney I had an opportunity of examining several phases of mediumship which will be of interest to the psychic reader. I called upon Mrs. Foster-Turner, who is perhaps the greatest all-round medium with the highest general level of any sensitive in Australia. I found a middle-aged lady of commanding and pleasing appearance with a dignified manner and a beautifully modulated voice, which must be invaluable to her in platform work. Her gifts are so many that it must have been difficult for her to know which to cultivate, but she finally settled upon medical diagnosis, in which she has, I understand, done good work. Her practice is considerable, and her help is not despised by some of the leading practitioners. This gift is, as I have explained previously in the case of Mr. Bloomfield, a form of clairvoyance, and Mrs. Foster Turner enjoys all the other phases of that wonderful power, including psychometry, with its application to detective work, the discerning of spirits, and to a very marked degree the gift of prophecy, which she has carried upon certain occasions to a length which I have never known equalled in any reliable record of the past.

Here is an example for which, I am told, a hundred witnesses could be cited. At a meeting at the Little Theatre, Castlereagh Street, Sydney, on a Sunday evening of February, 1914, Mrs. Turner addressed the audience under an inspiration which claimed to be W. T. Stead. He ended his address by saying that in order to prove that he spoke with a power beyond mortal, he would, on the next Sunday, give a prophecy as to the future of the world.

Next Sunday some 900 people assembled, when Mrs. Turner, once more under control, spoke as follows. I quote from notes taken at the time. "Now, although there is not at present a whisper of a great European war at hand, yet I want to warn you that before this year, 1914, has run its course, Europe will be deluged in blood. Great Britain, our beloved nation, will be drawn into the most awful war the world has ever known. Germany will be the great antagonist, and will draw other nations in her train. Austria will totter to its ruin. Kings and kingdoms will fall. Millions of precious lives will be slaughtered, but Britain will finally triumph and emerge victorious. During the year, also, the Pope of Rome will pass away, and a bomb will be placed in St. Paul's Church, but will be discovered in time and removed before damage is done."

Can any prophecy be more accurate or better authenticated than that. The only equally exact prophecy on public events which I can recall is when Emma Hardinge Britten, having been refused permission in 1860 to deliver a lecture on Spiritualism in the Town Hall of Atlanta, declared that, before many years had passed, that very Town Hall would be choked up with the dead and the dying, drawn from the State which persecuted her. This came literally true in the Civil War a few years later, when Sherman's army passed that way.

Mrs. Foster Turner's gift of psychometry is one which will be freely used by the community when we become more civilised and less ignorant. As an example of how it works, some years ago a Melbourne man named Cutler disappeared, and there was a considerable debate as to his fate. His wife, without giving a name, brought Cutler's boot to Mrs. Turner.

She placed it near her forehead and at once got *en rapport* with the missing man. She described how he left his home, how he kissed his wife good-bye, all the succession of his movements during that morning, and finally how he had fallen or jumped over a bridge into the river, where he had been caught under some snag. A search at the place named revealed the dead body. If this case be compared with that of Mr. Foxhall, already quoted, one can clearly see that the same law underlies each. But what an ally for our C. I. D. !

There was one pleasant incident in connection with my visit to Mrs. Foster Turner. Upon my asking her whether she had any psychic impression when she saw me lecturing, she said that I was accompanied on the platform by a man in spirit life, about 70 years of age, grey-bearded, with rugged eyebrows. She searched her mind for a name, and then said, "Alfred Russell Wallace." Doctor Abbott, who was present, confirmed that she had given that name at the time. It will be remembered that Mrs. Roberts, of Dunedin, had also given the name of the great Spiritualistic Scientist as being my coadjutor. There was no possible connection between Mrs. Turner and Mrs. Roberts. Indeed, the intervention of the strike had made it almost impossible for them to communicate, even if they had known each other—which they did not. It was very helpful to me to think that so great a soul was at my side in the endeavour to stimulate the attention of the world.

Two days before our departure we attended the ordinary Sunday service of the Spiritualists at Stanmore Road, which appeared to be most reverently and beautifully conducted. It is indeed pleasant to be present at a religious service which in no way offends one's taste or one's reason—which cannot always be said, even of Spiritualistic ones. At the end I was presented with a beautifully illuminated address from the faithful of Sydney, thanking me for what they were pleased to call "the splendidly successful mission on behalf of Spiritualism in Sydney." "You are a specially chosen leader," it went on, "endowed with power to command attention from obdurate minds. We rejoice that you are ready to consecrate your life to the spread of our glorious gospel, which contains more proof of the eternal love of God than any other truth yet revealed to man." So ran this kindly document. It was decorated with Australian emblems, and as there was a laughing jackass in the corner, I was able to raise a smile by suggesting that they had adorned it with the picture of a type of opponent with whom we were very familiar, the more so as some choice specimens had been observed in Sydney. There are some gentle souls in our ranks who refrain from all retort—and morally, they are no doubt the higher—but personally, when I am moved by the malevolence and ignorance of our opponents, I cannot help hitting back at them. It was Mark Twain, I think, who said that, instead of turning the other cheek, he returned the other's cheek. That is my unregenerate instinct.

I was able, for the first time, to give a bird's-eye view of my tour and its final results. I had, in all, addressed twenty-five meetings, averaging 2,000 people

in each, or 50,000 people in all. I read aloud a letter
from Mr. Carlyle Smythe, who, with his father, had
managed the tours of every lecturer of repute who had
come to Australia during the past thirty years. Mr.
Smythe knew what success and failure were, and he
said: "For an equal number of lectures, yours has
proved the most prosperous tour in my experience.
No previous tour has won such consistent success.
From the push-off at Adelaide to the great boom in
New Zealand and Brisbane, it has been a great dynamic
progression of enthusiasm. I have known in my
career nothing parallel to it."

The enemies of our cause were longing for my
failure, and had, indeed, in some cases most un-
scrupulously announced it, so it was necessary that
I should give precise details as to this great success,
and to the proof which it afforded that the public mind
was open to the new revelation. But, after all, the
money test was the acid one. I had taken a party
of seven people at a time when all expenses were
doubled or trebled by the unnatural costs of travel
and of living, which could not be made up for by
increasing the price of admission. It would seem a
miracle that I could clear this great bill of expenses
in a country like Australia, where the large towns
are few. And yet I was able to show that I had
not only done so, after paying large sums in taxation,
but that I actually had seven hundred pounds over.
This I divided among Spiritual funds in Australia,
the bulk of it, five hundred pounds, being devoted
to a guarantee of expenses for the next lecturer who
should follow me. It seemed to me that such a

lecturer, if well chosen, and properly guaranteed against loss, might devote a longer time than I, and visit the smaller towns, from which I had often the most touching appeals. If he were successful, he need not touch the guarantee fund, and so it would remain as a perpetual source of active propaganda. Such was the scheme which I outlined that night, and which was eventually adopted by the Spiritualists of both Australia and New Zealand.

On my last evening at Sydney, I attended a third séance with Charles Bailey, the apport medium. It was not under test conditions, so that it can claim no strict scientific value, and yet the results are worth recording. It had struck me that a critic might claim that there was phosphorescent matter inside the spectacle case, which seemed to be the only object which Bailey took inside the cabinet, so I insisted on examining it, but found it quite innocent. The usual inconclusive shadowy appearance of luminous vapour was evident almost at once, but never, so far as I could judge, out of reach of the cabinet, which was simply a blanket drawn across the corner of the room. The Hindoo control then announced that an apport would be brought, and asked that water be placed in a tin basin. He (that is, Bailey himself, under alleged control) then emerged, the lights being half up, carrying the basin over his head. On putting it down, we all saw two strange little young tortoises swimming about in it. I say "strange," because I have seen none like them. They were about the size of a half-crown, and the head, instead of being close to the shell, was at the end of a thin neck half as long as the body.

There were a dozen Australians present, and they all said they had never seen any similar ones. The control claimed that he had just brought them from a tank in Benares. The basin was left on the table, and while the lights were down, the creatures disappeared. It is only fair to say that they could have been removed by hand in the dark, but on examining the table, I was unable to see any of those sloppings of water which might be expected to follow such an operation.

Shortly afterwards there was a great crash in the dark, and a number of coins fell onto the table, and were handed to me by the presiding control as a parting present. They did not, I fear, help me much with my hotel bill, for they were fifty-six Turkish copper pennies, taken "from a well," according to our informant. These two apports were all the phenomena, and the medium, who has been working very hard of late, showed every sign of physical collapse at the close.

Apart from the actual production in the séance room, which may be disputed, I should like to confront the honest sceptic with the extraordinary nature of the objects which Bailey produces on these occasions. They cannot be disputed, for hundreds have handled them, collections of them have been photographed, there are cases full at the Stanford University at California, and I am bringing a few samples back to England with me. If the whole transaction is normal, then where does he get them? I had an Indian nest. Does anyone import Indian nests? Does anyone import queer little tortoises with long, thin necks? Is there a depot for Turkish copper coins in Australia? On the previous sitting, he got 100 Chinese ones. Those might be explained, since the Chinaman is not un-common in Sydney, but surely he exports coins, rather than imports them. Then what about 100 Babylonian tablets, with legible inscriptions in Assyrian, some of them cylindrical, with long histories upon them? Granting that they are Jewish forgeries, how do they get into the country? Bailey's house was searched once by the police, but nothing was found. Arabic papers, Chinese schoolbooks, mandarins' buttons, tropical birds —all sorts of odd things arrive. If they are not genu-ine, where do they come from? The matter is venti-lated in papers, and no one comes forward to damn Bailey for ever by proving that he supplied them. It is no use passing the question by. It calls for an answer. If these articles can be got in any normal way, then what is the way? If not, then Bailey has been a most ill-used man, and miracles are of daily occurrence in Australia. This man should be under the strict, but patient and sympathetic, control of the greatest scientific observers in the world, instead of being al-lowed to wear himself out by promiscuous séances, given in order to earn a living. Imagine our scientists expending themselves in the examination of shells, or the classification of worms, when such a subject as this awaits them. And it cannot await them long. The man dies, and then where are these experiments? But if such scientific investigation be made, it must be thorough and prolonged, directed by those who have real experience of occult matters, otherwise it will wreck itself upon some theological or other snag, as did Colonel de Rochas' attempt at Grenoble.

The longer one remains in Australia, the more one

is struck by the failure of State control. Whenever you test it, in the telephones, the telegraphs and the post, it stands for inefficiency, with no possibility that I can see of remedy. The train service is better, but still far from good. As to the State ventures in steamboat lines and in banking, I have not enough information to guide me. On the face of it, it is evident that in each case there is no direct responsible master, and that there is no real means of enforcing discipline. I have talked to the heads of large institutions, who have assured me that the conduct of business is becoming almost impossible. When they send an urgent telegram, with a letter confirming it, it is no unusual thing for the letter to arrive first. No complaint produces any redress. The maximum compensation for sums lost in the post is, I am told, two pounds, so that the banks, whose registered letters continually disappear, suffer heavy losses. On the other hand, if they send a messenger with the money, there is a law by which all bullion carried by train has to be declared, and has to pay a commission. Yet the public generally, having no standard of comparison, are so satisfied with the wretched public services, that there is a continued agitation to extend public control, and so ruin the well conducted private concerns. The particular instance which came under my notice was the ferry service of Sydney harbour, which is admirably and cheaply conducted, and yet there is a clamour that it also should be dragged into this morass of slovenly inefficiency. I hope, however, that the tide will soon set the other way. I fear, from what I have seen of the actual working, that it is only under exceptional conditions, and with very rigorous and high-principled direction, that the State control of industries can be carried out. I cannot see that it is a political question, or that the democracy has any interest, save to have the public work done as well and as economically as possible. When the capitalist has a monopoly, and is exacting an undue return, it is another matter.

As I look back at Australia my prayers—if deep good wishes form a prayer—go out to it. Save for that great vacuum upon the north, which a wise Government would strive hard to fill, I see no other external danger which can threaten her people. But internally I am shadowed by the feeling that trouble may be hanging over them, though I am assured that the cool stability of their race will at last pull them through it. There are some dangerous factors there which make their position more precarious than our own, and behind a surface of civilisation there lie possible forces which might make for disruption. As a people they are rather less disciplined than a European nation. There is no large middle or leisured class who would represent moderation. Labour has tried a Labour Government, and finding that politics will not really alter economic facts is now seeking some fresh solution. The land is held in many cases by large proprietors who work great tracts with few hands, so there is not the conservative element which makes the strength of the United States with its six million farmers, each with his stake in the land. Above all, there is no standing military force, and nothing but a small, though very efficient, police force to stand between organised government and some wild attempt of the extremists. There are plenty of soldiers, it is true, and they have been treated with extreme generosity by the State, but they have been reabsorbed into the civil population. If they stand for law and order then all is well. On the other hand, there are the Irish, who are fairly numerous, well organised and disaffected. There is no Imperial question, so far as I can see, save with the Irish, but there is this disquieting internal situation which, with the coming drop of wages, may suddenly become acute. An Australian should be a sober-minded man for he has his difficulties before him. We of the old country should never forget that these difficulties have been partly caused by his splendid participation in the great war, and so strain every nerve to help, both by an enlightened sympathy and by such material means as are possible.

Personally, I have every sympathy with all reasonable and practical efforts to uphold the standard of living in the working classes. At present there is an almost universal opinion among thoughtful and patriotic Australians that the progress of the country is woefully hampered by the constant strikes, which are declared in defiance of all agreements and all arbitration courts. The existence of Labour Governments, or the State control of industries, does not seem to alleviate these evil conditions, but may rather increase them, for in some cases such pressure has been put upon the Government that they have been forced to subsidise the strikers—or at least those sufferers who have come out in sympathy with the

OUR PARTY EN ROUTE TO THE JENOLAN CAVES, JANUARY 20TH, 1921, IN FRONT OF OLD COURT HOUSE IN WHICH BUSHRANGERS WERE TRIED.

original strikers. Such tactics must demoralise a country and encourage labour to make claims upon capital which the latter cannot possibly grant, since in many cases the margin of profit is so small and precarious that it would be better for the capitalist to withdraw his money and invest it with no anxieties. It is clear that the tendency is to destroy the very means by which the worker earns his bread, and that the position will become intolerable unless the older, more level-headed men gain control of the unions and keep the ignorant hot-heads in order. It is the young unmarried men without responsibilities who create the situations, and it is the married men with their women and children who suffer. A table of strikes prepared recently by the *Manchester Guardian* shows that more hours were lost in Australia with her 'five or six million inhabitants than in the United Kingdom with nearly fifty million. Surely this must make the Labour leaders reconsider their tactics. As I write the stewards' strike, which caused such extended misery, has collapsed, the sole result being a loss of nearly a million pounds in wages to the working classes, and great inconvenience to the public. The shipowners seem now in no hurry to resume the services, and if their delay will make the strikers more thoughtful it is surely to be defended.

On February 1st we started from Sydney in our good old *Naldera* upon our homeward voyage, but the work was not yet finished. On reaching Melbourne, where the ship was delayed two days, we found that a Town Hall demonstration had been arranged to give us an address from the Victorian Spiritualists, and wish us farewell. It was very short notice and there was a tram strike which prevented people from getting about, so the hall was not more than half full. None the less, we had a fine chance of getting in touch with our friends, and the proceedings were very hearty. The inscription was encased in Australian wood with a silver kangaroo outside and beautiful illuminations within. It ran as follows:

"We desire to place on permanent record our intense appreciation of your zealous and self-sacrificing efforts, and our deep gratitude for the great help you have given to the cause to which you have consecrated your life. The over-flowing meetings addressed by you bear evidence of the unqualified success of your mission, and many thousands bless the day when you determined to enter this great crusade beneath the Southern Cross. . . . In all these sentiments we desire to include your loyal and most devoted partner, Lady Doyle, whose self-sacrifice equals or exceeds your own."

Personally, I have never been conscious of any self-sacrifice, but the words about my wife were in no way an over-statement. I spoke in reply for about forty minutes, and gave a synopsis of the state of the faith in other centres, for each Australian State is curiously self-centred and realises very little beyond its own borders. It was good for Melbourne to know that Sydney, Brisbane, Adelaide and New Zealand were quite as alive and zealous as themselves.

At the end of the function I gave an account of the financial results of my tour and handed over £500 as a guarantee fund for future British lecturers, and

£100 to Mr. Britton Harvey to assist his admirable paper, *The Harbinger of Light.* I had already expended about £100 upon spiritual causes, so that my whole balance came to £700, which is all now invested in the Cause and should bring some good spiritual interest in time to come. We badly need money in order to be able to lay our case more fully before the world.

I have already given the written evidence of Mr. Smythe that my tour was the most successful ever conducted in his time in Australia. To this I may add the financial result recorded above. In view of this it is worth recording that *Life,* a paper entirely under clerical management, said: "The one thing clear is that Sir Conan Doyle's mission to Australia was a mournful and complete failure, and it has left him in a very exasperated state of mind." This is typical of the perverse and unscrupulous opposition which we have continually to face, which hesitates at no lie in order to try and discredit the movement.

One small incident broke the monotony of the voyage between Adelaide and Fremantle, across the dreaded Bight.

There have been considerable depredations in the coastal passenger trade of Australia, and since the State boats were all laid up by the strike it was to be expected that the crooks would appear upon the big liners. A band of them came on board the *Naldera* at Adelaide, but their methods were crude, and they were up against a discipline and an organisation against which they were helpless. One ruffian entered a number of cabins and got away with some booty, but was very gallantly arrested by Captain Lewellin himself, after a short hand-to-hand struggle. This fellow was recognised by the detectives at Fremantle and was pronounced to be an old hand. In the general vigilance and search for accomplices which followed, another passenger was judged to be suspicious and he was also carried away by the detectives on a charge of previous forgery. Altogether the crooks came out very badly in their encounter with the *Naldera,* whose officers deserve some special recognition from the Company for the able way in which the matter was handled.

Although my formal tour was now over, I had quite determined to speak at Perth if it were humanly possible, for I could not consider my work as complete if the capital of one State had been untouched. I therefore sent the message ahead that I would fit in with any arrangements which they might make, be it by day or night, but that the ship would only be in port for a few hours. As matters turned out the *Naldera* arrived in the early morning and was announced to sail again at 3 p.m., so that the hours were awkward. They took the great theatre, however, for 1 p.m., which alarmed me as I reflected that my audience must either be starving or else in a state of repletion. Everything went splendidly, however. The house was full, and I have never had a more delightfully keen set of people in front of me. Of all my experiences there was none which was more entirely and completely satisfactory, and I hope that it brought a very substantial sum into the local spiritual treasury. There was quite a scene in the street afterwards, and the motor could not start for the crowds who surrounded it and stretched their kind hands and eager faces towards us. It was a wonderful last impression to bear away from Australia.

It is worth recording that upon a clairvoyante being asked upon this occasion whether she saw any one beside me on the platform she at once answered "an elderly man with very tufted eyebrows." This was the marked characteristic of the face of Russell Wallace. I was told before I left England that Wallace was my guide. I have already shown that Mrs. Roberts, of Dunedin, gave me a message direct from him to the same effect. Mrs. Foster Turner, in Sydney, said she saw him, described him and gave the name. Three others have described him. Each of these has been quite independent of the others. I think that the most sceptical person must admit that the evidence is rather strong. It is naturally more strong to me since I am personally conscious of his intervention and assistance.

Apart from my spiritual mission, I was very sorry that I could not devote some time to exploring West Australia, which is in some ways the most interesting, as it is the least developed, of the States in the Federation. One or two points which I gathered about it are worth recording, especially its relation to the rabbits and to the sparrows, the only hostile invaders which it has known. Long may they remain so!

The battle between the West Australians and the rabbits was historical and wonderful. After the creatures had become a perfect pest in the East it was hoped that the great central desert would prevent them from ever reaching the West. There was no water for a thousand miles. None the less, the rabbits got across. It was a notable day when the West Australian outrider, loping from west to east, met the pioneer rabbit loping from east to west. Then West Australia made a great effort. She built a rabbit-proof wire screen from north to south for hundreds of miles from sea to sea, with such thoroughness that the northern end projected over a rock which fringed deep water. With such thoroughness, too, did the rabbits reconnoitre this obstacle that their droppings were seen upon the far side of that very rock. There came another day of doom when two rabbits were seen on the wrong side of the wire. Two dragons of the slime would not have alarmed the farmer more. A second line was built, but this also was, as I understand, carried by the attack, which is now consolidating, upon the ground it has won. However, the whole situation has been changed by the discovery elsewhere that the rabbit can be made a paying proposition, so all may end well in this curious story.

A similar fight, with more success, has been made by West Australia against the sparrow, which has proved an unmitigated nuisance elsewhere. The birds are slowly advancing down the line of the Continental Railway and their forward scouts are continually cut off. Captain White, the distinguished ornithologist, has the matter in hand, and received, as I am told, a wire a few weeks ago, he being in Melbourne, to the effect that two sparrows had been observed a thousand miles west of where they had any rights. He set off, or sent off, instantly to this way-side desert station in the hope of destroying them, with what luck I know not. I should be inclined to back the sparrows.

This Captain White is a man of energy and brains, whose name comes up always when one enquires into any question of bird or beast. He has made a remarkable expedition lately to those lonely Everard Ranges, which lie some distance to the north of the desolate Nularbor Plain, through which the Continental Railway passes. It must form one of the most dreadful wastes in the world, for there are a thousand miles of coast line, without one single stream emerging. Afforestation may alter all that. In the Everard Ranges Captain White found untouched savages of the stone age, who had never seen a white man before, and who treated him with absolute courtesy and hospitality. They were a fine race physically, though they lived under such conditions that there was little solid food save slugs, lizards and the like. One can but pray that the Australian Government will take steps to save these poor people from the sad fate which usually follows the contact between the higher and the lower.

From what I heard, West Australian immigrants are better looked after than in the other States. I was told in Perth that nine hundred ex-service men with their families had arrived, and that all had been fitted into places, permanent or temporary, within a fortnight. This is not due to Government, but to the exertions of a peculiar local Society, with the strange title of "The Ugly Men." "Handsome is as handsome does," and they seem to be great citizens. West Australia calls itself the Cinderella State, for, although it covers a third of the Continent, it is isolated from the great centres of population. It has a very individual life of its own, however, with its gold fields, its shark fisheries, its pearlers, and the great stock-raising plain in the north. Among other remarkable achievements is its great water pipe, which extends for four hundred miles across the desert, and supplies the pressure for the electric machinery at Kalgurli.

By a coincidence, the *Narkunda,* which is the sister ship of the *Naldera,* lay alongside the same quay at Fremantle, and it was an impressive sight to see these two great shuttles of Empire lying for a few hours at rest. In their vastness and majesty they made me think of a daring saying of my mother's, when she exclaimed that if some works of man, such as an ocean-going steamer, were compared with some works of God, such as a hill, man could sustain the comparison. It is the divine spark within us which gives us the creative power, and what may we not be when that is fully developed!

The children were fishing for sharks, with a line warranted to hold eighteen pounds, with the result that Malcolm's bait, lead, and everything else was carried away. But they were amply repaid by actually seeing the shark, which played about for some time in the turbid water, a brown, ugly, varminty creature, with fine lines of speed in its tapering body. "It was in Adelaide, daddy, not Fremantle," they protest in chorus, and no doubt they are right.

CHAPTER XII

IT was on Friday, February 11th, that we drew away
from the Fremantle wharf, and started forth upon
our long, lonely trek for Colombo—a huge stretch
of sea, in which it is unusual to see a single sail. As
night fell I saw the last twinkling lights of Australia
fade away upon our starboard quarter. Well, my job
is done. I have nothing to add, nor have I said anything which I would wish withdrawn. My furrow
gapes across two young Continents. I feel, deep in
my soul, that the seed will fall in due season, and that
the reaping will follow the seed. Only the work concerns ourselves—the results lie with those whose
instruments we are.

Of the many kindly letters which bade us farewell,
and which assured us that our work was not in vain,
none was more eloquent and thoughtful than that
of Mr. Thomas Ryan, a member of the Federal Legislature. "Long after you leave us your message will
linger. This great truth, which we had long thought
of as the plaything of the charlatan and crank, into
this you breathed the breath of life, and, as of old,
we were forced to say, 'We shall think of this again.

We shall examine it more fully.' Give us time—for the present only this, we are sure that this thing was not done in a corner. Let me say in the few moments I am able to snatch from an over-crowded life, that we realise throughout the land how deep and far-reaching were the things of which you spoke to us. We want time, and even more time, to make them part of ourselves. We are glad you have come and raised our thoughts from the market-place to the altar."

Bishop Leadbeater, of Sydney, one of the most venerable and picturesque figures whom I met in my travels, wrote, "Now that you are leaving our shores, let me express my conviction that your visit has done great good in stirring up the thought of the people, and, I hope, in convincing many of them of the reality of the other life." Among very many other letters there was none I valued more than one from the Rev. Jasper Calder, of Auckland. "Rest assured, Sir Arthur, the plough has gone deep, and the daylight will now reach the soil that has so long been in the darkness of ignorance. I somehow feel as if this is the beginning of new things for us all."

It is a long and weary stretch from Australia to Ceylon, but it was saved from absolute monotony by the weather, which was unusually boisterous for so genial a region. Two days before crossing the line we ran into a north-western monsoon, a rather rare experience, so that the doldrums became quite a lively place. Even our high decks were wet with spindrift and the edge of an occasional comber, and some of the cabins were washed out. A smaller ship would have been taking heavy seas. In all that great stretch of ocean we never saw a sail or a fish, and very few birds. The loneliness of the surface of the sea is surely a very strange fact in nature. One would imagine, if the sea is really so populous as we imagine, that the surface, which is the only fixed point in very deep water, would be the gathering ground and trysting place for all life. Save for the flying fish, there was not a trace in all those thousands of miles.

I suppose that on such a voyage one should rest and do nothing, but how difficult it is to do nothing, and can it be restful to do what is difficult? To me it is almost impossible. I was helped through a weary time by many charming companions on board, particularly the Rev. Henry Howard, reputed to be the best preacher in Australia. Some of his sermons which I read are, indeed, splendid, depending for their effect upon real thought and knowledge, without any theological emotion. He is ignorant of psychic philosophy, though, like so many men who profess themselves hostile to Spiritualism, he is full of good stories which conclusively prove the very thing he denies. However, he has reached full spirituality, which is more important than Spiritualism, and he must be a great influence for good wherever he goes. The rest he will earn later, either upon this side, or the other.

At Colombo I was interested to receive a *Westminster Gazette,* which contained an article by their special commissioner upon the Yorkshire fairies. Some correspondent has given the full name of the people concerned, with their address, which means that their little village will be crammed with chars-à-banc, and the peace of their life ruined. It was a rotten thing to do. For the rest, the *Westminster* inquiries seem to have confirmed Gardner and me in every particular, and brought out the further fact that the girls had never before taken a photo in their life. One of them had, it seems, been for a short time in the employ of a photographer, but as she was only a child, and her duties consisted in running on errands, the fact would hardly qualify her, as *Truth* suggests, for making faked negatives which could deceive the greatest experts in London. There may be some loophole in the direction of thought forms, but otherwise the case is as complete as possible.

We have just returned from a dream journey to Candy. The old capital is in the very centre of the island, and seventy-two miles from Colombo, but, finding that we had one clear night, we all crammed ourselves (my wife, the children and self) into a motor car, and made for it, while Major Wood and Jakeman did the same by train. It was a wonderful experience, a hundred and forty miles of the most lovely coloured cinema reel that God ever released. I carry away the confused but beautiful impression of a good broad red-tinted road, winding amid all shades of green, from the dark foliage of overhanging trees, to the light stretches of the half-grown rice fields. Tea groves, rubber plantations, banana gardens, and everywhere the coconut palms, with their graceful, drooping fronds. Along this great road streamed the people, and their houses lined the way, so that it was seldom that one was out of sight of human life. They were of

all types and colours, from the light brown of the real
Singalese to the negroid black of the Tamils, but all
shared the love of bright tints, and we were delighted
by the succession of mauves, purples, crimsons, ambers
and greens.   Water buffaloes, with the resigned and
half-comic air of the London landlady who has seen
better days, looked up at us from their mudholes, and
jackal-like dogs lay thick on the path, hardly moving
to let our motor pass.   Once, my lord the elephant
came round a corner, with his soft, easy-going stride,
and surveyed us with inscrutable little eyes.   It was the
unchanged East, even as it had always been, save for
the neat little police stations and their smart occupants,
who represented the gentle, but very efficient, British
Raj.   It may have been the merit of that Raj, or it may
have been the inherent virtue of the people, but in all
that journey we were never conscious of an unhappy
or of a wicked face.   They were very sensitive, speaking faces, too, and it was not hard to read the thoughts
within.

As we approached Candy, our road ran through the
wonderful Botanical Gardens, unmatched for beauty
in the world, though I still give Melbourne pride of
place for charm.   As we sped down one avenue an
elderly keeper in front of us raised his gun and fired
into the thick foliage of a high tree.   An instant later
something fell heavily to the ground.   A swarm of
crows had risen, so that we had imagined it was one
of these, but when we stopped the car a boy came running up with the victim, which was a great bat, or
flying fox, with a two-foot span of leathery wing.   It
had the appealing face of a mouse, and two black,

round eyes, as bright as polished shoe buttons. It was wounded, so the boy struck it hard upon the ground, and held it up once more, the dark eyes glazed, and the graceful head bubbling blood from either nostril. "Horrible! horrible!" cried poor Denis, and we all echoed it in our hearts. This intrusion of tragedy into that paradise of a garden reminded us of the shadows of life. There is something very intimately moving in the evil fate of the animals. I have seen a man's hand blown off in warfare, and have not been conscious of the same haunting horror which the pains of animals have caused me.

And here I may give another incident from our Candy excursion. The boys are wild over snakes, and I, since I sat in the front of the motor, was implored to keep a look-out. We were passing through a village, where a large lump of concrete, or stone, was lying by the road. A stick, about five feet long, was resting against it. As we flew past, I saw, to my amazement, the top of the stick bend back a little. I shouted to the driver, and we first halted, and then ran back to the spot. Sure enough, it was a long, yellow snake, basking in this peculiar position. The village was alarmed, and peasants came running, while the boys, wildly excited, tumbled out of the motor. "Kill it!" they cried. "No, no!" cried the chauffeur. "There is the voice of the Buddhist," I thought, so I cried, "No! no!" also. The snake, meanwhile, squirmed over the stone, and we saw it lashing about among the bushes. Perhaps we were wrong to spare it, for I fear it was full of venom. However, the villagers remained round the spot, and they had sticks, so perhaps the story was not ended.

Candy, the old capital, is indeed a dream city, and we spent a long, wonderful evening beside the lovely lake, where the lazy tortoises paddled about, and the fireflies gleamed upon the margin. We visited also the old Buddhist temple, where, as in all those places, the atmosphere is ruined by the perpetual demand for small coins. The few mosques which I have visited were not desecrated in this fashion, and it seems to be an unenviable peculiarity of the Buddhists, whose yellow-robed shaven priests have a keen eye for money. Beside the temple, but in ruins, lay the old palace of the native kings.

I wish we could have seen the temple under better conditions, for it is really the chief shrine of the most numerous religion upon earth, serving the Buddhist as the Kaaba serves the Moslem, or St. Peter's the Catholic. It is strange how the mind of man drags high things down to its own wretched level, the priests in each creed being the chief culprits. Buddha under his Boh tree was a beautiful example of sweet, unselfish benevolence and spirituality. And the upshot, after two thousand years, is that his followers come to adore a horse's tooth (proclaimed to be Buddha's, and three inches long), at Candy, and to crawl up Adam's Peak, in order to worship at a hole in the ground which is supposed to be his yard-long footstep. It is not more senseless than some Christian observances, but that does not make it less deplorable.

I was very anxious to visit one of the buried cities further inland, and especially to see the ancient Boh tree, which must surely be the doyen of the whole vegetable kingdom, since it is undoubtedly a slip taken from Buddha's original Boh tree, transplanted into Ceylon about two hundred years before Christ. Its history is certain and unbroken. Now, I understand, it is a very doddering old trunk, with withered limbs which are supported by crutches, but may yet hang on for some centuries to come. On the whole, we employed our time very well, but Ceylon will always remain to each of us as an earthly paradise, and I could imagine no greater pleasure than to have a clear month to wander over its beauties. Monsieur Clemenceau was clearly of the same opinion, for he was doing it very thoroughly whilst we were there.

From Colombo to Bombay was a dream of blue skies and blue seas. Half way up the Malabar coast, we saw the old Portuguese settlement of Goa, glimmering white on a distant hillside. Even more interesting to us was a squat battleship making its way up the coast. As we came abreast of it we recognised the *Malaya*, one of that famous little squadron of Evan Thomas's, which staved off the annihilation of Beatty's cruisers upon that day of doom on the Jutland coast. We gazed upon it with the reverence that it deserved. We had, in my opinion, a mighty close shave upon that occasion. If Jellicoe had gambled with the British fleet he might have won a shattering victory, but surely he was wise to play safety with such tremendous interests at stake. There is an account of the action, given by a German officer, at the end of Freeman's book "With the *Hercules* to Kiel," which shows clearly that the enemy desired Jellicoe to close with them, as giving

DENIS WITH A BLACK SNAKE AT MEDLOW BATH.

them their only chance for that torpedo barrage which they had thoroughly practised, and on which they relied to cripple a number of our vessels. In every form of foresight and preparation, the brains seem to have been with them—but that was not the fault of the fighting seamen. Surely an amateur could have foreseen that, in a night action, a star shell is better than a searchlight, that a dropping shell at a high trajectory is far more likely to hit the deck than the side, and that the powder magazine should be cut off from the turret, as, otherwise, a shell crushing the one will explode the other. This last error in construction seems to have been the cause of half our losses, and the *Lion* herself would have been a victim, but for the self-sacrifice of brave Major Harvey of the Marines. All's well that ends well, but it was stout hearts, and not clear heads, which pulled us through.

It is all very well to say let bygones be bygones, but we have no guarantee that the old faults are corrected, and certainly no one has been censured. It looks as if the younger officers had no means of bringing their views before those in authority, while the seniors were so occupied with actual administration that they had no time for thinking outside their routine. Take the really monstrous fact that, at the outset of a war of torpedoes and mines, when ships might be expected to sink like kettles with a hole in them, no least provision had been made for saving the crew! Boats were discarded before action, nothing wooden or inflammable was permitted, and the consideration that life-saving apparatus might be non-inflammable does not seem to have presented itself. When I wrote to the Press, pointing this out with all the emphasis of which I was capable—I was ready to face the charge of hysteria in such a cause—I was gravely rebuked by a leading naval authority, and cautioned not to meddle with mysteries of which I knew nothing. None the less, within a week there was a rush order for swimming collars of india rubber. *Post hoc non propter,* perhaps, but at least it verified the view of the layman. That was in the days when not one harbour had been boomed and netted, though surely a shark in a bathing pool would be innocuous compared to a submarine in an anchorage. The swimmers could get out, but the ships could not.

But all this comes of seeing the white *Malaya,* steaming slowly upon deep blue summer seas, with the olive-green coast of Malabar on the horizon behind her.

I had an interesting conversation on psychic matters with Lady Dyer, whose husband was killed in the war. It has been urged that it is singular and unnatural that our friends from the other side so seldom allude to the former occasions on which they have manifested. There is, I think, force in the objection. Lady Dyer had an excellent case to the contrary—and, indeed, they are not rare when one makes inquiry. She was most anxious to clear up some point which was left open between her husband and herself, and for this purpose consulted three mediums in London, Mr. Vout Peters, Mrs. Brittain, and another. In each case she had some success. Finally, she consulted Mrs. Leonard, and her husband, speaking through Feda, under control, began a long conversation by saying, "I have already spoken to you through three mediums, two women and a man." Lady Dyer had not given her name upon any occasion, so there was no question of passing on information. I may add that the intimate point at issue was entirely cleared up by the husband, who rejoiced greatly that he had the chance to do so.

Bombay is not an interesting place for the casual visitor, and was in a state of uproar and decoration on account of the visit of the Duke of Connaught. My wife and I did a little shopping, which gave us a glimpse of the patient pertinacity of the Oriental. The sum being 150 rupees, I asked the Indian's leave to pay by cheque, as money was running low. He consented. When we reached the ship by steam-launch, we found that he, in some strange way, had got there already, and was squatting with the goods outside our cabin door. He looked askance at Lloyd's Bank, of which he had never heard, but none the less he took the cheque under protest. Next evening he was back at our cabin door, squatting as before, with a sweat-stained cheque in his hand which, he declared, that he was unable to cash. This time I paid in English pound notes, but he looked upon them with considerable suspicion. As our ship was lying a good three miles from the shore, the poor chap had certainly earned his money, for his goods, in the first instance, were both good and cheap.

We have seen the Island of Elephanta, and may the curse of Ernulphus, which comprises all other curses, be upon that old Portuguese Governor who desecrated it, and turned his guns upon the wonderful stone carvings. It reminds me of Abou Simbel in Nubia, and the whole place has an Egyptian flavour. In a vast hollow in the hill, a series of very elaborate bas-reliefs have been carved, showing Brahma, Vishnu and Siva, the old Hindoo trinity, with all those strange satellites, the bulls, the kites, the dwarfs, the elephant-headed giants with which Hindoo mythology has so grotesquely endowed them. Surely a visitor from some wiser planet, examining our traces, would judge that the human race, though sane in all else, was mad the moment that it touched religion, whether he judged it by such examples as these, or by the wearisome iteration of expressionless Buddhas, the sacred crocodiles and hawk-headed gods of Egypt, the monstrosities of Central America, or the lambs and doves which adorn our own churches. It is only in the Mohammedan faith that such an observer would find nothing which could offend, since all mortal symbolism is there forbidden. And yet if these strange conceptions did indeed help these poor people through their journey of life—and even now they come from far with their offerings—then we should morally be as the Portuguese governor, if we were to say or do that which might leave them prostrate and mutilated in their minds. It was a pleasant break to our long voyage, and we were grateful to our commander, who made everything easy for us. He takes the humane view that a passenger is not merely an article of cargo, to be conveyed from port to port, but that his recreation should, in reason, be considered as well.

Elephanta was a little bit of the old India, but the men who conveyed us there from the launch to the shore in their ancient dhows were of a far greater antiquity. These were Kolis, small, dark men, who held the country before the original Aryan invasion, and may still be plying their boats when India has become Turanian or Slavonic, or whatever its next avatar may be. They seem to have the art of commerce well developed, for they held us up cleverly until they had extracted a rupee each, counting us over and over with great care and assiduity.

At Bombay we took over 200 more travellers.

We had expected that the new-comers, who were mostly Anglo-Indians whose leave had been long overdue, would show signs of strain and climate, but we were agreeably surprised to find that they were a remarkably healthy and alert set of people. This may be due to the fact that it is now the end of the cold weather. Our new companions included many native gentlemen, one of whom, the Rajah of Kapurthala, brought with him his Spanish wife, a regal-looking lady, whose position must be a difficult one. Hearne and Murrell, the cricketers, old playmates and friends, were also among the new-comers. All of them seemed perturbed as to the unrest in India, though some were inclined to think that the worst was past, and that the situation was well in hand. When we think how splendidly India helped us in the war, it would indeed be sad if a serious rift came between us now. One thing I am very sure of, that if Great Britain should ever be forced to separate from India, it is India, and not Britain, which will be the chief sufferer.

We passed over hundreds of miles of absolute calm in the Indian Ocean. There is a wonderful passage in Frank Bullen's "Sea Idylls," in which he describes how,

after a long-continued tropical calm, all manner of
noxious scum and vague evil shapes come flickering
to the surface. Coleridge has done the same idea,
for all time, in "The Ancient Mariner," when "the very
sea did rot." In our case we saw nothing so dramatic,
but the ship passed through one area where there was
a great number of what appeared to be sea-snakes,
creatures of various hues, from two to ten feet long,
festooned or slowly writhing some feet below the surface. I cannot recollect seeing anything of the kind in
any museum. These, and a couple of Arab dhows,
furnished our only break in a thousand miles. Certainly, as an entertainment the ocean needs cutting.

In the extreme south, like a cloud upon the water,
we caught a glimpse of the Island of Socotra, one of
the least visited places upon earth, though so near to
the main line of commerce. What a base for submarines, should it fall into wrong hands! It has a
comic-opera Sultan of its own, with 15,000 subjects,
and a subsidy from the British Government of 200
dollars a year, which has been increased lately to 360,
presumably on account of the higher cost of living.
It is a curious fact that, though it is a great place of
hill and plain, seventy miles by eighteen, there is only
one wild animal known, namely the civet cat. A
traveller, Mr. Jacob, who examined the place, put
forward the theory that one of Alexander the Great's
ships was wrecked there, the crew remaining, for he
found certain Greek vestiges, but what they were I
have been unable to find out.

As we approached Aden, we met the *China* on her
way out. Her misadventure some years ago at the

Island of Perim, has become one of the legends of the sea. In those days, the discipline aboard P. & O. ships was less firm than at present, and on the occasion of the birthday of one of the leading passengers, the officers of the ship had been invited to the festivity. The result was that, in the middle of dinner, the ship crashed, no great distance from the lighthouse, and, it is said, though this is probably an exaggeration, that the revellers were able to get ashore over the bows without wetting their dress shoes. No harm was done, save that one unlucky rock projected like a huge spike, through the ship's bottom, and it cost the company a good half-million before they were able to get her afloat and in service once more. However, there she was, doing her fifteen knots, and looking so saucy and new that no one would credit such an unsavoury incident in her past.

Early in February I gave a lantern lecture upon psychic phenomena to passengers of both classes. The Red Sea has become quite a favourite stamping ground of mine, but it is much more tolerable now than on that terrible night in August when I discharged arguments and perspiration to a sweltering audience. On this occasion it was a wonderful gathering, a microcosm of the world, with an English peer, an Indian maharajah, many native gentlemen, whites of every type from four great countries, and a fringe of stewards, stewardesses, and nondescripts of all sorts, including the ship's barber, who is one of the most active men on the ship in an intellectual sense. All went well, and if they were not convinced they were deeply interested, which is the first stage. Somewhere there are great forces which are going to carry on this work, and I never address an audience without the feeling that among them there may be some latent Paul or Luther whom my words may call into activity.

I heard an anecdote yesterday which is worth recording. We have a boatswain who is a fine, burly specimen of a British seaman. In one of his short holidays while in mufti, in Norfolk, he had an argument with a Norfolk farmer, a stranger to him, who wound up the discussion by saying: "My lad, what you need is a little travel to broaden your mind."

The boatswain does his 70,000 miles a year. It reminded me of the doctor who advised his patient to take a brisk walk every morning before breakfast, and then found out that he was talking to the village postman.

A gentleman connected with the cinema trade told me a curious story within his own experience. Last year a psychic cinema story was shown in Australia, and to advertise it a man was hired who would consent to be chained to a tombstone all night. This was done in Melbourne and Sydney without the person concerned suffering in any way. It was very different in Launceston. The man was found to be nearly mad from terror in the morning, though he was a stout fellow of the dock labourer type. His story was that in the middle of the night he had heard to his horror the sound of dripping water approaching him. On looking up he saw an evil-looking shape with water streaming from him, who stood before him and abused him a long time, frightening him almost to death. The man was so shaken that the cinema company had to send him for a voyage. Of course, it was an unfair test for anyone's nerves, and imagination may have played its part, but it is noticeable that a neighbouring grave contained a man who had been drowned in the Esk many years before. In any case, it makes a true and interesting story, whatever the explanation.

I have said that there was an English peer on board. This was Lord Chetwynd, a man who did much towards winning the war. Now that the storm is over the public knows nothing, and apparently cares little, about the men who brought the ship of State through in safety. Some day we shall get a more exact sense of proportion, but it is all out of focus at present. Lord Chetwynd, in the year 1915, discovered by his own personal experiments how to make an explosive far more effective than the one we were using, which was very unreliable. This he effected by a particular combination and treatment of T.N.T. and ammonia nitrate. Having convinced the authorities by actual demonstration, he was given a free hand, which he used to such effect that within a year he was furnishing the main shell supply of the army. His own installation was at Chilwell, near Nottingham, and it turned out 19,000,000 shells, while six other establishments were erected elsewhere on the same system. Within his own works Lord Chetwynd was so complete an autocrat that it was generally believed that he shot three spies with his own hand. Thinking the rumour a useful one, he encouraged it by creating three dummy graves, which may, perhaps, be visited to this day by pious pro-Germans. It should be added that Lord Chetwynd's explosive was not only stronger,

[281]

but cheaper, than that in previous use, so that his labours saved the country some millions of pounds.

It was at Chilwell that the huge bombs were filled which were destined for Berlin. There were 100 of them to be carried in twenty-five Handley Page machines. Each bomb was capable of excavating 350 tons at the spot where it fell, and in a trial trip one which was dropped in the central courtyard of a large square building left not a stone standing around it. Berlin was saved by a miracle, which she hardly deserved after the irresponsible glee with which she had hailed the devilish work of her own Zeppelins. The original hundred bombs sent to be charged had the tails removed before being sent, and when they were returned it was found to be such a job finding the right tail for the right bomb, the permutations being endless, that it was quicker and easier to charge another hundred bombs with tails attached. This and other fortuitous matters consumed several weeks. Finally, the bombs were ready and were actually on the machines in England, whence the start was to be made, when the Armistice was declared. Possibly a knowledge of this increased the extreme haste of the German delegates. Personally, I am glad it was so, for we have enough cause for hatred in the world without adding the death of 10,000 German civilians. There is some weight, however, in the contention of those who complain that Germans have devastated Belgium and France, but have never been allowed to experience in their own persons what the horrors of war really are. Still, if Christianity and religion are to be more than mere words, we must be content that Berlin was not laid in ruins at a time when the issue of the war was already decided.

Here we are at Suez once again. It would take Loti or Robert Hichens to describe the wonderful shades peculiar to the outskirts of Egypt. Deep blue sea turns to dark green, which in turn becomes the very purest, clearest emerald as it shallows into a snow-white frill of foam. Thence extends the golden desert with deep honey-coloured shadows, stretching away until it slopes upwards into melon-tinted hills, dry and bare and wrinkled. At one point a few white dwellings with a group of acacias mark the spot which they call Moses Well. They say that a Jew can pick up a living in any country, but when one surveys these terrible wastes one can only imagine that the climate has greatly changed since a whole nomad people were able to cross them.

In the Mediterranean we had a snap of real cold which laid many of us out, myself included. I recall the Lancastrian who complained that he had swallowed a dog fight. The level of our lives had been disturbed for an instant by a feud between the children and one of the passengers who had, probably quite justly, given one of them a box on the ear. In return, they had fixed an abusive document in his cabin which they had ended by the words, "With our warmest despisings," all signing their names to it. The passenger was sportsman enough to show this document around, or we should not have known of its existence. Strange little souls with their vivid hopes and fears, a parody of our own. I gave baby a daily task and had ordered her to do a map of Australia. I found her weeping in the evening. "I did the map," she cried, between her sobs, "but they all said it was a pig!" She was shaken to the soul at the slight upon her handiwork.

It was indeed wonderful to find ourselves at Marseilles once more, and after the usual unpleasant *douane* formalities, which are greatly ameliorated in France as compared to our own free trade country, to be at temporary rest at the Hôtel du Louvre.

A great funeral, that of Frederic Chevillon and his brother, was occupying the attention of the town. Both were public officials and both were killed in the war, their bodies being now exhumed for local honour. A great crowd filed past with many banners, due decorum being observed save that some of the mourners were smoking cigarettes, which "was not handsome," as Mr. Pepys would observe. There was no sign of any religious symbol anywhere. It was a Sunday and yet the people in the procession seemed very badly dressed and generally down-at-heel and slovenly. I think we should have done the thing better in England. The simplicity of the flag-wrapped coffins was however dignified and pleasing. The inscriptions, too, were full of simple patriotism.

I never take a stroll through a French town without appreciating the gulf which lies between us and them. They have the old Roman civilisation, with its ripe mellow traits, which have never touched the Anglo-Saxon, who, on the other hand, has his raw Northern virtues which make life angular but effective. I watched a scene to-day inconceivable under our rule. Four very smart officers, captains or majors, were seated outside a café. The place was crowded, but there was room for four more at this table on the sidewalk, so presently that number of negro privates came along and occupied the vacant seats. The officers smiled most good humouredly, and remarks were exchanged between the two parties, which ended in the high falsetto laugh of a negro. These black troops seemed perfectly self-respecting, and I never saw a drunken man, soldier or civilian, during two days.

I have received English letters which announce that I am to repeat my Australian lectures at the Queen's Hall, from April 11th onwards. I seem to be returning with shotted guns and going straight into action. They say that the most dangerous course is to switch suddenly off when you have been working hard. I am little likely to suffer from that.

CHAPTER XIII

ONE long stride took us to Paris, where, under the friendly and comfortable roof of the Hôtel du Louvre, we were able at last to unpack our trunks and to steady down after this incessant movement. The first visit which I paid in Paris was to Dr. Geley, head of the Institut Metaphysique, at 89, Avenue Niel. Now that poor Crawford has gone, leaving an imperishable name behind him, Geley promises to be the greatest male practical psychic researcher, and he has advantages of which Crawford could never boast, since the liberality of Monsieur Jean Meyer has placed him at the head of a splendid establishment with laboratory, photographic room, lecture room, séance room and library, all done in the most splendid style. Unless some British patron has the generosity and intelligence to do the same, this installation, with a man like Geley to run it, will take the supremacy in psychic advance from Britain, where it now lies, and transfer it to France. Our nearest approach to something similar depends at present upon the splendid private efforts of Mr. and Mrs. Hewat MacKenzie, in the Psychic College at 59, Holland Park, which deserve the support of everyone who realises the importance of the subject.

I made a *faux pas* with the Geleys, for I volunteered to give an exhibition of my Australian slides, and they invited a distinguished audience of men of science to see them. Imagine my horror when I found that my box of slides was in the luggage which Major Wood had taken on with him in the *Naldera* to England. They were rushed over by aeroplane, however, in response to my telegram, and so the situation was saved.

The lecture was a private one and was attended by Mr. Charles Richet, Mr. Gabrielle Delanne, and a number of other men of science. Nothing could have gone better, though I fear that my French, which is execrable, must have been a sore trial to my audience. I gave them warning at the beginning by quoting a remark which Bernard Shaw made to me once, that when he spoke French he did not say what he wanted to say, but what he could say. Richet told me afterwards that he was deeply interested by the photographs, and when I noted the wonder and awe with which he treated them—he, the best known physiologist in the world—and compared it with the attitude of the ordinary lay Press, it seemed a good example of the humility of wisdom and the arrogance of ignorance. After my lecture, which covered an hour and a quarter, we were favoured by an extraordinary exhibition from a medium named Aubert. This gentleman has had no musical education whatever, but he sits down in a state of semi-trance and he handles a piano as

I, for one, have never heard one handled before. It is a most amazing performance. He sits with his eyes closed while some one calls the alphabet, striking one note when the right letter sounds. In this way he spells out the name of the particular composer whom he will represent. He then dashes off, with tremendous verve and execution, upon a piece which is not a known composition of that author, but is an improvisation after his manner. We had Grieg, Mendelssohn, Berlioz and others in quick succession, each of them masterly and characteristic. His technique seemed to my wife and me to be not inferior to that of Paderewski. Needles can be driven through him as he plays, and sums can be set before him which he will work out without ceasing the wonderful music which appears to flow through him, but quite independently of his own powers or volition. He would certainly cause a sensation in London.

I had the honour next day of meeting Camille Flammarion, the famous astronomer, who is deeply engaged in psychic study, and was so interested in the photos which I showed him that I was compelled to leave them in his hands that he might get copies done. Flammarion is a dear, cordial, homely old gentleman with a beautiful bearded head which would delight a sculptor. He entertained us with psychic stories all lunch time. Madame Bisson was there and amused me with her opinion upon psychic researchers, their density, their arrogance, their preposterous theories to account for obvious effects. If she had not been a great pioneer in Science, she might have been a remarkable actress, for it was wonderful how her face took off the various types. Certainly, as described by her, their far-fetched precautions, which irritate the medium and ruin the harmony of the conditions, do appear very ridiculous, and the parrot cry of "Fraud!" and "Fake!" has been sadly overdone. All are agreed here that spiritualism has a far greater chance in England than in France, because the French temperament is essentially a mocking one, and also because the Catholic Church is in absolute opposition. Three of their bishops, Beauvais, Lisieux and Coutances, helped to burn a great medium, Joan of Arc, six hundred years ago, asserting at the trial the very accusations of necromancy which are asserted to-day. Now they have had to canonise her. One would have hoped that they had learned something from the incident.

Dr. Geley has recently been experimenting with Mr. Franek Kluski, a Polish amateur of weak health, but with great mediumistic powers. These took the form of materialisations. Dr. Geley had prepared a bucket of warm paraffin, and upon the appearance of the materialised figure, which was that of a smallish man, the request was made that the apparition should plunge its hand into the bucket and then withdraw it, so that when it dematerialised a cast of the hand would be left, like a glove of solidified paraffin, so narrow at the wrist that the hands could not have been withdrawn by any possible normal means without breaking the moulds. These hands I was able to inspect, and also the plaster cast which had been taken from the inside of one of them. The latter showed a small hand, not larger than a boy's, but presenting the characteristics of age, for the skin was loose and formed transverse folds. The materialised figure had also, un-asked, left an impression of its own mouth and chin, which was, I think, done for evidential purposes, for a curious wart hung from the lower lip, which would mark the owner among a million. So far as I could learn, however, no identification had actually been effected. The mouth itself was thick-lipped and coarse, and also gave an impression of age.

To show the thoroughness of Dr. Geley's work, he had foreseen that the only answer which any critic, however exacting, could make to the evidence, was that the paraffin hand had been brought in the medium's pocket. Therefore he had treated with cholesterin the paraffin in his bucket, and this same cholesterin reap-peared in the resulting glove. What can any sceptic have to say to an experiment like that save to ignore it, and drag us back with wearisome iteration to some real or imaginary scandal of the past? The fact is that the position of the Materialists could only be sus-tained so long as there was a general agreement among all the newspapers to regard this subject as a comic proposition. Now that there is a growing tendency towards recognising its overwhelming gravity, the evi-dence is getting slowly across to the public, and the old attitude of negation and derision has become puerile. I can clearly see, however, that the Materialists will fall back upon their second line of trenches, which will be to admit the phenomena, but to put them down to material causes in the unexplored realms of nature with no real connection with human survival. This change of front is now due, but it will fare no better than the old one. Before quitting the subject I should have added that these conclusions of Dr. Geley concerning the paraffin moulds taken from Kluski's materialisation are shared by Charles Richet and Count de Gramont of the Institute of France, who took part in the experiments. How absurd are the efforts of those who were not present to contradict the experiences of men like these.

I was disappointed to hear from Dr. Geley that the experiments in England with the medium Eva had been largely negative, though once or twice the ectoplasmic flow was, as I understand, observed. Dr. Geley put this comparative failure down to the fantastic precautions taken by the committee, which had produced a strained and unnatural atmosphere. It seems to me that if a medium is searched, and has all her clothes changed before entering the séance room, that is ample, but when in addition to this you put her head in a net-bag and restrict her in other ways, you are producing an abnormal self-conscious state of mind which stops that passive mood of receptivity which is essential. Professor Hyslop has left it on record that after a long series of rigid tests with Mrs. Piper he tried one sitting under purely natural conditions, and received more convincing and evidential results than in all the others put together. Surely this should suggest freer methods in our research.

I have just had a sitting with Eva, whom I cannot even say that I have seen, for she was under her cloth cabinet when I arrived and still under it when I left, being in trance the whole time. Professor Jules Courtier of the Sorbonne and a few other men of science were present. Madame Bisson experiments now in the full light of the afternoon. Only the medium is in darkness, but her two hands protrude through the cloth and are controlled by the sitters. There is a flap in the cloth which can be opened to show anything which forms beneath. After sitting about an hour this flap was opened, and Madame Bisson pointed out to me a streak of ectoplasm upon the outside of the medium's bodice. It was about six inches long and as thick as a finger. I was allowed to touch it, and felt it shrink and contract under my hand. It is this substance which can, under good conditions, be poured out in great quantities and can be built up into forms and shapes, first flat and finally rounded, by powers which are beyond our science. We sometimes call it Psychoplasm in England, Richet named it Ectoplasm, Geley calls it Ideoplasm; but call it what you will, Crawford has shown for all time that it is the substance which is at the base of psychic physical phenomena.

Madame Bisson, whose experience after twelve years' work is unique, has an interesting theory. She disagrees entirely with Dr. Geley's view, that the shapes are thought forms, and she resents the name ideoplasm, since it represents that view. Her conclusion is that Eva acts the part which a "detector" plays, when it turns the Hertzian waves, which are too short for our observation, into slower ones which can become audible. Thus Eva breaks up certain currents and renders them visible. According to her, what we see is never the thing itself but always the reflection of the thing which exists in another plane and is made visible in ours by Eva's strange material organisation.

It was for this reason that the word Miroir appeared in one of the photographs, and excited much adverse criticism. One dimly sees a new explanation of mediumship. The light seems a colourless thing until it passes through a prism and suddenly reveals every colour in the world.

A picture of Madame Bisson's father hung upon the wall, and I at once recognised him as the phantom which appears in the photographs of her famous book, and which formed the culminating point of Eva's mediumship. He has a long and rather striking face which was clearly indicated in the ectoplasmic image. Only on one occasion was this image so developed that it could speak, and then only one word. The word was "Esperez."

We have just returned, my wife, Denis and I, from a round of the Aisne battlefields, paying our respects incidentally to Bossuet at Meaux, Fenelon at Château Thierry, and Racine at La Ferté Millon. It is indeed a frightful cicatrix which lies across the brow of France—a scar which still gapes in many places as an open wound. I could not have believed that the ruins were still so untouched. The land is mostly under cultivation, but the houses are mere shells, and I cannot think where the cultivators live. When you drive for sixty miles and see nothing but ruin on either side of the road, and when you know that the same thing extends from the sea to the Alps, and that in places it is thirty miles broad, it helps one to realise the debt that Germany owes to her victims. If it had been in the Versailles terms that all her members of parliament and journalists should be personally conducted, as we have been, through a sample section, their tone would be more reasonable.

It has been a wonderful panorama. We followed the route of the thousand taxi-cabs which helped to save Europe up to the place where Gallieni's men dismounted and walked straight up against Klück's rear-guard. We saw Belleau Wood, where the 2nd and 46th American divisions made their fine début and showed Ludendorff that they were not the useless soldiers he had so vainly imagined. Thence we passed all round that great heavy sack of Germans which had formed in June, 1918, with its tip at Dormans and Château Thierry. We noted Bligny, sacred to the sacrifices of Carter Campbell's 51st Highlanders, and Braithwaite's 62nd Yorkshire division, who lost between them seven thousand men in these woods. These British episodes seem quite unknown to the French, while the Americans have very properly laid out fine graveyards with their flag flying, and placed engraved tablets of granite where they played their part, so that in time I really think that the average Frenchman will hardly remember that we were in the war at all, while if you were to tell him that in the critical year we took about as many prisoners and guns as all the other nations put together, he would stare at you with amazement. Well, what matter! With a man or a nation it is the duty done for its own sake and the sake of its own conscience and self-respect that really counts. All the rest is swank.

We slept at Rheims. We had stayed at the chief hotel, the Golden Lion, in 1912, when we were en route to take part in the Anglo-German motor-car competition, organised by Prince Henry. We searched round, but not one stone of the hotel was standing. Out of 14,000 houses in the town, only twenty had entirely escaped. As to the Cathedral, either a miracle has been wrought or the German gunners have been extraordinary masters of their craft, for there are acres of absolute ruin up to its very walls, and yet it stands erect with no very vital damage. The same applies to the venerable church of St. Remy. On the whole I am prepared to think that save in one fit of temper, upon September 19th, 1914, the guns were never purposely turned upon this venerable building. Hitting the proverbial haystack would be a difficult feat compared to getting home on to this monstrous pile which dominates the town. It is against reason to suppose that both here and at Soissons they could not have left the cathedrals as they left the buildings around them.

Next day, we passed down the Vesle and Aisne, seeing the spot where French fought his brave but barren action on September 13th, 1914, and finally we reached the Chemin des Dames—a good name had the war been fought in the knightly spirit of old, but horribly out of place amid the ferocities with which Germany took all chivalry from warfare. The huge barren countryside, swept with rainstorms and curtained in clouds, looked like some evil landscape out of Vale Owen's revelations. It was sown from end to end with shattered trenches, huge coils of wire and rusted weapons, including thousands of bombs which are still capable of exploding should you tread upon them too heavily. Denis ran wildly about, like a terrier in a barn, and returned loaded with all sorts of trophies, most of which had to be discarded as overweight. He succeeded, however, in bringing away a Prussian helmet and a few other of the mort portable of his treasures. We returned by Soissons, which interested me greatly, as I had seen it under war conditions in 1916. Finally we reached Paris after a really wonderful two days in which, owing to Mr. Cook's organisation and his guide, we saw more and understood more, than in a week if left to ourselves. They run similar excursions to Verdun and other points. I only wish we had the time to avail ourselves of them.

A tragic intermezzo here occurred in our Paris experience. I suddenly heard that my brother-in-law, E. W. Hornung, the author of "Raffles" and many another splendid story, was dying at St. Jean de Luz in the Pyrenees. I started off at once, but was only in time to be present at his funeral. Our little family group has been thinned down these last two years until we feel like a company under hot fire with half on the ground. We can but close our ranks the tighter. Hornung lies within three paces of George Gissing, an author for whom both of us had an affection. It is good to think that one of his own race and calling keeps him company in his Pyrenean grave.

Hornung, apart from his literary powers, was one of the wits of our time. I could brighten this dull chronicle if I could insert a page of his sayings. Like Charles Lamb, he could find humour in his own physical disabilities—disabilities which did not prevent him, when over fifty, from volunteering for such service as he could do in Flanders. When pressed to have a medical examination, his answer was, "My body is like a sausage. The less I know of its interior, the easier will be my mind." It was a characteristic mixture of wit and courage.

During our stay in Paris we went to see the Anglo-French Rugby match at Coulombes. The French have not quite got the sporting spirit, and there was some tendency to hoot whenever a decision was given for the English, but the play of their team was most excellent, and England only won by the narrow margin of 10 to 6. I can remember the time when French Rugby was the joke of the sporting world. They are certainly a most adaptive people. The tactics of the game have changed considerably since the days when I was more familiar with it, and it has become less dramatic, since ground is gained more frequently by kicking into touch than by the individual run, or even by the combined movement. But it is still the king of games. It was like the old lists, where the pick of these two knightly nations bore themselves so bravely of old, and it was an object lesson to see Clement, the French back, playing on manfully, with the blood pouring from a gash in the head. Marshal Foch was there, and I have no doubt that he noted the incident with approval.

I had a good look at the famous soldier, who was close behind me. He looks very worn, and sadly in need of a rest. His face and head are larger than his pictures indicate, but it is not a face with any marked feature or character. His eyes, however, are grey, and inexorable. His kepi was drawn down, and I could not see the upper part of the head, but just there lay the ruin of Germany. It must be a very fine brain, for in political, as well as in military matters, his judgment has always been justified.

There is an excellent clairvoyante in Paris, Madame Blifaud, and I look forward, at some later date, to a personal proof of her powers, though if it fails I shall not be so absurd as to imagine that that disproves them. The particular case which came immediately under my notice was that of a mother whose son had been killed from an aeroplane, in the war. She had no details of his death. On asking Madame B., the latter replied, "Yes, he is here, and gives me a vision of his fall. As a proof that it is really he, he depicts the scene, which was amid songs, flags and music." As this corresponded with no episode of the war, the mother was discouraged and incredulous. Within a short time, however, she received a message from a young officer who had been with her son when the accident occurred. It was on the Armistice day, at Salonica. The young fellow had flown just above the flags, one of the flags got entangled with his rudder, and the end was disaster. But bands, songs and flags all justified the clairvoyante.

Now, at last, our long journey drew to its close. Greatly guarded by the high forces which have, by the goodness of Providence, been deputed to help us, we are back in dear old London once more. When we look back at the 30,000 miles which we have traversed, at the complete absence of illness which spared any one of seven a single day in bed, the excellence of our long voyages, the freedom from all accidents, the undisturbed and entirely successful series of lectures, the financial success won for the cause, the double escape from shipping strikes, and, finally, the several inexplicable instances of supernormal, personal happenings, together with the three-fold revelation of the name of our immediate guide, we should be stocks and stones if we did not realise that we have been the direct instruments of God in a cause upon which He has set His visible seal. There let it rest. If He be with us, who is against us? To give religion a foundation of rock instead of quicksand, to remove the legitimate doubts of earnest minds, to make the invisible forces, with their moral sanctions, a real thing, instead of mere words upon our lips, and, incidentally, to reassure the human race as to the future which awaits it, and to broaden its appreciation of the possibilities of the present life, surely no more glorious message was ever heralded to mankind. And it begins visibly to hearken. The human race is on the very eve of a tremendous revolution of thought, marking a final revulsion from materialism, and it is part of our glorious and assured philosophy, that, though we may not be here to see the final triumph of our labours, we shall, none the less, be as much engaged in the struggle and the victory from the day when we join those who are our comrades in battle upon the further side.

THE END